"In this riveting tale, [...] takes us back to a time when Americans fought on distant shores and dreamed of the wives, husbands, and sweethearts they left behind. We witness WWII first-person through an extraordinary collection of letters written by Army Air Corps Lt. James Richard Jones to his fiancée, Elnora Bartlett. Supplemented by Ms. Armstrong's meticulous research, *Wings and a Ring* will renew your faith in the human spirit and the extraordinary, enduring power of love."

—Merline Lovelace, author

Catch Her If You Can, A Samantha Spade Mystery, January 2011

Danger in the Desert, Silhouette Romantic Suspense, January 2011

Strangers When We Meet, Silhouette Romantic Suspense, June 2011

Crusader Captive, Harlequin Historicals, July 2011

Double Deception, Silhouette Romantic Suspense, August 2011

"Reading *Wings and a Ring* brought back many memories of when I was in the service. I especially enjoyed hearing about the popular music of the time and remember waiting to dock at the next port to collect mail and records sent from home. The mission descriptions really complete the story. I would have liked to have kissed that girl!"

—Glenn McDuffie, forensically verified *Kissing Sailor*: V-J Day, August 14, 1945, Times Square

René Palmer Armstrong

Wings and a Ring

Letters of War and Love from a WWII Pilot

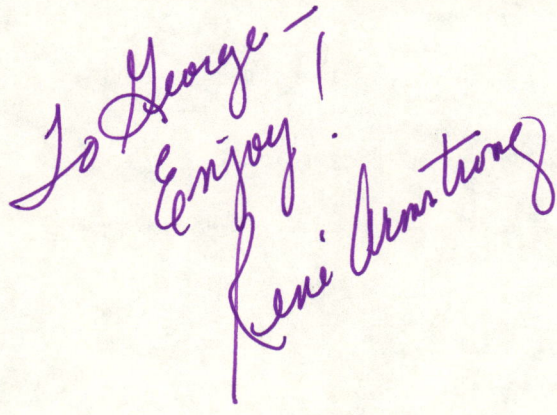

Tate Publishing & Enterprises

Wings and a Ring
Copyright © 2011 by Rene' Palmer Armstrong. All rights reserved.

No part of this publication may be reproduced, stored in a retrieval system or transmitted in any way by any means, electronic, mechanical, photocopy, recording or otherwise without the prior permission of the author except as provided by USA copyright law.

The opinions expressed by the author are not necessarily those of Tate Publishing, LLC.

Published by Tate Publishing & Enterprises, LLC
127 E. Trade Center Terrace | Mustang, Oklahoma 73064 USA
1.888.361.9473 | www.tatepublishing.com

Tate Publishing is committed to excellence in the publishing industry. The company reflects the philosophy established by the founders, based on Psalm 68:11,
"The Lord gave the word and great was the company of those who published it."

Book design copyright © 2011 by Tate Publishing, LLC. All rights reserved.
Cover design by Shawn Collins
Interior design by Joel Uber
Edited by Aubrey Kinat

Published in the United States of America

ISBN: 978-1-61346-310-9
1. History: Military, World War II
2. Biography & Autobiography: Historical
11.06.28

WINGS
AND A
RING

DEDICATION

345TH BOMBARDMENT GROUP

Photo of original "Warpath" courtesy of Lloyd Sullivan.

To the wonderful men of the 345th Bombardment Group *Air Apaches*, I dedicate this book to commemorate all that you did during WWII to keep the United States of America free. Your sacrifices and gumption are the fabric that is woven into the history of these great United States. Amidst the atrocities of war, your *git-r-done* attitude and your sense of humor provided the fuel to bring this story alive. Stories of your generation's deeds have been told many times over, but my dream is to convey your everyday story so we can learn that, even in our most difficult hours, life moves on and romance will always find a way.

Bombardment Squadrons of the 345th Bombardment Group: 498th *Falcons*, 499th *Bats Outa' Hell*, 500th *Rough Raiders*, 501st *Black Panthers* (AKA *Tree Top Terrors*)

I love you guys!

The Central Texas (Centex) Wing

Commemorative Air Force, San Marcos, Texas

*Photo of Yellow Rose crew courtesy of Jim Liles,
The Centex Wing, CAF, San Marcos, TX.*

A special thanks to the forward-thinking volunteers who so generously keep the memories alive by providing a participatory museum of the historic aircraft of WWII.

One of their warbirds is a B-25J Mitchell bomber, christened the *Yellow Rose*, providing visitors with hands-on experience of what it was like for James Richard Jones and hundreds of like pilots and crews as they flew over New Guinea in the early days of the Southwest Pacific Area.

www.centexwing.com

ACKNOWLEDGMENTS

Glenna Racer-Riggan
Friend extraordinaire—Thanks for keeping me on track and on task. Your help in transcribing the first half of the letters allowed us to spend hours on the phone as we discovered this beautiful story. Your heart of gold stands out as a beacon of light to all who know you.

Suzie Jones Neff
Daughter of J.R. and Elnora Jones—Thanks for sharing your parents' love story to inspire and educate a new generation of readers on the personal realities of war. The insight you provided breathed life into the soul of this book.

Lawrence J. Hickey
Historian and author—your sacrificial efforts to document the true story of war is overwhelming and inspiring.

Lloyd Sullivan
Photographer extraordinaire—your attention to detail in enhancing the pictures in this book is significant in telling their story.

Melvin Best
WWII veteran and member of the 345th Bombardment Group from its activation to its deactivation—your willingness to share your personal stories is like icing on the cake.

Marshall Riggan
WWII veteran who served as a radar operator in the Fifth Air Force in New Guinea and father-in-law of Glenna Racer-Riggan—Thanks for providing pictures for the book.

Glee Smith
WWII veteran and Delta Tau Delta fraternity brother of J.R. Jones—Thanks for your service to the Kansas State Legislature and The University of Kansas.

Stacy Baker, Tate Publishing & Enterprises, LLC—your belief in my work meant the world to me. Thanks for providing the vehicle to make my dream come true.

Countless friends—you have endured hours of listening to me going crazy, telling you of the endless facts I learned in the process of writing this book and about the greatest generation and their wartime stories.

Kenton D. Armstrong
Husband and declared *Licensed Dumpster-Diver*—your finding the letters started this amazing journey. Thanks for standing by me and supporting me in my efforts—always and forever.

Most of all, I would also like to thank my Lord and Savior, Jesus Christ, for allowing me the opportunity to work on this book. As a two-time cancer survivor, God's not finished with me yet!

TABLE OF CONTENTS

Foreword	15
Introduction	19
Who Were These Sweethearts?	25
Zowie, Out Walks Miss Bartlett and My Eyes Popped Out a Foot!	39
A Fateful Decision: December 1941	45
The Same Music Was Playing	49
Look Out for the Measles	57
New Guinea: Warfront and Tokyo Rose	63
The Jungle: 501st, Movies and the Music Continues	79
The Big Treat: Fresh Potatoes and a Haircut	97
A Falling Bomb Doesn't Whistle: It Roars	113
I Guess Irving Berlin Was Right	125
How About a Date This Evening?	141
Wings and a Ring: The Long-Awaited Picture	153
If This is Sunday, I'll Eat My Hat	163
Comin' In On a Wing and a Prayer	181
Look Out: Yank Driving!	195
That Pink Paper is Beginning to Get to Me	203
A Movie, an Air Raid, More Rain, and a Game of Golf	221

Lord, I Must Be the Only One of the Bunch Not Married	235
Finally a Pilot: Bombing, More Bombing, a Drink, and Debriefing	243
Flying, but at What Price: The Fate of the Tree Top Terrors	261
The Fruitcake Will Probably Pass On This Evening	267
They Changed the Rules: Hopes of Home Seem So Far Away	281
Enough of the Hardships of the War	285
The Music Became So Potent: Kostelanetz to Jazz	297
A Purple Heart and Precious Little Sleep	311
The Wayward Footlocker	321
The Chow Hound: Eating in Style Again	327
Air Medal: Courage and Devotion to Duty	347
The Front Line and the Frat Brothers	355
The Long Boat Ride Home: Daydreams of a Certain Redhead Running Through My Mind	377
Mrs. Jones, Meet the New Mrs. Jones	381
The Rest of the Story	387
Journey of Discovery	403
Afterword	419
Bibliography	427
Contact Information	429

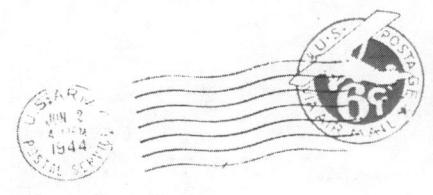

FOREWORD

The wartime letters between GIs and family are undoubtedly the most forgotten and undocumented records of war. Letters to family, friends, wives, and lovers were the lifeline of these brave souls to a world far away from the torrents of battle. These valuable artifacts that detail the human side of war are very often shuffled to the attic, forgotten or relegated to a junk store where their fate is most certain. Along with these discarded and forgotten letters are stories of joy, hardship, triumphs, and the everyday life-experiences of the millions of GIs who served and fought not only in WWII, but in all conflicts. Thousands of stories will go by the wayside, unnoticed, undocumented—except this one.

This is the story of one bunch of letters that narrowly escaped the ultimate fate. They were pulled back from the brink by a casual visit to a Texas City junk store, but only to sit in a storage area for four more years. Once discovered for the second time and reviewed, the letters revealed a story that not only describes the daily affairs of a brave young WWII pilot, but of the ongoing romance to the fiancée he left back in the states. This is the story of Lt. James R. Jones, better known as J.R., a B-25 pilot assigned to the 501st Squadron of the 345th Bombardment Group—the legendary Air Apaches. J.R., and hundreds of pilots and air crews

like him, flew the missions and brought the war to the Japanese using new, radical tactics and employing the most heavily armed aircraft of WWII, a modified B-25 outfitted with numerous guns and bombs. These gutsy pilots attacked Japanese strongholds and shipping lines at wave-top level from New Guinea to the Philippines, using this weapon to devastating effects, but at an extraordinarily high toll. While the 345th expended munitions at astronomic rates and destroyed more shipping than any other unit in the South Pacific, they also lost the most crews. During the 16 months the 345th was active over 712 men did not return.

Faced with these insurmountable odds, J.R. manages to keep his cool during his 50 combat missions as evidenced by the letters he sends to Elnora, his fiancée. J.R.'s letter writing, over 1,500 handwritten pages in the course of three years, enables him to establish a single-minded goal to make it out of the meat grinder known as the Southwest Pacific Theater. The "wartime censors" prohibited J.R. from writing about the daily experience of war, but by reading carefully between the lines and comparing the missions and daily logs to his letters, you can sense his struggle and determination to achieve his ultimate goal, to wed the redhead he left back in Texas.

While reviewing *Wings and a Ring* it brought back many memories of my own father's letters from the same conflict and the very same squadron, the 501st. Ironically, the combat tours of Lt. J.R. Jones and my father, Lt. Ed Bina, crossed paths in the same jungles, on the same airstrips, and perhaps on the same missions, but we'll never know. I saw a unique resemblance in the letters of both pilots though as they both wrote about similar experiences and observations, such as the extreme living conditions, lousy chow, long hours at work, the makeshift entertainment, the desire to see their families again, and to get back to the real world and pursue their dreams and ambitions.

With *Wings and a Ring* Ms. Armstrong brings a new and unique twist to the personal accounts of WWII veterans, a view of the wartime theater seen vicariously through the veteran's eyes by a seldom seen artifact, GI's letters. Ms. Armstrong brings the romance of J.R. and Elnora to life in a masterful way. She and J.R. lay out the story so well that in many instances I found myself in New Guinea sitting on a cot across from J.R. watching him write his letters while the radio was playing Sinatra or a ditty by Glenn Miller. Between the two of them, Ms. Armstrong and J.R. did a fine job of putting the reader in the middle of the theater.

In many instances GI's letters are filed away in a dusty trunk or dilapidated box in the corner of a closet or garage. The letters of my Dad are tucked away safely, waiting to be scanned and eventually to be passed down and shared as part of a family heirloom. Most families I'm sure say with confidence "I'll get something done with those this winter…," but there they remain, forgotten. The letters of J.R. were brought back from a near certain fate of destruction by someone who not only saw a wartime diary of a pilot, but also of a long-distance romance that needed to be told to the world.

Wings and a Ring gives a fascinating and rare account of what life was like during wartime operations. It gave me a greater depth of understanding and feel for the challenges that J.R., my dad, and thousands of others went through on a daily basis. I encourage succeeding generations to take interest in works like *Wings and a Ring* as it brings a very personal and human element to the daily grind of wartime operations, and that these men, including J.R., were determined to succeed regardless of the cost. Most importantly it shows that life didn't stop because of the war, but rather life went on in spite of the war.

James Bina
President, 345th Bombardment Group Association
Second Generation

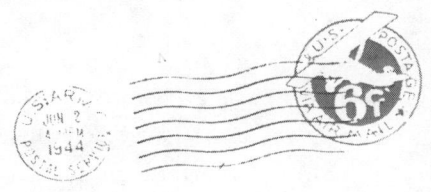

INTRODUCTION

Photo of James Richard Jones courtesy of Suzie Jones Neff.

Romance has a voice of its own. Somehow, it has to be heard over the everyday voice—the trials of making a living and just getting by. Wartime romance is yet another voice that demands to be heard over orders and duty stations, and being sent over there.

Theirs was a wartime romance whose voice was heard fifty-eight years later as it cried out to be listened to, demanding that someone pay attention to a long-lost affair. The discovery of the letters in a junk store in Texas City, Texas, was ordained by a dying woman's profound statement to her daughter: "I hope someday someone writes a book about these letters, because it is a love story that needs to be told."

When my husband, Ken, found a box of 295 letters, he knew they were a record of something special, but little did he realize just how profound a piece of history he had acquired until we transcribed these words into a document. Sitting down and reading the over fifteen-hundred handwritten pages took me on the journey of discovery of a time that was gentler and kinder, even in the midst of war. The time period of 1941-1944 allowed people to fall in love and marry even though they might have only known each other for a few, short, glorious days.

Photo of Helen Elnora Bartlett courtesy of Suzie Jones Neff.

Thus began a journey to discover who these two young people were, who met on a blind date, communicating to each other over three years in the only way that this era could afford—through love letters that encompassed two continents and the ravages of war.

Censorship is something that seems so foreign to the average twenty-first century American. However, this was wartime and *"loose lips might sink ships"* was the standard for censorship in WWII. In his letters, James Richard Jones (J.R.) could only state that he flew today, for if he spoke of details, they would literally be cut out of his letters. Armed with that understanding, he only had to experience the loss of his words to the scissors of the censors once. From then on, he stuck to the rules while communicating his love to Helen Elnora Bartlett (Elnora).

Providence has a way of speaking to you, enabling you to find the truth behind extraordinary circumstances. As I began the journey of discovery, Col. Henry A. Kortemeyer, member of the 345th Bombardment Group said, "buy Lawrence J. Hickey's book, *The Warpath Across the Pacific*, and it will give you an understanding of what your pilot went through." Wanting to find out more, I eagerly purchased the book and devoured it. The pictures were amazing, but the stories I found there jumped off the pages and became alive right before me.

Photo of B-25 cockpit courtesy of the Lawrence J. Hickey Collection.

In my naivety, I picked up the phone and called the publisher, hoping to get to speak to the author. I explained my desire to discover the history of the 345th Bombardment Group by speaking to a man who has the single largest private collection of pictures of the Southwest Pacific Area. I wanted to see where J.R. flew and fought. I wanted to understand the wartime conditions he so aptly described in his letters to Elnora. What I didn't expect was to receive from Mr. Hickey copies of the mission logs, intelligence reports, and unit history of the time period of August, 1943, through August, 1944, when J.R. was in New Guinea.

Enhanced with official, now declassified, government documents, the story of the love affair of James Richard Jones and Helen Elnora Bartlett unfolds as he writes to his sweetheart from the jungles of New Guinea. Now I understood what J.R. went through in the eyes of history.

Extending an Invitation

At the end of their story, I have included my own, added solely because J.R. and Elnora's daughter, Suzie Jones Neff, challenged me to include it in this work. I wanted to remain true only to their story, but she said the book wouldn't be complete without my journey.

I invite you to read between the lines and see the conflict that J.R. surely felt as he writes of his unending love for his redhead amidst the realities of bombs, bugs, and never-ending rain and mud. These realities of war can somehow coexist with the gentleness of romance.

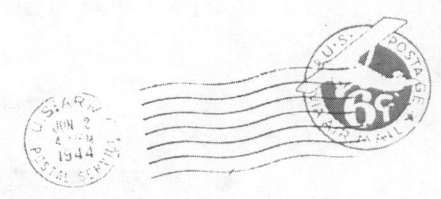

WHO WERE THESE SWEETHEARTS?

"JUST A DANCE, A SONG, AN EVENING OF LAUGHTER, AND THERE IT WAS."

Thus begins the story of the wartime romance of J.R. and Elnora. A blind date with a redhead would forever change the course of life for this Indiana farm boy.

James Richard Jones

Photo of James Richard Jones courtesy of Suzie Jones Neff.

James Richard Jones (J.R.) was just an average boy growing up on a small farm in Indiana. Playing baseball and riding bikes were the typical everyday activities. As J.R. was entering his teen years, he quickly discovered how lucky he was that his family would have access to the necessities once the Great Depression hit. Farming proved to be a hard way of making a living, and the migration of the population from rural to urban had begun. The doors were opened to a new way of living for J.R., and an education was just the vehicle he needed to join the masses as they quickly marched toward the city.

*Photo of J.R. Jones courtesy of University Archives,
Spencer Research Library, University of Kansas Libraries.*

Though small in stature, J.R. was a big man on campus at Kansas University, Lawrence, Kansas [now commonly known as The University of Kansas]. He matriculated in the fall of 1938 and earned a scholarship as a track star, eventually holding the Big Six track record for the broad jump. A college student's life was so different than his mother's family background of farming in Indiana. His mother had encouraged him to stretch his wings and be what he dreamed. J.R. decided to pursue finance with an ultimate goal of attending law school.

*Photo of Delta Tau Delta fraternity brothers
courtesy of the Delta Tau Delta Educational Foundation.
J.R. is seated at the piano on the right.*

J.R. started college when America was not yet involved in WWII. There was nothing standing in the way of achieving his goals, short of his own discipline to work hard and study smart. Life at college in the late 1930s and early 1940s held many distractions, particularly in the form of fraternity life. Though on a scholarship, he needed money to support his decision to live in a fraternity house, and J.R. decided to work off his expenses by serving meals and cleaning dining tables at the Delta Tau Delta Fraternity House. Glee clubs, panty raids, practical jokes, and sneaking a drink were the typical culprits that competed for study time. Dances were the highlight of the social scene and were headed up by big bands such as Tommy Dorsey's Orchestra.

WINGS AND A RING

Photo of Delta Tau Delta Fraternity at Kansas
University 1939–40 courtesy of University Archives,
Spencer Research Library, University of Kansas Libraries.
James Richard "J.R." Jones (2nd row from bottom, 2nd from left)
Charles "Smooch" Soller (3rd row from bottom, 4th from left)
Paul "Shields" Haerle (2nd row from top, last on right)

Photo of officers of Delta Tau Delta at Kansas University courtesy of the Delta
Tau Delta Educational Foundation.
Charles "Smooch" Soller is in the middle with
James Richard "J.R." Jones to his right.

J.R. often spoke of Mother Landes, the housemother of the Delta Tau Delta Fraternity House. She made sure her boys were well taken care of and the fraternity house was in good order. She was truly like a mother to the boys and spent many hours talking with them. She was someone to come to, not only for counsel in problems of everyday life but also in the affairs of the heart. Glee Smith, a fellow fraternity brother of J.R., told me that the girls often spent more time talking and playing cards with Mother Landes than they did with their dates. I can only imagine the sense of gratitude that many a mother felt for Mother Landes, since their baby boys were so far away from home.

One of J.R.'s fraternity brothers, Paul "Shields" Haerle, was in love with a Texas gal named Daurice Smith. Being adventuresome souls, J.R. and another fraternity brother, Charles "Smooch" Soller, made the trip with Shields to Houston to visit Daurice. It was during this trip in August of 1941 that J.R. met Elnora.

Helen Elnora Bartlett

Elnora was very outgoing and never met a stranger, but in every way, she was frighteningly charming. She may never have uttered a curse word, but she had the ability to bless you out in sixteen-letter words; being a redhead makes you a little different.

She was the absolute pride of her father, Brady Bartlett. He used to take her to his insurance office to show her off. But since he had black hair and her mother was a blonde, he quickly grew tired of the redheaded milkman jokes. When he had had enough, her father grew a beard to show that it too was red.

Even though she was usually at the bottom of any mischief going on, she was very mindful that she was never to embarrass her parents by her behavior. She absolutely insisted on being treated like a lady. Suzie remembered her mother relating that once her dad got fresh with her and she *cold-cocked* him—Elnora's words.

The Bartlett family was somewhere between upper middle class and society. Elnora grew up during the depression and her family's wealth was impacted greatly by the stock market crash. But, just as in the South after the Civil War, there was a lot of genteel, high-society poor. Her father was a Shriner; her mother belonged to the Eastern Star, Junior League, Daughters of the American Revolution, and United Daughters of the Confederacy. She could draw and paint well. She also took ballet lessons from the time she was six. She was a talented, if not accomplished, toe dancer. She could not sing a note, as her voice was too deep, but she was always enthralled with J.R.'s musical ability. They both loved music.

RENÉ PALMER ARMSTRONG

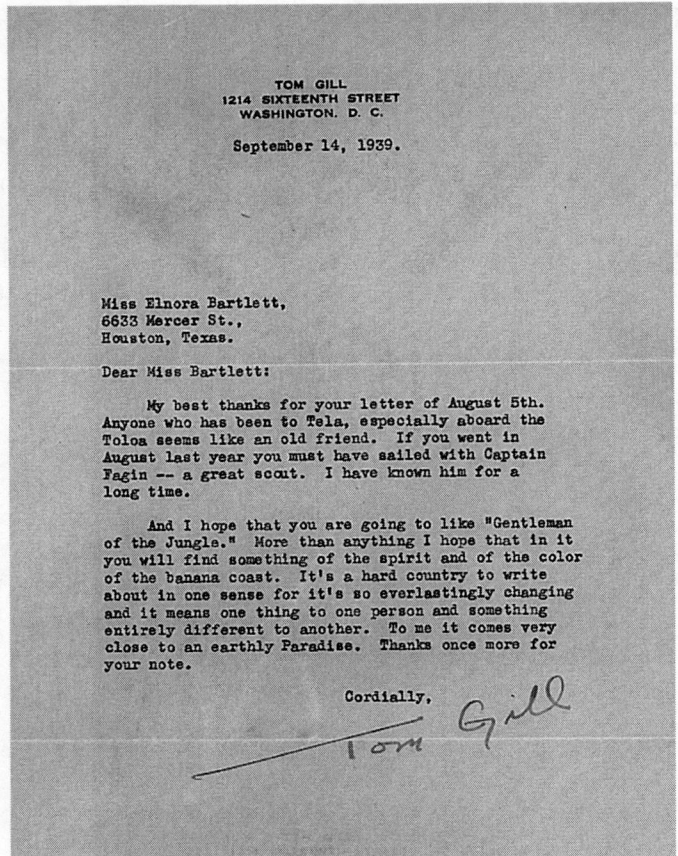

Photo of Tom Gill letter courtesy of Lloyd Sullivan.

The Bartletts traveled extensively when she was young. They took cruises and also visited Cuba. She met Tom Gill, author of *Gentleman of the Jungle*, on one of her trips, as she accompanied her Aunt Wilhelmena to the banana trade coast of Latin America aboard the ship Toloa. As an impressionable young lady, she fell in love with the Latin culture and dark-skinned, dark-eyed, young men. This trip had a lasting impact on her, as it was love at first sight for her when she saw the dark-haired, dark-eyed J.R. Jones on that fateful blind date in 1941.

Elnora was just an average child with a few advantages. The family had a lake house, somewhere near Athens, Texas, that backed up to Clint Murchison's family's property [founder of the Dallas Cowboys football team]. They used to swim together, and their daughter can remember Elnora speaking with Clint every now and then on the phone.

She constantly ran around with two growing-up friends, Mary Lee and Jane. She took ballet lessons, rode horses and attended her mother's teas and garden parties, and various Shriner social functions.

Elnora went to school with Marvin Zindler. His family owned Zindler's Menswear in Houston. Suzie, Elnora's daughter, informed me they went from elementary school through high school together, and used to ride horses down the dirt path now known as Houston's Bellaire Boulevard. She had a quarter-horse named Beauty that was mean as a snake, a biter and a kicker, and would intentionally puff up to make the saddle slide off if you didn't elbow her before cinching it. Elnora's father used to have to catch her and re-break her if she wasn't ridden for a few weeks. Beauty was the perfect horse for Elnora because Elnora was meaner. She and a few friends, Marvin included, used to ride up and down in the Bellaire area of Houston on land that used to be pastures in the 20s and 30s. Elnora told Suzie that once, Marvin and Jimmy, while racing their horses, ended up jumping into some poor lady's front yard and right into her flower beds.

Elnora drove a car at age ten; they let them do that back then. Elnora drove Marvin down to Allen's Landing to stage a shooting competition, somewhere around the ripe old age of ten or eleven. Marvin bragged that his new rifle could outshoot Elnora's father's bone-handled, silver-plated .45. Since Elnora never backed off a challenge in her life, they decided they would settle the matter right then and there. Suzie never did know who won, but she would probably bet on her mom, as she was a dead shot with the .45 and a wrist rocket slingshot. Suzie believes her mother's maid, Jane, tattled on them about the shootout. Elnora's father was at work and, when he heard what was going on, he left work and found them, then read them the riot act. However, it didn't seem to have affected either one of them.

Note: Marvin Zindler was a Houston-area television celebrity. His investigative reporting on the infamous Chicken Ranch near La Grange, Texas, made him famous with the Broadway and film musical *The Best Little Whorehouse In Texas*, giving him nation-wide exposure. Unfortunately, I learned of their connection too late, as Mr. Zindler died in 2007. I can only imagine the stories I could have gleaned from him, and I believe that he could have provided me with pictures of some of their youthful adventures. Those of us who grew up in the Houston area will always remember his famous byline—*Maaaarvin Zindler, Eeeeyewitness News*!

Elnora was not allowed to date individually while in high school. She either had to have a family escort, usually her brother, or attend gatherings at the homes of people whom Elnora's mother approved. She also went in a group with Jane and Mary Lee. Before Elnora was allowed to attend a party at someone's house, Mrs. Jones had to know their *pedigree*.

Elnora graduated from Mirabeau B. Lamar Senior High School, Houston in the spring of 1939. While looking through the 1939 Lamar yearbook, *The Orenda*, I found a picture of Elnora in a formal dress. She belonged to Le Cercle Français, a club to promote interest in French and to provide extra-curricular activity for the students of the language. Along with J.R.'s letters to Elnora, I also found numerous invitations to teas, coffees, luncheons, and garden parties marking graduation celebrations of some of her classmates. Following graduation, Elnora enrolled in Texas State College for Women (now Texas Woman's University) in Denton, Texas, but transferred to Texas Technological College (now Texas Tech University) in Lubbock, Texas, majoring in home economics.

Elnora met J.R. before Pearl Harbor was bombed. After that life-changing event, Elnora finished her spring semester at college and then went to work as a secretary at Brown Shipbuilding Company in Houston. This company fabricated sub chasers and landing craft for the U.S. Navy. In some small way, this was Elnora's sacrifice for the war effort. J.R.'s letters indicate that she was good at what she did, as he noted in one of his letters that she received a raise, and he joked that perhaps he should consider letting her make the money while he sat at home living in the lap of luxury.

Elnora's days were filled with work, but her evenings were often filled with parties attended by flyboys from nearby Ellington Field, a training facility for flyboys and bombardiers. Her striking red hair and bright green eyes had quite an impact upon all she met. Her beauty did not go unnoticed. Even though Elnora had only been on two dates with J.R. in August of 1941, she had an idea that he would be someone special in her life. However, being the beautiful belle that she was, it turns out that she had another date that evening, and their day two was cut short, much to the chagrin of J.R. It appears that he found out about it and enjoyed poking a few jabs at her as he recounts their initial days together! She must have been one striking young lady, with just enough daredevil in her to attempt two dates in one evening.

During one of my visits with their daughter, Suzie, she spoke of the infamous front porch mentioned in the day two recap. Elnora's parents' bedroom was located directly over the front porch. The story goes that when a young man was bringing Elnora home and the good-byes were taking a little too long, Mr. Bartlett would let his shoe drop on the wooden bedroom floor above, signaling to Elnora that it was time for the young man to leave.

Unfortunately, due to a family fire, only a few pictures remain of Elnora and they are not of good enough quality to present here. When their daughter's house burned to the ground, the only wall standing was the one with the two pictures shown in the introduction. The fire chief called the survival of those two pictures nothing short of miraculous. Their original frames still show signs of soot.

THE CIRCLE OF FRIENDS

In order to fully understand the story in *Wings and a Ring*, I want to introduce some of the key players. Life has a way of pushing one toward his destiny. Interactions with casual acquaintances and close personal friends mold us into the people we become, impacting us for a lifetime.

Elnora attended Lamar High School with Roger Smith. Roger had a younger sister named Daurice. It was Daurice Smith who introduced J.R. and Elnora. From my research, I found that the Smiths had a ranch somewhere to the west of Houston. It must have been a wonderful place, even having a register for visiting guests. J.R. also speaks of *Technicolor* moving pictures recording some of their time at the ranch, signaling the fact that the Smith family was a family of means, able to have, for the times, such expensive technology.

Mrs. Vivian L. Smith took it upon herself to be the personal matchmaker for J.R. and Elnora. She wanted to make sure they had every opportunity to get together. At a time when casual/pleasure driving was not allowed and gas rationing was enforced, J.R. would fly into Ellington Field in Houston, and Mrs. Smith saw to it that Elnora was able to meet him. A young couple in love couldn't have asked for a better friend.

Roger Smith was also a pilot in WWII and became a prisoner of war in Italy. J.R. mentions Roger throughout his letters and showed great concern that his friend had been captured. Roger eventually was released and returned home, graduating from Rice University in Houston.

ZOWIE, OUT WALKS MISS BARTLETT AND MY EYES POPPED OUT A FOOT!

The two years of J.R.'s letters written from October 1941 through July 1943 are not all included in this book. Obviously I was not present to know first-hand what happened, but by studying excerpts from his letters and using his actual words when possible, I have recapped the events and emotions that occurred.

Their letters are the platform on which this story is built. Remember, they were together only eleven days from the time they met until the time he flew to New Guinea. Since he couldn't physically be with her, his letters became his courting tools as he tried to woo her with his words. His competition was everywhere with nearby Ellington Field being a hub of activity for aviators and bombardiers. A male friend of mine who read the letters called J.R. one love sick puppy. J.R. was truly smitten by Elnora and did his best to convey his love. Keep in mind, since this was wartime, he was not able to tell her some of his activities and the details of his training due to censorship.

Blind Date with a Redhead

Day One: Saturday, August 30, 1941, Houston, Texas

A blind date can be a great adventure or a terrible disaster. J.R. had gone out on another blind date the night before he met Elnora, and she practically drank him under the table, but he admired her for her enormous beer capacity. He figured if he had an extremely attractive date the night before, he couldn't possibly do so well the next night. He also had misgivings about redheads, stating they were either "extremely good looking or extremely *good God!*"

He didn't know quite what to expect, but he told himself that it was only for an evening and that at least he could be civil to the girl. The laugh was on him as he went to the door and, *zowie*, out walks Miss Bartlett and his eyes popped out a foot. Never had he wanted so strongly for an evening not to end. So began an evening that stood out in his mind to him as few others had.

He was clearly smitten by her, and when she flashed that devastating smile of hers his way, he wilted. He wondered if she exerted such charm on all men, or just him.

They went to the Southern Diner Club in Houston, Texas. He said in his letter, "We'd dance, I'd step back to talk to you, you'd smile such a pretty smile. I said to myself, 'look out J.R. you're going,' then you'd smile again, and I didn't have to be convinced." He remembered everything about that evening, right down to the last detail. He told her she was the one beautiful dream he had when he was wide awake.

I learned it was not only love at first sight for J.R., but it was also the same for Elnora. They kissed on their first date and J.R. had never done that before. He felt right then and there she was to be a part of his future. Their favorite song was "Everything I Love," and he asked her, "When you hear the band play 'Everything I Love,' think of me. If you do, the next time we meet, I'll be no stranger."

The following is an excerpt from one of Elnora's letters that was not mailed to J.R.:

> "You speak of a memory of a very lovely evening—that one evening and all the memories will remain with me forever. You thought I was thinking of someone else when I mentioned 'Everything I Love,' didn't you—or am I wrong again?
>
> "It was a carefree laugh and a clasp of hands with a promise of tomorrow, but tomorrow hasn't come yet."

A Lazy Sunday Afternoon at the Smith Ranch

Day Two: Sunday, August 31, 1941, Houston, Texas

Their second day together proved to be quite challenging, not because of their parting kiss the night before, but because he was so frustrated he was having to take her home early. He wanted so badly to tell her what he felt for her, but he knew it was best to leave such things unsaid. Their day on the Smith Ranch was pure torture because he wanted to get her alone, but was unable to do so. He thought if he could have held time back with his bare hands, he would have done just that.

He remembered word-by-word what was said, but he didn't dare say what was on his heart. He didn't want Elnora to think he was one of those one-night stand gentlemen. He told her that he spent most of his high school days flittering from pillar to post and that he knew she had a lot more of college left before her. He encouraged her to drag every ounce of enjoyment out of college that she could, realizing that when one is away from it, nothing can replace it. He stated, "Give all of the men a good run for their money, but love none until that day comes when you decide *he* is the one. You will find that distance will end more loves than a third person can ever do."

I discovered he wanted them to be more than friends, but he also didn't want them to move toward marriage, because he didn't believe that marrying, going off to war, and perhaps being killed was what he wanted for Elnora—he didn't want to make her a widow. He told her, "Have a good time. You can be in love with someone and never be near him, and still have a great deal of fun. You may forget me as quickly as you met me, but I doubt if I let you." J.R. felt he had met the best girl in Texas, and he wanted to remember her and love her for who she was.

As he brought her home early on that Sunday, he wondered if he would ever see her again. If only he had known that she was smitten in the same manner he was. Her front porch seemed to be their beginning and end.

Returning to Kansas University for his senior year, J.R. made it through rush week, but then received his induction notice only two days before school began. He was inducted on September 26, 1941, at Ft. Harrison in South Bend, Indiana, and he was sent from Ft. Harrison to Camp Wallace, Texas. He spent forty-two hours on a train before arriving on October 2, 1941, and after that many hours, he would have been happy even to have gotten off in hell. He wasn't quite sure that he hadn't. He lovingly referred to Camp Wallace as Swamp Wallace; it was mostly marshlands with lots of mosquitoes and continual hot and humid weather.

As a private in the army, he received $21.00 a month; after all the deductions, he wound up with $15.52. He quickly came to realize that infantry life and peeling potatoes was not what he wanted to do. He told Elnora that he hadn't committed any social errors, but it was merely his time to peel spuds, joking that his fingers were plenty tired and that he was developing a good set of dishpan hands. He also had improved quite a bit with a rifle under Uncle Sam's tutelage. He started to work in an office, and that type of work kept him from doing K.P. [kitchen police]. He didn't like marching, comparing it to monotonous plodding up and down on flat country without even an anthill to break against the horizon.

On December 2, 1941, he wrote to Elnora that he had requested a transfer to the U.S. Army Air Corps to be a pilot. Little did he know that five days later, his world, along with our nation, would be turned upside down with the Japanese bombing of Pearl Harbor. He was at the Smith Ranch on that Sunday, December 7th, when he heard about the bombing, and he expressed to Elnora that he knew he would be leaving quickly for pilot training. He sent his regrets that he couldn't whip up an interesting conversation in his letter, but upon his return to the barracks, there was such an uproar that it was very difficult for him to think.

A FATEFUL DECISION: DECEMBER 1941

CHRISTMAS EVE AND ELNORA

DAY THREE: WEDNESDAY, DECEMBER 24, 1941,
HOUSTON, TEXAS, AND CAMP WALLACE, HITCHCOCK, TEXAS

Scan of Camp Wallace stationary courtesy of Lloyd Sullivan.

It was Christmas Eve and all J.R. really wanted for Christmas was to be with Elnora. Their last day together in August had been difficult for him. The questions in his mind were quickly put aside as soon as he had his arms around her. All he could remember was that one brief Christmas Eve when the whole world seemed to stand still and nothing else seemed to matter. She was a magnet to him, and he knew her attraction would draw him back to her once this war was over. With the attack on Pearl Harbor, everyone's life had changed, and he knew he would be leaving soon to begin flight training. Elnora's friend, Roger, felt the same way as J.R., and they were both full of the spirit to fly for the United States. He told Elnora there should be someone like her for every man to come back to, even though they had but a few sweet evenings together.

The song "White Christmas" was certainly popular with the soldiers. J.R. reminisced there would be more people away from home that Christmas than there had ever been before.

He and Elnora went to see a show, but he concluded it was a foolish waste of time because he had his mind so thoroughly on Elnora—he didn't see much of it.

The Only Real Christmas Present

Day Four: Thursday, December 25, 1941, Houston, Texas, and Camp Wallace, Hitchcock, Texas

J.R. was aware that Elnora was sizing him up to see if he was the same guy, and his fears were again dismissed when he realized she did care for him.

He thought of their relationship, short though it was. He wanted desperately to propose to her. Even when he would be commissioned, he could never ask anyone to marry him. He just couldn't bring himself to believe it was right to marry and then leave a wife, perhaps to die. He told Elnora he often pondered the thought, and then asked her if she thought she could ever be happy under such circumstances.

As the day drew to an end, he told her she was the nicest Christmas present he had ever received and wished he could get it again next year. He boldly told her the only *real* Christmas present was her love.

Tomorrow Hasn't Arrived Yet

Day Five: Friday, December 26, 1941, Houston, Texas, and Camp Wallace, Hitchcock, Texas

J.R. and Elnora went dancing at the Hi-Hat the last night they were together. That night they went around the dance floor, and he had her in his arms, looking at her and telling himself how wonderful he thought she was. He wished this was the way every night would be when they were together. He had fire in his eyes and in his heart, and that inevitably meant a redhead. Neither of them said much that last night—they just sat and drank and were lost in their own thoughts.

He wanted to get her alone and talk with her about his emotions and their future. He envisioned they could have a couple of drinks and start to chat. There would be quiet music in the background, music that haunts your mind. He imagined it would have been delightful to make her laugh, to tell her all the things they never had time for. However, he thought they knew each other very well, in spite of their brief time together.

Both of them loved music and often wrote in their letters about the latest record they had heard. One of the songs was "You Made Me Love You" by Harry James. J.R. commented that it really was a beauty, but the title wasn't very applicable to them. He told her one time when he was in New Orleans, he got himself very comfortably situated in a bar. There, they had a record machine that required an operator to play the selections. With over a thousand selections, he really had a hey-day.

J.R. had only a few days before shipping out to Maxwell Field, Alabama, and it was torture for him not to be able to spend them with Elnora. If the time had been his own, he would have been with her. It was such a sinking feeling for him to know she was such a short distance away and he could not take advantage of it.

At the back gate of Camp Wallace, J.R. kissed Elnora good night and said, "So long, I'll see you tomorrow." Tomorrow hadn't arrived yet, but that look on her face lingered with him. It was cold walking back to the barracks, and his mind was full of strange thoughts. He still could hardly believe he had come across someone such as Elnora.

Elnora's letter to J.R. that she never mailed after Christmas, 1941:

> Oh, but I miss your slaphappy wit and your kisses, and I know I'll miss you more than I will ever know and more than you can imagine before I see you again.
>
> I can hardly wait for your next letters, for the last was so wonderful. If I read it once, I know I have read it ten times.

Soon after their three days together, J.R. traveled by train to Maxwell Field, feeling quite important traveling first-class and receiving three dollars a day for food. This was not bad compared to what he had been doing.

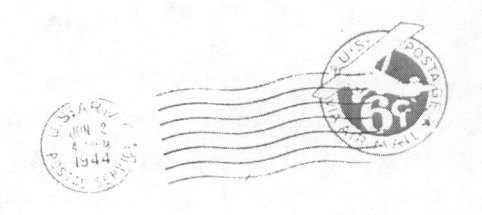

THE SAME MUSIC WAS PLAYING

From Maxwell Field, J.R. was sent to the Air Corps Training Detachment in Bennettsville, South Carolina, where J.R. progressed through his flight training and completed his first solo flight on July 22, 1942. It is my understanding that, to pilots, the first solo flight is a real milestone. Elnora was proud of his accomplishments and provided him with an identification bracelet to commemorate that important date. J.R. soon began to call this bracelet a *crash bracelet* and spoke quite often of it in his letters.

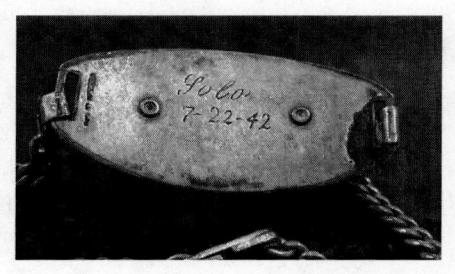

Photo of J.R.'s crash bracelet courtesy of Lloyd Sullivan.
[J.R. Jones – first solo flight 7-22-42.]

Unlike J.R., many couples decided to marry before they were shipped off to war. Marie Richter of Port O'Connor, Texas, now ninety years old, told me she married her sweetheart, Lee, the day before he received his wings, which really was against army policy. While stationed in Tampa, Florida, to receive advanced flying, Lee and other crew members were required to do nocturnal flight training. Unfortunately, some guys would never return from these training exercises. To help calm the nerves of the wives during these nighttime exercises, the war-brides joined together at the movies to watch the latest releases and then returned to the base, waiting for their husbands to come home. When the last flight had landed and one of the planes did not return, the group would surround the grieving widow and support her in her loss. Marie shared the following saying, "One a day in Tampa Bay." It must have been overwhelming for these young brides to experience this kind of loss at such an early age.

J.R. received additional training at Shaw Field and Moody Field in Sumter, South Carolina, and eventually was stationed at Greenville Army Air Base in Greenville, South Carolina. After receiving his wings in December, 1942, he spent Christmas at home with his parents in Indiana. He then began to receive his training in many different disciplines, including aerial gunnery. He thought it was odd that he was trained in this way, as he believed he would be flying the B-25 Mitchell, a medium bomber. However, history would soon record he would be joining an amazing group that would use the B-25 in innovative ways never seen before. This advance training was frustrating to J.R. because many of his friends were shipped out soon after receiving their wings. He wanted to complete his service and return to his redhead.

All the Right Questions and All the Right Answers

Day Six: Saturday, May 22, 1943, Ellington Field and the Hi-Hat, Houston, Texas

Photo of J.R. Jones courtesy of Suzie Jones Neff.

With this delay in being shipped out, J.R seized the opportunity to see Elnora again. That last night at Camp Wallace, he said he would see her tomorrow. He had no idea how far into the future tomorrow would be—December 26, 1941, all the way to May 22, 1943. He was able to schedule a training flight to Ellington Field. He called her at 5:30 p.m. from Lake Charles, Louisiana, to make a date and flew many miles to meet her at 7:00 p.m. A rainstorm was forecasted, and since he had looked so forward to seeing her, he wasn't about to let something like that stop him.

The intensity of the rainstorm had him a little more than worried and he was about to divert to San Antonio, Texas, when he found a hole to come through. He flew right over her house and felt like jumping out there—he couldn't wait to see her.

How excited he was to see Elnora and Mrs. Smith as they drove to meet him and his crew. He thought they would never get out to the field. They picked him up at the main gate of Ellington Field—only a few miles from where he had been dropped off two Decembers ago. Perhaps that it is why it seemed like only a day had passed since they had last seen each other.

He never ceased to be amazed at how completely natural that evening was; even though it seemed like it was the shortest evening on record, it was just like he had imagined it would be. J.R. stated, "As a pilot would say, when I first saw you again—I *spun in*." He saw a very contented, yet smug look on Elnora's face. He asked her all of the right questions and she gave him all of the right answers. He proposed to her at Ellington Field in front of Mrs. Smith and his crew. He couldn't believe that he was now engaged to this lovely girl, and that she managed to floor all of his crew. He came out with a future wife—Elnora Jones.

As they drove into town together in Mrs. Smith's car, he wanted to kiss her, but between the rain and the four other fellows in the car, he didn't have much of a chance. He got tickled thinking about the way she acted—looking so happy but not saying a word. He kept expecting her to go up in a cloud of smoke or something. When they went out to dance, all he could do was stare at her.

Nothing seemed to have changed very much in his absence. When they walked in the Hi-Hat, the same music was playing as it was before. He felt as if he had never been away. The band played "Don't Get Around Much Anymore"—which seemed to be his theme. "Missed the Saturday Dance"—he actually didn't miss it. "Couldn't Stand It Without You"—he knew she had spoiled him for anyone else.

He got to thinking about something that struck him oddly. When he flew to Houston, Elnora was wearing low heels. It occurred to him that she might have been afraid that she would have been taller than him. However, that she was taller and slimmer was the first thing he had noticed. He pondered if she would have cared if he had been an inch or two shorter; would she have put up with him anyhow?

The same music was playing: The Hi-Hat, Houston, Texas.

According to Dorothy Trahan, now eighty-six years old, the Hi-Hat was the happening place to be. I had the pleasure of speaking with Mrs. Trahan. Dorothy grew up in Houston and she said if you went anywhere, you went to the Hat, as it was fondly known by the youngsters at the time. She said you always remember your first dates and one of the most thrilling experiences of her mid-teen years was to dance the jitterbug all night long at the Hat. The Hat was the in place for the younger crowd; no gray hairs were found there. Unlike the Plantation, a larger night club with live music, the Hat only had a jukebox. The building was a wooden structure with a large dance floor in the middle. The jukebox was located at the opposite end from the entrance and the tables aligned the dance floor two-deep, close to the outside walls. She stated the Hat was like heaven, and even though you might have been too young, it was every girl's ambition to date a young man who could get you into the Hat. Dorothy married at age seventeen on August 29, 1942. WWII had been declared, and the boys were going off to war. All the girls married their sweethearts before they left, not knowing if their husbands would return. The concept today seems so romantic; the reality is that many would be made widows and life would never be the happy, carefree times they knew while dancing at the Hat.

My Mind Is Very Clear and So Is the Future

Day Seven: Sunday, May 23, 1943, Ellington Field, Houston, Texas

It is amazing that J.R. remembered what Elnora wore on that Sunday morning, the day after he proposed to her. He recounted how lovely she looked in her white dress. It baffled him that she could look so wonderful after staying up half the night, that she was the same beautiful woman as when he left her the evening before. He even asked if she did it with mirrors or something.

When she and Mrs. Smith drove out to Ellington to tell him good-bye, he asked her if she realized the consequences of his visit. He thought it would be easier for them having made the big decision. Now his mind was very clear and so was the future. They would have to get used to the idea that they were going to be apart. He reminded her how hard it would have been for them to say good-bye if they had been together for several days; in fact, it would have been nearly impossible. As he left, he questioned how he was lucky enough to become engaged to the beautiful girl whose pictures always sat on his desk.

He said good-bye to his pretty redhead. I'm sure he wondered if he would ever see her again. How would he get her the ring? He certainly wanted to place it on her hand. Would that chance present itself in the future? Leaving her that day must have been one of the hardest things he ever had to do. He had won her hand, but he would have to keep their love strong in his letters.

Mrs. Smith certainly played cupid for this lovesick couple. Remember, wartime rationing was in effect and gasoline was hard to come by. Pleasure driving was not something the average

American could afford. However, due to their family wealth and influence in Houston society, Mrs. Smith always found a way to get Elnora and J.R. together. J.R. was indebted to Mrs. Smith and thankful for the hand of friendship she extended to them.

All too soon, he returned to dear old Greenville. However, their wish had come true. He now believed the old adage that it only took a short time to change the course of one's life.

The ring purchasing process had him baffled to no end. He was lost in a maze of prices, points, and designs. He confessed the only thing he ever noticed about an engagement ring was whether a girl was wearing one if he wanted to ask her for a date. He was hoping that Elnora would have the same trouble and he wished the ring were on her finger at that instant. He hoped it was what she pictured in her mind and that it would fit her.

All he could offer her was his promise and the ring, as nothing else in his life could be promised due to the war. J.R. told her that even a diamond couldn't fully express what he thought of her, but he hoped it would help. He had never proposed to anyone before, and he didn't even part with his fraternity pin in college. About the only thing she had to worry about was Ubangi and Eskimo women, but as for his worries—well the combination of wings and a ring should keep the cadets off.

The only string attached to the ring was J.R. It was all paid for and he had done the best he could under the circumstances. However, as far as he was concerned, the Hope Diamond would be too small for Elnora, for he loved her so.

LOOK OUT FOR THE MEASLES

J.R. wrote Elnora expressing that it was possible he would be granted a few days of leave. It would take a lot of luck to enable them to see each other with her being in Houston and him being in Greenville, South Carolina. He boldly suggested they meet by train in Montgomery, Alabama, a place he had loved while being stationed there in his cadet days and a place he mentioned often in his letters to Elnora. He couldn't help but worry about her job situation. If she met him in Montgomery, he was afraid the absence from her job might cost her the job, and he would hate it very much if that happened. Elnora contrived a plan to fake having the measles.

He also knew they wouldn't have much time for plans, and he told her he would call or wire her as soon as he found out anything definite, asking her to keep her fingers crossed and pray. He desperately wanted to deliver the ring in person, and if it meant traveling all the way to Houston to stay only one day, he was willing to do it.

Elnora wrote back that she thought she could make Montgomery, and J.R. imagined he could get someone to fly him to a town close by so he could catch a train without too much difficulty. He also told Elnora "to look out for the measles."

Montgomery and You

Days Eight, Nine, and Ten: Wednesday, Friday, June 9-11, 1943, Montgomery, Alabama

J.R. was overjoyed in the way Elnora dropped everything to meet him in Montgomery. He recalled that all he asked for was a few hours, and somehow they got a few days.

According to their daughter, Suzie, J.R. had a dry wit and loved to play practical jokes. In recounting their meeting in Montgomery, he said he would never forget the expression on Elnora's face when he didn't mention the ring for about a half hour. She looked as if she could have committed murder at the time. He wouldn't have blamed her, but it was so much fun for him to tease her. He thanked God he was able to give the ring to her and see her eyes light up. Best of all, it fit, so it couldn't have been anyone else's.

J.R. stayed at the Jefferson Davis Hotel in downtown Montgomery, Alabama, and Elnora stayed at the Fosters' home. It was common practice in WWII for people to open their homes to visitors in towns with military bases, as hotel rooms were usually reserved for the troops. Mrs. Foster even wrote to Elnora's mother telling her how much in love the young couple was. J.R. recalled that they must have appeared pretty far gone to Mrs. Foster, but it was rough trying to live a year in five days and wondering if your plans would ever have a chance to turn out.

They spent their time seeing the city of Montgomery, going to the Maxwell Field officer's club and the Drum Room. J.R. remembered the way the hostess smiled at them when they came in, thinking that she could tell they were in love just by looking at them. He questioned what they talked about those evenings—all he could remember was looking at her out of the corner of his eye just to make sure she was there, and he would find her looking back at him. He told her that her hair positively amazed him in the sunlight. He had never been able to tell her in a letter how lovely he thought she was. Seeing her again almost put him at a loss for words.

They both loved music, and they loved to dance. J.R. hoped his dancing didn't disappoint Elnora, since he was out of practice of late.

It is not clear, from their letters, if J.R. and Elnora ever *got together*; however, J.R. made the following statement in one of his letters:

> So you like to think of that last night in Montgomery—funny, so do I. There'll come a day and look out. In your letter, you referred to the horse play we'll be doing some day. It's odd, but I was thinking about that last night. We'll never have a dull moment, darling. You can count on that. From the sound of your letters, I think I had better be getting back to you pretty soon. What's the matter, dear? Do you need a little lovin' same as me? You mentioned Montgomery a little too often, and don't think I don't get the general idea. It's killing me Elnora, and I'm ready at any time.

No day was ever to be as blue for J.R. as that Saturday when he left Montgomery. They knew what they wanted, and three years was much too long to wait.

They didn't marry on his leave, and the boys back in Greenville who had seen Elnora called J.R. a fool. He guessed he wasn't very smart to let her get away from Montgomery without tying her down.

The Most Lonesome Guy in the World

Day Eleven: Saturday, June 12, 1943,
Greenville Army Air Base, South Carolina

J.R. had been unconscious ever since he left Elnora that morning. When he was packing, he would start to do something and immediately forget what he was doing, calling himself a hopeless case. They had agreed that she would not come to the train station, but he kept looking anxiously for her to turn up. It would have been unbearable for both of them, though, if she had.

Once he returned to Greenville on Sunday, all he could think about was writing her a note, letting her know he was the most lonesome guy in the world. He felt he was dying by the inch. Coincidentally, the letters she had sent prior to leaving for Montgomery were waiting for him once he got back to the base. He got a kick out of them because she left out words and punctuation, and he suggested she must have really been in a lather. He also received a letter from Mrs. Smith written just before she went down to see Elnora off. He thought Mrs. Smith was so very sweet, and he wished he could have seen that going away party.

He so desperately missed Elnora that he took all of the letters she had written to him while he was in Greenville and spent the better half of the afternoon and evening rereading them. Reading those letters made it seem as if they had always been engaged and were both looking forward to marriage.

Over the next few days, he received the letters and telegrams she sent to him on her trip back to Houston. He daydreamed she was getting close to New Orleans, and she must be very tired. He would not feel at ease until he received the telegram informing him she had made it home. He hoped she was able to get a Pullman [private sleeping compartment].

When he finally received the telegram, he wrote her that he was looking forward to the day when, as a married couple, they would be visiting Houston and she would refer to *home* as being with him. He also asked her how she was going to like being called Mrs. Jones.

When Elnora returned to work, it must have been a little awkward, but obvious, with no visible measles marks and sporting an engagement ring on her finger. J.R. wrote he was relieved that the measles gag went over well, and it was a wonder the ring didn't give her away. He also said that since she could pull a stunt like that on her boss and get away with it, he'd better watch her closely.

He told Elnora how lucky they were to have a few days of leave together. Air Forces Headquarters had just issued an order that there would be no more leaves for combat crews who had completed their training. The twelve crews with which he was associated were leaving for their overseas assignments, and he was not going with them. He was upset until he found out that six more crews were leaving in about two weeks and that he was to lead them across, as his aircrew would be the only one with a navigator. He knew that would put a lot of responsibility on his crew, but he also hoped it would mean he would get one of the new aircraft making the crossing.

Wednesday, June 16, 1943, Greenville Army Air Base, South Carolina

J.R. wrote a thank you letter to Mrs. Foster for being such a gracious host to them.

> My dear Mrs. Foster,
> I'm back with my bomber again and, I must say, I much prefer Elnora. I do want to thank you and your husband

for all your kindness to Elnora and me. It was all too good to be true.

I'm not leaving here as soon as I thought, but it shouldn't be more than two or three weeks before I leave. I'll be a happy lad to get out of this place too.

Perhaps the next time we meet, Elnora and I will be the hosts. At least I hope so. At present, this war is rather a handicap.

Let me thank you again—I'll never be able to repay you. Tell your husband and Suzan hello, and until we meet again, I remain
	Sincerely yours,
	J.R. Jones

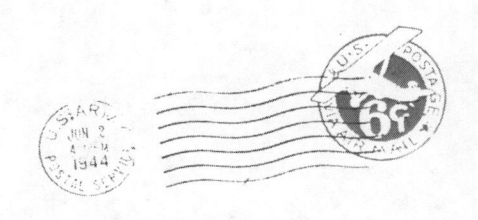

NEW GUINEA: WARFRONT AND TOKYO ROSE

Information regarding mission logs, unit histories, and intelligence reports were taken from official, now declassified, government documents provided by Lawrence J. Hickey and found at the official website of the 345th Bombardment Group at: www.345thbombgroup.org

J.R.'s name was not listed on the mission logs until he was assigned the position of pilot. At times, I have included missions based upon comments in his letters stating that he flew that day or would be getting up early the next day to fly.

J.R.'s letters, interspersed with portions of these mission logs, unit histories, and intelligence reports of the 345th Bombardment Group, follow. For the sake of brevity, not all of his overseas letters were included and not every line in his letters was used. I have taken the liberty to correct spelling and grammatical errors, and have included only those letters that illustrate the everyday life of a wartime pilot in the Southwest Pacific Area.

Thursday, June 24, 1943, Greenville Army Air Base, South Carolina

Scan of Greenville Army Air Base stationary courtesy of Lloyd Sullivan.

Elnora my darling,

I was informed last night of a bit of news that may interest you. As soon as I leave Greenville, I will be strictly incommunicado till I reach my destination. In other words, it may be a month or more before you hear from me. I may not even be able to call you from Greenville. I'll have no idea where I'll be going, and I can't be sure till I get there. Probably the only way you will know I'm gone will be my silence. If there is any way to quickly notify you after arriving, I'll do it. You know that, darling; above all please don't worry. It won't help anyone. Mother will be the only one able to notify you if anything happens to me. You have my home address, don't you? The government won't notify you unless you are my wife. So don't worry, darling, everything will be all right. It's bound to be.

I'm glad you liked the picture, my dear. If it pleased you, I can ask nothing more, for it was meant for you and no one else. If, as you say, I'm always watching you, it must be rather embarrassing at bedtime; isn't it, darling? What do you do—turn me to the wall?

I stare at these beautiful pictures of you and these snapshots of us by the hour. Heaven knows what it will be like over there. Knowing that you love me, though, and that you are more lovely than a picture can ever be is one dream I've had come true. Now I'm looking forward to another one. You couldn't guess what it is, can you?

I must close, my love, as the hour of twelve is here. I have much more to tell you, and I intend to do it tomorrow. I'd like to tonight, but I don't think I could do it adequately. I can say though very truthfully—I love you very much.

Always, J.R.

Note the time lapse between the previous letter dated June 24, 1943, and the next letter dated August 21, 1943—almost two months. I'm sure Elnora was distraught knowing J.R. was entering the war zone. Elnora was elated to finally receive the letter and surmise where he was stationed. His unit could have been sent to either warfront. Much comfort was derived knowing he had made the long plane trip across the ocean safely.

Melvin Best, a member of the 345th from its activation to its deactivation, told me their unit was originally scheduled to go to a cold-weather climate [probably England] and was issued cold-weather gear. However, on April 5, 1943, their orders were changed. Maj. Gen. George C. Kenney, commander of the Allied Air Forces in the Southwest Pacific Area (SWPA) and the Fifth Air Force, had some novel ideas about how to engage the Japanese and convinced Col. Clinton U. True to join him in the SWPA. Was the cold weather gear truly an indication of where they would be sent or a clever way to mislead the enemy regarding their intentions? Melvin reported that, once they got to Port Moresby, huge piles of cold-weather gear were discarded in heaps and left to rot in the humid tropics of New Guinea.

Saturday, August 21, 1943

My dearest Elnora,

Perhaps I can elucidate a bit further in this letter, as V-mail rather cramps my style even though it is faster. As I said, I'm *down under* and that's no joke. This is as far under as I hope to get. I haven't seen too much of this country, but I haven't appreciated too much what I have seen.

Brisbane is a rather large city, and fairly nice, but the best part of Australia is Sydney. I've heard it's rather nice, and I'm sure I'll find out some day. These small towns are a sight for sore eyes. They are very reminiscent of our West of seventy years ago. The townspeople seem to have a fondness for orange and yellow houses, and their architecture is from another world. It lets you know in no uncertain terms that you are no longer in the U.S.

All the homes and places of business are very dirty and unkempt. It's really not a very pleasant effect. Everything looks as if it could use a good bath. Most of all, you notice the smell of these small towns. As you enter one, a very peculiar odor assails you and refuses to go away until you leave. Each store has its own special smell, none of which can actually be classified as delectable. I am stationed, at present, outside of one such small town, so I should know.

The people are fairly friendly, but I don't believe the Australian soldiers care too much for us. They are really a wild lot and aren't too particular who they fight. For lack of anything else to do, they will fight each other. I've seen several excellent bar room brawls already that further remind one of the Wild West. I'll tell you more about that later on.

The trains are really something here, too. They look like toys and make about twenty miles an hour. I had to take a blasted trip on one and it nearly killed me. The really small trains are hilarious though—big whistle, small train. It looked like something out of a Walt Disney show.

As far as the country—you never saw so much space with so few people on it. Australia is as big as the U.S. and Mexico, and has only about five million inhabitants so that spreads pretty thin. I'd really hate to get lost in some of it.

Where I am now looks a lot like west Texas and the climate is like Arizona. It's very comfortable. It's winter here now, so I suppose it will get much warmer—in fact, I'm sure it will.

That's another confusing point—here as you go south it gets colder and as you go north it gets warmer. That's what I get for crossing the equator—it was warm too. Also, I gained a day when I crossed the date line. Lord, I'll never get this straightened out.

The monetary system here gave me a bad time for a while, but I'm catching on rapidly now. I can get a glass of beer for six pence, two glasses for a shilling, four for a florin, and forty for a pound. See, it's all very simple when you drink beer! Of course, if I have to buy something else then I'm stuck all over again. The beer is excellent and what a wallop it has. It's bad enough by the glass, but in bottles it's terrific, as they only sell it in quarts. It's rather hard to get though, so we just mainly talk about it.

Most of the women I've seen here have as much sex appeal as a dead herring. They just don't know the American beauty secrets. Quite different from the U.S., the prettiest girls are in uniform here.

I haven't any idea how big the Royal Australian Air Force is, but they have the prettiest uniform of anyone. It's about the bluest blue I ever saw. I hope they have some airplanes to go with the uniform.

The first three days I spent at this station, I lived in a hangar that was open at both ends and I nearly froze at night, so I took to sleeping in long underwear. I look like the man on the flying trapeze in that stuff. Now that I have the luxury of a tent, all is beautiful.

I'm not doing a great deal now. Just going to school a bit and that's all. This, however, is the first opportunity I've had to write in a long time.

I haven't received any letters yet and how I miss hearing from you, darling. I hope I get a lot when I do. I'm sure I have mail somewhere, but heaven only knows when it will catch up with me. I believe I'll be able to write regularly now.

I must say goodnight, my dear, as it's late for this part of the world. It's impossible to say how much I miss you now, but I hope you know. I looked at that ring today and it made everything seem all right. It can't be so long until it's yours. I'll write again tomorrow—good night, darling, and I love you.

Always, J.R.

Photo of B-25 Mitchells at Townsville, Australia, courtesy of the Lawrence J. Hickey Collection.

August 21, 1943: Eighteen aircraft of the 501st Bombardment Squadron returned to Port Moresby, New Guinea, from Townsville, Australia, with modifications made to change them from medium bombers to strafers and low-altitude bombers.

Three new aircraft were added to the squadron; one of these new aircraft was flown over by James Richard Jones when he joined the 345th Bombardment Group.

In order to fully understand the military significance of the 345th Bombardment Group, one must read their story in an incredible book, *Warpath Across The Pacific: The Illustrated History of the 345th Bombardment Group During WWII*, written by Lawrence J. Hickey of the International Historical Research Associates at www.airwar-worldwar2.com

INTRODUCTION OF "WARPATH ACROSS THE PACIFIC":

> Around a small skeleton of trained Air Corps personnel—only a handful of them pre-war regulars—1,600 young men from America's schools, factories and farms would be transformed from eager but inexperienced young graduates of the Air Corps training camps into an efficient military organization equipped with an example of America's most modern aviation technology, the North American B-25 *Mitchell* bomber.
>
> The 345th Bomb Group trained as a medium bombardment unit. With the normal course of events, it would have served out the war flying its missions from eight to twelve thousand feet, making a valuable but not extraordinary contribution to America's victory in the Pacific war.
>
> But fate was in the making. In Australia, at the rear base of the 5th Air Force, Maj. Paul I. 'Pappy' Gunn, an engineer and a tinkerer, was about to unleash a devastating tool for eliminating Japan's ability to make and sustain war

in the Southwest Pacific. By removing the bombardier-navigator from his greenhouse compartment in the nose of a B-25 medium bomber, Gunn found he could install eight forward-firing .50 caliber machine guns in the aircraft. Thus was born the low-level B-25 strafer, a weapon which would revolutionize warfare in the Southwest Pacific and unleash the hell-raising aerial hot-rodder that lived in the soul of many young Air Corps medium-bombardment pilots.

The strafer was an ingenious weapon for neutralizing enemy airpower on the ground and devastating Japan's strategic shipping lanes across the Southwest Pacific. Using this tool, the planes of the 345th Bomb Group ripped their way across the southeastern reaches of the Japanese empire, strafing and bombing into ruin everything in their path. So great was their fear of attack by these planes that Japanese merchant seaman sometimes took to the lifeboats rather than face an attack."

Thursday, August 26, 1943

Dearest Elnora,

Another day and not much accomplished. The days go rather rapidly, but they would go faster if I would receive some mail, since it's nearly two months now. It takes about a month to get mail. At the rate I'm going, I'll be home before I hear from you. I hope you have received my letters. They will probably turn up at all sorts of odd times.

It gets dark so blasted early here that it's tough to finish a letter before we go on candlelight. It's rather tough trying to write by one. It must have given Abe Lincoln a bad time.

Last night was a big night for me. It was one of those rare occasions that they sell beer, and I managed to take on two bottles before they sold out, very potent stuff. Afterwards, a movie—William Powell and Hedy Lamar in *Crossroads*, nothing but the latest! Any show would entertain me these days.

My social life is really something. I even had a date the other night. She was a nurse and, believe it or not, from Lubbock. Actually, I didn't see much of her during the evening as the wolves were terrific at the Officer's Club. I didn't mind though as I wasn't particularly intrigued, just something to do in the long evenings.

We are stationed near a small town and what a burg it is. The Red Cross has a place fixed up for the Americans, and it is quite nice. You can really get excellent meals there. Speaking of food, tonight we had liver, and I hate it with a passion. It seems that most people do, but the Army keeps right on serving it. There isn't much else in the town worth mentioning except an open-air picture show. The reason it's an open air show is because the roof burned off sometime back and they've never taken the trouble to replace it—besides, it never rains much around here anyway.

One of the boys has already gotten him a baby kangaroo for a pet. What queer tastes some people have. It certainly is an odd-looking critter for a friend.

It seems a long time since Montgomery already. I hate to think what would have happened if it hadn't been for those lucky months of May and June. I don't believe I've ever heard a voice as surprised as your mother's that first night I called. It's probably a good thing you weren't at home or I wouldn't have gotten a word out of you. Then when I did get you, you thought someone was kidding you. Very embarrassing to say the least, but it seems I finally convinced you. If I didn't, you're engaged to a stranger.

I guess I'd better close, darling, as the lights are getting very bad. I'll write again very soon, but I'd do much better if I would hear from you. Good night, dear. I love you and miss you more than I can say.

Always love, J.R.

Many may question the fact that both J.R. and Elnora continued to go out on dates with other people, even after they were engaged. For Elnora, having a date merely meant accompanying a soldier to a USO sponsored type of event. Ladies of the upper circles of society were encouraged to do their patriot part by providing weary soldiers with the opportunity to dance and socialize. Even though it must have been difficult for J.R., it was he who encouraged her to go out and have a good time. Above all, he did not want to make Elnora a widow, and he didn't want her to regret not having a good time if she thought she had to stay home after they were engaged. It was love at first sight for both of these young souls, and it was their love that gave J.R. his reason to fight hard and hurry home. Elnora did decide to quit dating as J.R. pointed out in one of his letters, much to his delight, for it was her decision and not his request. J.R. did go out with Australian young ladies on his leaves. He matter-of-factly records this in his letters to Elnora. Both must have been confident in their love for each other, or their relationship would not have withstood this kind of testing.

Special Intelligence Report:
Natives, August 25, 1943

To: Base Intelligence Officer, APO 929.

On the morning of August 23rd, approximately 0430/K, a party of perhaps 15-20 natives were seen traveling along the road between the Laloki River Bridge and Schwimmer Aerdrome. These natives were apparently leaving our area, as they were all heavily laden with bundles, some of which were seen to be Government Issue Bags, such as the A/C A-3 and B-4 bags. Upon being challenged by an Air Corps Officer, the natives immediately ran away and took cover in nearby brush and grass. One native was caught with items in his possession, as shown on the enclosure herewith.

1—A-3 Bag, wool—contents
    2 blankets
    3 mosquito bar nets
    1 pr. khaki pants
    3 towels
    1 undershirt, cotton
    2 pr. white cotton socks
    1 cotton sock
    1 O.D. [olive drab] sock
    1 fatigue jacket
    1 can tooth powder
    1 pipe
    1 can tobacco
    1 A/C sleeve patch

1—Musette Bag—contents
    1 mattress cover
    2 bed sheets
    2 towels
    11 handkerchiefs
    2 lengths of cotton cloth
    1 undershirt, cotton
    2 cans of brown shoe polish
    1 pipe
    1 can body powder
    1 pr. sun glasses (left lens cracked)
    1 box matches (China)

1—Musette Bag—contents
    1 towel
    9 handkerchiefs
    1 pr. heavy underdrawers, cotton
    1 white cotton jacket

1 pr. O.D. pants
1 pr. khaki pants—short
1 khaki shirt
2 black ties
1 G.I. belt
1 harmonica
1 cotton undershirt
4 pr. cotton shorts
3 pkg. cigarettes—1 Phillip Morris, 1 Old Gold, 1 Capstan
1 O.D. cap
Evert W. K. Andrau
Captain, Air Corps,
Intelligence Officer

Tuesday, August 31, 1943

Dearest Elnora,

This is the last day of August, and I've really covered some territory. It seems like a dream mostly, I guess it is August 30 where you are. It's very easy to recall where I was two years ago at that date. In fact, the Smiths have it on film. I also recall seeing the San Jacinto monument stag. Anyhow, that was a nice afternoon at the ranch. Now all the boys who were present are in the Army; Daurice is married, and you and I—I wish to God we were and hope we will be. We'll see another August before that and perhaps another Christmas.

The boys have a little motto about getting home. They say, "The Golden Gate by '48". That doesn't sound too cheerful, but I don't think it will actually be that long. I say that with my fingers crossed.

I saw a red-hot picture show Monday night. It was Hopalong Cassidy in something or other; and in the newsreel, the British were about to take Tunisia. Nothing but the latest around here! Yesterday I read a New York newspaper dated July 20. Just two days after I left Greenville. Dates don't really mean a good deal here, except those you remember and pay day.

Cigarettes are rationed here and that is a pain in the neck; just a carton every ten days. It's a tight fight, but it can be done. You have to line up for nearly everything around here—ice cream and beer if you get there early. Liquor is nearly non-existent. I would trade plenty now for one good Coke. I really miss those things. I hear that some places you can get them occasionally. I only hope that is true.

We get Glenn Miller recordings direct from Tokyo. It's a propaganda program and they really play some hot stuff. We listen to the music and put up with the rest. It's mighty fine of them to entertain us. You should hear some of the tall tales they put out.

Tokyo [Rose] is now playing "There's No Place Like Home"—very heartrending. Now it's Glenn Miller and "Sunrise Serenade." It really beats me.

I imagine that before too long I'll be going where the war is. That is always something else to look forward to. I should have plenty to tell our children, anyhow. At least I should be busy and that helps no end.

As to why the Japs should want bloody Australia is more than I can see, but it's none of my business. It is really wild country to fly over, and I guess it's really something where they are fighting. All I know is what I read in the papers, and they are plenty old.

I really got a zoot haircut yesterday. It was by a local barber, or hairdresser as they call them here. Now I'm right back where I started. What I dislike most about it is the fact that my hat doesn't fit anymore.

I think I'll close darling and save some material for a future letter. If I ever get some mail from you, I can be a red-hot correspondent again. Some fellows got some mail today, but not I. I won't give up yet, but in two more months, I'm liable to get a little anxious.

Good night, dear—I hope you didn't have to go to San Jacinto by yourself. I take that back knowing what that could lead to. I'll write again shortly, darling. I love you, and I miss you—too much.

My love, J.R.

Tokyo Rose was not a real person, but rather a name given to several English-speaking women who either volunteered or were coerced to broadcast propaganda to the troops on a program called *The Zero Hour*, which was broadcasted from 6:00-7:15 every evening except Sunday.

In my December, 2010, meeting with Melvin Best, 345th member, I asked him if Tokyo Rose's broadcasts had any adverse effect on the group's moral. He related that, on the contrary, they looked forward to her 6:00 p.m. broadcast each day. He explained that they knew they were being effective in their bombing raids by some of the things she would say. The most notable of her comments, one about the 498th Bomb Squadron (Falcons), was the one in which she called them the *yellow-nosed bastards*. The 498th Falcons' nose art was that of the head of a Falcon, and the yellow nose/beak was very prominent. Her comment was made after the infamous November 2, 1943, attack on Simpson Harbor, Rabaul.

For additional information on the 345th Bombardment Group, please go to the following website: www.345thbombgroup.org

"The boys have a little motto about getting home. They say 'The Golden Gate by '48.'" These words were written by J.R. in his letter of August 31st. Pilots flying planes to New Guinea left McClellan Field in Sacramento, California, and flew past the Golden Gate Bridge. It was the last soil of the continental United States they would see as they flew across the Pacific toward Hawaii. It must have been difficult for them to know that they might never see that sight again, and that they were leaving behind their families and friends and the only way of life most of them had ever known. Certainly, they would not return the same persons they had been before they experienced the ravages of war. Melvin Best related that the flyboys took great delight in buzzing the Golden Gate as they headed off to war, even though this was very much frowned upon by the War Department and city officials.

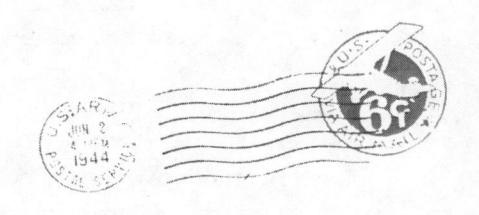

THE JUNGLE: 501ST, MOVIES, AND THE MUSIC CONTINUES

Thursday, September 9, 1943

Dearest Elnora,

Well I've been chasing around again. I can't seem to stay put very long. It's really very discouraging as far as postal service goes. Also my possessions are strung half way around the world. I wonder if it will ever all catch up with me. I'll probably have to buy everything new some day.

It seems that no matter where you go, the officers will have a club. I have really seen some beauties since I've been gone. Over here, the Army nurse seems to have undergone a change for the better. I have seen quite a few good-looking numbers about. It makes a pleasant atmosphere anyhow.

I haven't accomplished much the past few days. I find it difficult to write, because I have nothing to go on, and there's so much we're not permitted to say. Two months is rather a long time to be shut off with no word from you, my dear. I had an idea it would be at least this long, but now I'm afraid it's going to be longer.

A funny thing happened yesterday. I was lying about half-asleep on my cot when I thought I heard some very familiar music. I didn't know whether I was dreaming or my ears were playing tricks on me. I got up to make sure, and it finally dawned on me it was a radio in the next barracks. It was a local station playing a recording of "My Prodigal." It was the last record I ever expected to hear in this part of the world. It's all very confusing. I wish they wouldn't sneak up on me next time.

I saw a rather good show last night. It was Shirley Temple and Laraine Day in *Kathleen*. Miss Day convinced me that I now know three beautiful redheads, and you know who heads the list. If not, look at your left hand.

I'm still wondering what happened to my rivals. Also, I never found out your brother's reaction. So many things. If I can get a few epistles, I may be a decent correspondent again. As it is, I feel as if I've been in this blasted country forever.

Here again. This is several days later, and I've moved again. I'm now in what is known as the South Pacific area. In other words, I can't say definitely, but I can tell you I'm up where the fireworks begin.

It really is something here. I wouldn't have believed it possible. We have an officer's club in the middle of nowhere. It's really amazing. The jungle is terrifically dense, and Lord how I'd hate to be forced down in it.

I'll tell you more as I go along. Believe it or not, I have just finished listening to the *Hit Parade*. I haven't heard it since we were together in Montgomery. It's an odd feeling out here. "All or Nothing at All" and "In the Blue of Evening"—God, Elnora, how I wonder what you are doing now. No word from you, no nothing. I know I have some mail from you as some fellows saw it in Australia.

I'm in a swell gang, but as I'm newest, I guess I'll start at the bottom again. You know, darling, no matter how long you are in the Air Corps, you are always starting over again. Ah, well, you're never too old to learn. I feel I have so much to tell you, yet it all seems so mixed up. Perhaps I'll get it all straightened up some day, maybe never till I see you again, but I'll do my best.

At present, this letter-writing proposition is driving me nuts. I know it isn't your fault. I'll probably be swamped when it comes through. All I need to do is look at your picture and this blasted war doesn't seem so bad. You know, my pretty redhead, you're a wonderful gal. Now Tokyo [Rose] gives forth Artie Shaw and "Moonglow." If you have any of these records, just play them and imagine me in the jungle. I'm going to close, darling, before this becomes too big for an envelope. Night, my dear—I love you so much—

Always love, J.R.

P.S. This is the address.

Lt. James R. Jones 0-794421
501st B.S. 345th BG
APO 929 c/o Postmaster
San Francisco, CA

*Photo of 501st Bomb Squad. board
courtesy of the Lawrence J. Hickey Collection.*

Censorship is basically an unknown concept to the modern-day twenty-first century person. We are very lucky in the United States that we do not have our mail opened and read every time we send a letter. However, during WWII, censorship was imposed on both the soldiers and their families. The saying *"loose lips might sink ships"* was truly the case, and any mention of the location of a soldier could have grave consequences. There were no permanent/felt-tip markers in the 1940s, so censors would take scissors and actually cut out words or even sentences from a soldier's letter. J.R. only experienced the scissors of the censors once. I can only imagine how much time was spent reading each letter for every serviceman and woman, and then cutting out things that didn't pass their censorship. J.R. often was assigned this duty, and he complained many times, in his letters to Elnora, that not only was this a tedious task but also that he found the letters to be just flat boring.

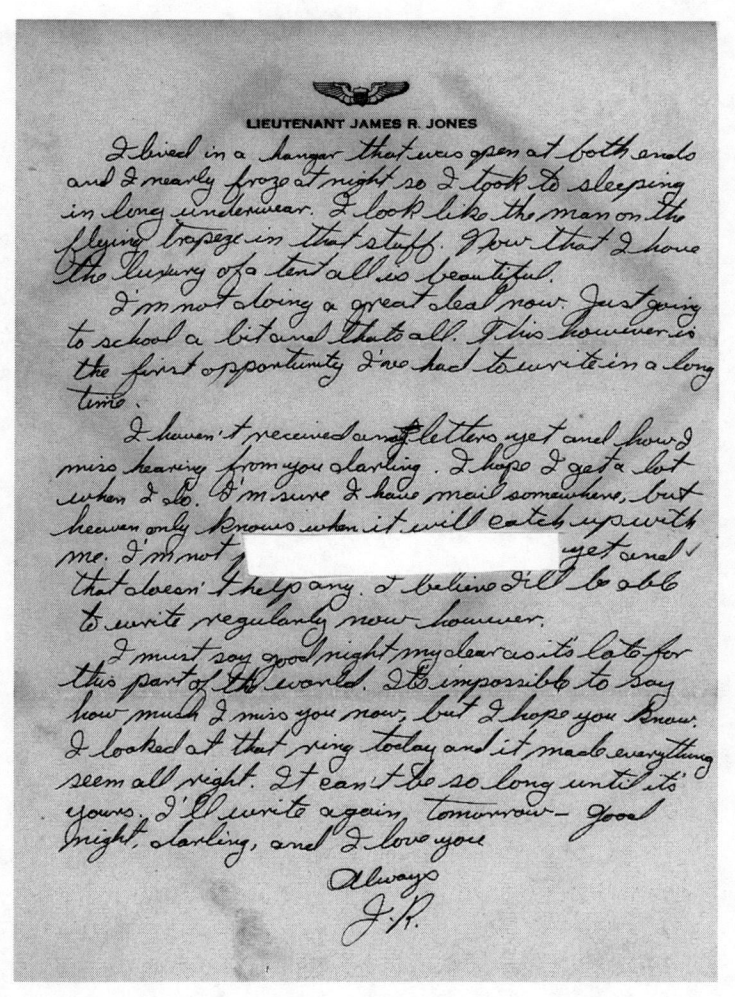

Scan of J.R.'s letter with censor's cut out area courtesy of Lloyd Sullivan.

Friday, September 10, 1943

Dearest Elnora,

Perhaps this letter will have a bit more continuity—at least I hope it will. These will be the last three sheets of stationary I have. I have another box in my luggage, but God knows when I'll get it.

The days haven't consisted of too much since I arrived here. I know they are plenty hot and it's so dusty, I'm always covered with a film of it. They say when it rains everything immediately turns to mud. I imagine that will be pleasant. I know the bugs, spiders, etc. are something to be reckoned with. I have really seen some rare specimens wandering around.

We have started to track down our mail in hopes that it will get here some day. All the boys here get it quite regularly. You should have quite a few letters from me by now that have been written in various parts of the world.

I live in quite a state of luxury here. The food is good and much better than I had expected. A native boy makes our bed, cleans our tents, and does our laundry for a nominal fee. All this came as a surprise too. Perhaps I should bring one home for a houseboy for us. It might, however, be a little difficult to get clothes on him.

We have our officer's club, which is called the Panther Room, or have I told you all this? It really is a classy place and the best around this place. It makes the evenings very pleasant. We have a radio, phonographs, books, dice table, and many other things you probably wouldn't expect to find out here. Last, but not least, we have our bar. We can get a few drinks during the evenings—just enough to remind you that there are such things.

One of the boys who came over with me saw your picture tonight and said you looked familiar. He had gone to Ellington, and he said he had seen you at some tea dance. He remembered the red hair and said you wore pearls. You must have made quite an impression on him, darling. I wonder if those cadets back there have any idea what they are getting into.

There are great many hazards here other than the enemy. The weather is something to behold, and the country surrounding isn't exactly a park. I really feel for the ground troops. What a job they must have!

I'm going to have to get some clean clothes soon or start wearing the dirty ones over again. I'll have to put the native boy to work tomorrow I suppose. We don't have much spare time during the day. At least we haven't yet.

They seem to have quite a few records by Harry James around here. It feels good to hear music like that. I haven't danced to a big band since I left college. There was that time at Maxwell Field, but there were too many people to enjoy it. He's playing "I Cried For You." We have so much to do some day. Everything will be new to us, and everything we do is bound to be fun. It is great pleasure to look forward to the day we won't have to say good-bye any more.

I had better close, darling, as I'm running short of paper, and I'm afraid I must get up very early. I can always look forward till the next day, because there is always a chance I'll have a letter from you. I'll probably drop dead when I do. I must say goodnight, my dear—I love you and miss you so.

Always my love—J.R.

Photo of upscale living quarters in New Guinea courtesy of Marshall Riggan.

MISSION FFO 255-O: SEPTEMBER 13, 1943

This was the first official mission for James Richard Jones. Twelve A/P [airplane] of this squadron were ordered to bomb and strafe the village of Tari, Labu Island, and the south bank of the Markham River lying between these two points, and provided ground support to the troops. Tari Village was left in flames due to direct hits and strafing. The mission was successful with no loss of plane or crew.

MONDAY, SEPTEMBER 13, 1943

Dearest Elnora,
   I've just had my beliefs in the jungles verified. A sixteen and one-half foot python was just killed a short distance from the officer's club. Lord, how I'd hate to wake up and find one of those babies in bed with me. I'll probably really have wild dreams tonight. I haven't even had a drink either.

I've just returned from a movie. It was some thriller about the *Falcon*. I spent the bulk of my time slapping mosquitoes. These are the fiercest I've seen yet. They had a pretty good short with Al Donohue supplying the music. Sweet music is really a treat here.

Also I've finally gotten my hand into the war a bit. As usual I'm at the bottom working my way up again. This sure gets tiresome, but I guess you get used to it sooner or later. They say when you get too old to learn, it's time to die.

I'm finding it a little difficult to get used to the wild animal situation around here. I prefer my exhibit in the zoo and not around my home. I imagine you would have gone for that critter I just saw. I don't know which I'd prefer—being shot at by the Japs or swallowed by that gargantuan we have on display.

Today is the 13th—last month it was Friday 13th. I had a good scare then. It was in mid Pacific. Oh well, I guess I'll have to tell you about that some other time.

Did I tell you about the party we had in the club Saturday night? We got a band, and it was plenty good. We had some sort of punch that absolutely paralyzed. Of course, nurses supplied the feminine interest, at least they did for some.

I'm now beginning to look eagerly in the mailbox every evening. I've never really expected to get mail up till now. Darling, if I don't hear from you one of these days—well, I guess I'll just have to wait, but I don't want to. I know the days will go much faster when I do get word from you. I'm really beginning to feel now that I am on the other side of the world. It's been a good deal of fun up to now, but it's beginning to be hard work. I won't mind that as long as I get back to where you are. That seems to be all most of the fellows live for. I know when I left you in Montgomery I left a good deal behind; in fact, everything that I ever want to remember. When I was a cadet at Maxwell Field, I used to think how I would like to show you the place. Well, we seem to have gotten a good many of our wishes to date. It takes time as we've found, but it works.

I'm so blamed tired, my darling, that I must close. This has been a rather rugged day for this lad. I guess I'll have to toughen up gradually. I imagine you think I've forgotten how to write letters, but I can't seem to do a thing without hearing from you. See, you're a very necessary gal to me, or haven't I told you before? Night my dear, I love you so very much, and I wish to God this were over. So long, engaged woman.

Always, I love you, J.R.

Wednesday, September 15, 1943—V-mail

My darling Elnora,

Today at last it happened—loads of letters. I felt as if a part of my life just caught up with me. I never was as happy and then the first letter about Roger Smith. I knew about it. He's been on my mind for weeks. I hated to read it. I pray to God it isn't true.

This is all the stationary I have. I have so much to say, but I won't do it this way. I was so glad, my dear, that you have met my mother if only by letter. How did you fair?

Also I was very glad to hear that your brother has been home. I know you must be happy indeed. He has a very beautiful sister, and I happen to be very much in love with her. I only wish I could have seen him, but I shall some day.

It has taken me a very long time to read my mail, and it was a marvelous evening. Now I will be able to really do my best. So many letters, darling—you just remember that I am mad about you. Dear, I must close this, but I promise I'll write a letter tomorrow that will be the best ever.

Night darling—I love you.
Always, J.R.

V-mail, or Victory mail, was a one-paged microfilmed letter that was supposed to ensure quicker delivery of correspondence for the soldiers.

It was an ingenious method by reducing the size of letter and placing it onto microfilm, providing an easy way to transport the letters. The rolls of film were sent to different facilities and developed at a receiving station near the intended addressee. Individual facsimiles of the letters were reproduced and then delivered to the addressee.

J.R. clearly did not like this method and chose to use it only on several occasions.

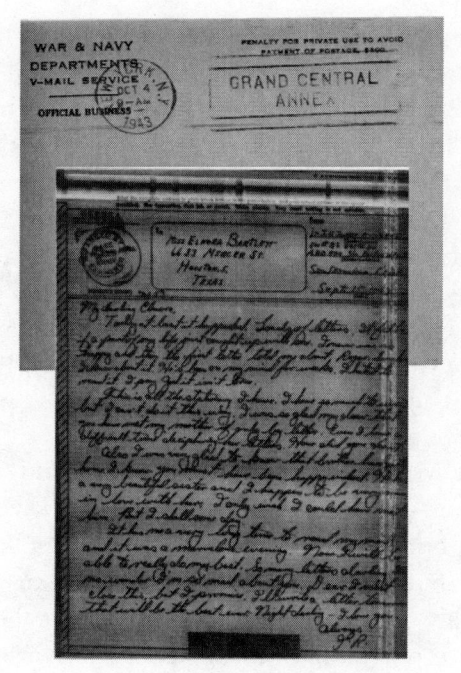

Scan of V-mail courtesy of Lloyd Sullivan.

September 15, 1943

The official opening day was held with many notables in attendance, including Gen. Ramey, commander of the Fifth Bomber Command; Lt. Col. True and Maj. Fridge with 345th Group Hqs.; and Maj. Fain and Lt. Gallagher, 501st Commanding Officer and adjutant respectively. The boys had a swell time. Three Red Cross women attended the big affair. Drinks were served continuously. Music was furnished by members of the 27th Air Depot and the 5th Bomber Command presented stage acts that were enjoyed by all. All in all, the opening night was a big success.

Thursday, September 16, 1943

My dearest Elnora,

How do you like this fancy stationery? It's all I can rake up at present, but it's writing space. I'm starting out to answer all your letters. Several seem to be missing, as you mentioned several things in passing and made no further reference to them. Your letters begin right after the storm in Houston and end with one saying you are sending some snapshots, but I'll have to wait for them. Your first letter was dated July 27. Mother mentioned that a friend of yours saw me in California. Who was it? You didn't say anything about it in any of your letters. They wouldn't let us write there so we just fooled around.

I know Mrs. Smith must feel terrible and have a good idea of how I feel about this whole thing. I wish I could be there, but I don't suppose I could help much. I must write her, but I hardly know what to say. I thought I would be the only one writing by candlelight, but the storm in Houston seems to have made you do likewise. We have electric light that is better than in Australia.

Say, I saw *Stormy Weather* the other night, and it really was good. The funny part was that it began to rain during the show, but it wasn't very serious. *Mr. Lucky* was showing too, but I saw that at Lake Field in Phoenix, Arizona, coming across the U.S. They get fairly recent shows around here.

I was glad you sent me Shield's letter. He should still be in medical school, but I guess that's the breaks. I'd like to talk to some of my old friends again.

I received two of the enlarged photos. They turned out rather well. I thank you so much for them, my darling. I imagine my letters seem rather sparse those first two months, but running around as we were made it rather difficult to write, or say anything for that matter. You got my letters from Hawaii rather quickly.

So, you've been reading *Army Wife*. I expect most of what you read will apply only during peacetime, but that's a pleasant thought.

So Roger got D.F.C. [Distinguished Flying Cross]? It's quite an honor and doesn't come cheaply. It seems rather apparent now, doesn't it? He must have been a good man in his outfit. I hope to God he turns up. It all seems so impossible, but I know all too well it can happen.

I should have liked to have seen you roughing it while you had no lights. That would have been a good time for me to have landed in Houston. I would have had to stay a while then and that would have been tough.

Women exasperate me. You and my mother write each other, and the only fact that I get in on is that you told her Roger was missing and your brother was coming home. I seem to be full of spare letters this evening. I hope you keep it up. Mother detests writing letters, but I know she won't miss out on you. You'll really get a whack out of her. She is threatening to join the WACs [Women's Army

Corps] or something. I think that small town is about to get the best of her.

I would very much enjoy meeting someone over here that knew you. Perhaps I am closer to your friend than you think. If you gave me his APO and outfit I could run him down in a hurry if he's around here. I hope you didn't send him my first address, as he'd never guess where that is.

I've answered quite a few of your letters. Now I can write you forever. It's very plain to me why I love you so. I particularly enjoyed that letter that contained the ads. Your hair is still as red as ever, my dear. I've never seen anything like it or you either for that matter.

Someone is really loading the phonograph with sentimental music. I find myself listening and daydreaming instead of writing. Would I ever like to go to a big dance, but it will probably be many a moon before I'll be doing that.

I guess I should be closing this so I can get it all in one envelope. I still have reams I could write you about, but I must send Mother a word. I tried V-mail, but it doesn't satisfy me greatly.

I'll be glad when you start using my present address, as service will be a good deal quicker. I'm really looking forward to those new snapshots—I've kicked myself a hundred times for not having a camera over here.

I must say goodnight, darling. If you only knew how much your letters meant to me. I thought they'd never get here, but I knew it wasn't your fault. Here, I've written five pages and on all of them, all I want to say is I love you and how I wish time would fly. I'll write again shortly.

Always—I love you, J.R.

Friday, September 17, 1943

My dearest Elnora,

I'm still reading your letters and answering them bit by bit. I'll be terribly behind, but you can't realize what all that mail meant. You must have written nearly every day. I wish I could have done the same, but I've been a few places where writing is pretty impossible.

Tokyo [Rose] is now supplying the music and propaganda to match. I wonder where they get all the records. It really is heart rendering when they play "Home Sweet Home."

I was just thinking how much spare time you'll have when you don't have to write me anymore. With all your correspondence though, I'll probably have to read a book while you write someone else.

I'd still like to know who saw me in California and then told you about it. I can't find anything about it in your letters, but Mother told me. I can't for the life of me think who it could have been, and it's been puzzling me ever since. I wish you could have been in California with me. We could have really had a time there. That is a plenty happy-go-lucky state.

The days here seem to get warmer as they go along. It is just spring here now, and I hate to think what summer will be like. I also am aware, however, that Houston can really scorch at this time of year. I don't believe I've ever been as uncomfortable as those first weeks at Wallace. I guess you just gradually adjust your life to whatever turns up.

I should think by now, darling, they would have given you a life membership at the Hat [Hi-Hat, a nightclub in Houston]. It is certainly an unimposing-looking affair, but I must admit it was a pretty wonderful place when I was there with you. In fact, I don't recall ever looking around much while I was there.

I didn't finish this last night as the lights went out, and I had to go to bed—a very pleasant pastime. My time hasn't been too fully occupied lately so I get plenty of that stuff. I expect we'll get back to work shortly.

I just ran into a good buddy of mine today. I thought he was on the other side so I was really surprised to see him. We were in flying school all the way from the Old Mill till Shaw Field. I guess they will turn up periodically.

When I was a Cadet at Maxwell Field, I never dreamed then that someday I'd be sitting with you at that officer's club. We used to look very enviously at that swimming pool. I'd really like to be stationed some place like that some day.

This letter has had more interruptions. I just finished taking in a show, and it was raining too. Sounds sort of crazy, doesn't it?

Already I'm wishing I'd get some more mail and so soon after that last bunch. Anything you do interests me. Even if you tell me you just walked around the block.

When you get out some place like this, I begin to wonder if someone lovely as you really existed. It doesn't seem possible, but I have some very tangible proof of it. Why, I've even got a picture of me standing by you. Those two nights in Houston and four days in Montgomery, I couldn't take my eyes off of you. Even in a show, I looked more at you than the screen. After a siege in two jungles, I'll probably have a wild look in my eye. Can you blame me?

You'll be a married gal then by the name of Jones—you'd better be. What a good thought that is. I think Mildred [Mrs. Foster—where they stayed during the four days in Montgomery] half expected us to get married while we were there. She was really wonderful to us. Only time can tell if we're right, but I'm sure of it now. I knew I was ten seconds after I saw you again.

I must close, darling. I hope you are hearing from me regularly now. I'll do my best, but when the mail doesn't get through, just remember I love you always and miss you more than I ever thought possible.

Always—my love, J.R.

Scan of cartoon from original "Warpath" courtesy of Lloyd Sullivan.

Sunday, September 19, 1943

My dearest Elnora,

Hello, darling—this is Sunday and not very eventful either. I've spent a good deal of it sleeping and eating and reading. Sounds like hard work, doesn't it?

It must have done your family and yourself much good to have seen your brother again. Your letters bespeak it very plainly. I'm only too sorry I couldn't have been there to meet him and dispel any doubts he may have about me. But, as you once said, anyone who doesn't like it can go jump in the river. I can't really think of any logical reason why they should. We'll take care of all that some day.

Perhaps if I had been there, you would have gotten him a date and we could have all had a good time dancing. I would have readily done that, and I would have taken Mrs. Smith because she's my secret love down there. If she wasn't already married, you wouldn't stand a chance. Of course, I don't know, as that red hair is pretty potent and so is the girl under it.

God, but I've felt miserable about Roger being missing—why do things like this have to happen to such wonderful people?

It's growing rather late, and I have to close. I'm wondering how long it takes for you to receive my letter from here. I counted all the letters I received last week and there were 43. Rather unbelievable, but I knew you were there every day, darling. If you keep that up, perhaps it won't seem like such a long time over here. Night dear—

I love you—always, J.R.

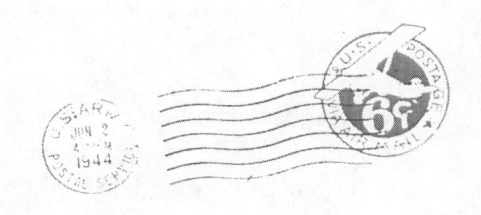

THE BIG TREAT: FRESH POTATOES AND A HAIRCUT

Tuesday, September 21, 1943

Dearest Elnora,

Hooray, I received three more letters from you and quite a few from Mother. You seem rather blue, as you hadn't heard from me lately. I can guess why, but think how I felt for two and half months. Your last letter is dated August 26, nearly a month ago. I'll receive them a bit faster when you start writing to my above address.

I certainly hope by the time you get this one that you are hearing from me often. I told you a long time ago that I didn't mean to let you forget me, and you should know by now I wasn't kidding.

I heard the remark of the century yesterday. I have told you about the dances we have at the club and the native boys hanging around outside watching and listening to the music. Some of the boys speak fair English as they have gone to mission schools. Anyhow, the boy that works for one of the fellows asked his boss the next morning,

"You have good time—hang on woman—get dizzy." That remark nearly brought down the house. As I know your love for dancing, I thought you would appreciate how the native boys view it. Also they have taught him to call Tokyo [Rose] several classic names that, needless to say, I shan't mention.

In one of your letters, you mentioned that time that I got under your skin slightly when I was kidding you on the bus. I became aware of it suddenly myself then, so I shut up. I shouldn't ever worry about my being angry with you. I'd probably never let you know if I were.

I often wondered how much you really know about me. The same applies to me, but I think I know all I need ever know. I hope you'll never be disappointed. It can't always be easy, but who would ever expect that. We both have a lot to learn, but that will be all the more fun.

We had a big treat at dinner today—real butter and fresh potatoes. It was amazing! These dehydrated foods aren't too appetizing. It's rather hard to get many fresh foods here. It gets slightly monotonous too, but it's not bad. It's edible, and that's more than I could say for some of the messes I've seen in the States. I don't imagine I'd do much complaining back there, however.

I've got an itch that's about to drive me dippy. I think it's the heat, but it's enough to drive you slaphappy.

It rained last night but good, and God, the mud! This morning the dust was blowing hard as ever. What a country. This dust makes it terribly difficult to keep clean. Another nature note—I found a huge spider in my shoe yesterday morning. It's futile between the bugs and mud. We've been warned however to shake out our clothes and shoes.

I think I'll close, darling, as it's late and they would like to close the club. Be back soon. Know what? I love you and I can't help it, but I do.

Always—my love, J.R.

*Photo of 499th's Bat's Outa' Hell Club
courtesy of the Lawrence J. Hickey Collection.*

THURSDAY, SEPTEMBER 23, 1943

Dearest Elnora,

These past two days have seemed extra long for some reason. I guess it's because we have had to get up very early. I don't mind getting up early, but it can be over done at times.

I haven't received any more letters lately, so I'm still awaiting those snapshots. You really shouldn't have mentioned sending them and then I wouldn't be so impatient. I'm really very anxious to see them, though, and if I don't get some more soon then others will be threadbare. I still get a bang when I look at our Foster family. If people weren't acquainted with the facts, they would certainly think it strange that you only wear one ring.

I haven't seen any good shows lately, have you? You must keep me posted on such things. I can hardly wait till they start playing "White Christmas" on the radio here. I'll probably tear out my hair. The boys I talked to in the States say it was really enough to make you go dippy last year. I imagine this will be a very torrid Christmas this year.

About the only good book I've read lately is *Only the Stars Are Neutral* by Quentin Reynolds. I doubt if you'd like it however. Also I read *Assignment in Brittany*, a pretty good thriller. I suppose you saw the picture.

Also, I have been broadening myself by playing Wagner on the phonograph. By the way, did I tell you I saw Disney's *Fantasia* while in Australia? I enjoyed it greatly except for the theater itself. The floor was literally covered with peanut shells. I'd certainly hate to come in there barefooted. Also the Aussies like to eat ice cream during the show. It beats anything I've ever seen. They smoke any place in the theater and you never know the lights were out. All in all, it's quite an experience—you enjoy the surroundings almost as much as the film.

I haven't too much more in the way of news. All I know is I miss you like the dickens, and oh how I'd like to be in Houston or any place that you are. It's going to be double lonely out in this wilderness before I get home. It's new now, but I can see where it will get rather tiring.

I think I'll close, darling, and get to bed, as it's up early again tomorrow. Night dear—I love you.

Always, J.R.

Sunday, September 26, 1943

Dearest Elnora,

I suppose you are tired of this stationary, but you should be thankful it's provided or I wouldn't have any at all.

I haven't heard from you lately, but I imagine I will soon. I got a letter from Mother yesterday dated September 14. It was in answer to a letter I had written in Australia, so it only took a month round trip. You can readily see why I'm expecting to hear from you soon.

Even on Sunday here you can tell the difference in days. I think I liked those college Sundays best of all. We always had a good time then. Of course, in the Army now, there isn't supposed to be any difference between Sunday and any other day, but there is.

My mind seems to be wandering slightly. All in all, I haven't done a good deal today. I cleaned my pistol and that's about the extent of it. It was really a scorcher today. I should be able to stand that Houston weather fine after this.

I wish I could find something good to read. We should be getting a new supply of literature soon. Every time someone returns from leave, they bring something.

I'm beginning to be in desperate need of a haircut. As we have no regular barber, the boys cut each other's hair and you are liable to see anything these days. I guess I'll just have to take my chances on someone soon. I guess it really doesn't make too much difference here.

I'm getting low on ink. I hope I don't run out before I finish this letter. I'm awfully restless this evening and I don't feel like doing much of anything. I think I'll close, darling, as we must arise very early on the morrow. Give everyone my best and tell yourself that I love you very much—must be that red hair.

Always—I love you, J.R.

Photo of Marshall Riggan receiving a hair cut courtesy of Marshall Riggan.

Mission FFO 269-J: September 27, 1943

Twelve A/P on first strike in Wewak area. Dagua A/D [airdrome—air base] is the target. Results excellent—target left in flames, smoke, and explosion. 14,750 X .50 cal. and 1750 x. .30 cal. rounds expended in strafing. Buildings at Marienburg and Agoram strafed. Lt. Moore, while approaching his target, saw a Zero coming in from 7 o'clock and passing in front of him making a left bank. Airplane [Zero] was pulling up and when hit was at an altitude of 150 ft. Bursts caused one of the wheels to dropout from the wings, and several pieces were seen falling off in addition. The airplane was seen falling into the water while smoking. Two probable enemy A/P are claimed destroyed.

Wednesday, September 29, 1943

My dearest Elnora,

The mail is beginning to dribble in slowly, but surely. Just like the good old days—I received three today dated Aug. 19 and 20 and Sept. 11.

Of course, the best news was concerning Roger. It took a great weight off my mind and I know Mrs. Smith must be terribly happy. It's no joke to have the enemy on your tail and those red circles really show up on a Jap's plane. I don't imagine Roger will enjoy his visit at the expense of the Italian government. I just hope he hasn't been sent to Germany. Tell Mrs. Smith hooray for our side. She might have known that a Texan is too ornery to be killed!

I have had a recurrence of this blasted itch and it's about to drive me nuts. I have no idea what causes it, but it's a might uncomfortable.

I have finally dug up a mattress so I can begin to live again. I can hardly wait to go to bed this evening. Sleep is the best thing I do these days. I have been reading Willkie's *One World* for lack of nothing else to do. For my exercise, I have taken up ping-pong with a vengeance. In this climate, a fast game of aforesaid sport and you're really shot.

I received your airmail letters just as quickly as the V-mail. They try to get all our mail to us as rapidly as possible and I'm doing pretty well now. Your letters mean more than ever these days. You have no idea how I appreciate them darling.

Shields [Delta Tau Delta Fraternity brother] is a pretty lucky boy to be going to Illinois University. How do people get away with such things? I hope he gets a good deal out of it. It sounds pretty good to me.

We have an album of Strauss waltzes by Kostelanetz, and it is the loveliest music I know. We also have the *Show Boat* album. What a pleasure those records are here.

How come the wolves are no longer snapping at your heels? Does the ring scare them? I hope. I'll be more than glad when you own the other one. Actually, you do already if you consider it that way.

Another raise, darlin'? It sounds good to me. You may have to support me some day. I'm not proud! Maybe I'll have to be your secretary or something by that time.

I went to a show this evening and what did the star do but eat a large steak before my eyes. I must have been drooling something fierce. Nearly all we eat is canned food. I'll hate the sight of a can before this is over. I'm making myself hungry with all this talk so I'd better shut up.

Your brother must not have received much leave. Most of it was probably spent in traveling as leaves usually are.

I think I had better close, my darling, as this is all the paper I have at present. Tell your Mother and Mrs. Smith hello. Lord how I miss you already. I hope you know how much I love you for then you'll never be able to doubt it.

Always—I love you, J.R.

Photo of Delta Tau Delta Fraternity at Kansas University courtesy of University Archives, Spencer Research Library, University of Kansas Libraries. J.R. Jones is the third from the left on the middle row. Paul "Shields" Haerle is the first person on the left on the top row.

Friday, October 1, 1943

My dearest,

I got another stack of mail yesterday. It ranged from August 1 to Sept. 14. I think I have nearly all of it now. I'm really the envy of the bunch.

What I most enjoyed was the pictures—that close up of you really set me on my heels. Lord, but you looked lovely. A very nice looking brother you have my dear. Of course, my good buddies tried to convince me that you were hood winking me and that guy wasn't your brother at all—I might add that they were from Texas and hate to see a Yankee steal one of their beautiful women. Are you sure you haven't gained weight, darling? I wonder, but of course you realize I'm teasing. I get into trouble with Mother about the same subject. You'd die to see her pull in the stomach when we have our picture taken together. Then she begins to tell me about when she was a girl that she was as slender as I am and that someday I'll begin to settle.

All in all, you've been wonderful in writing. Getting all those letters was like falling in love all over again. I do every time I hear from you. Oh, those pictures of you—I can remember when I didn't have any and now I have quite a collection.

I was most pleased when you told me the whereabouts of all my friends. You didn't mention my best friend Jay Voran. You would probably have despaired had you known the two of us in college. It was enough to discourage anyone. You'll probably know all of them someday and decide they are all crazy.

You and Mother seem to be getting along famously. I wouldn't be surprised to hear any day that she has taken up welding or something. She's allergic to small towns and I think she's about to blow a gasket in New Castle.

I know Mrs. Smith must feel like a new woman since the news about Roger. I wish I could have been there to help celebrate. What a day it will be when we all gather out on their ranch and really have the time of our lives. At least I won't be taking you home early for another date. You'll have a permanent one then and your name won't be Bartlett anymore.

Everything we do should be a great adventure. We've got so much ahead of us. You'll never know how much I think about that. It won't make much difference where we are as long as we're together. I never thought much about Montgomery as a town until I was there with you. Then it seemed like the best place on earth. Many a Saturday night I used to walk those streets wondering what I'd find to do. It seemed very simple with you along. You'd make anything perfect.

I must close darling. I'll write more tomorrow. I have a good deal to do before turning. I've been daydreaming throughout this letter. I've said so many things to you there that aren't in this letter. I love you so much my darling. I'll always try to keep you aware of that. I know you are by your letters. Good night darling—

I love you—with all my heart. J.R.

Sunday, October 3, 1943

My dearest Elnora,

Good old happy Sunday—there's nothing like them. We had quite a party last night. A couple of guys walked in wearing tails and I nearly dropped dead. It later developed that they were part of the evening's entertainment. It certainly seemed strange to see something like that out here. What a good feeling it would be to crawl into something like that again. We used to gripe about so many formal dances in college—it's hard to believe.

I had a great treat this evening—a real bottle of Coke and it tasted lovely. We also got some more beer, but that Coke looked the best to me. It's odd what small things you miss.

Glenn Miller is giving forth this evening—it's "String of Pearls" and a short time ago "Daydreaming." As quickly as the popularity of music changes, I soon won't know what you're talking about.

I was just thinking about something last night, but the thought has occurred to me quite a few times before. If at all possible, let's try to spend a few days in New Orleans. We could really have a wonderful time there. It's a perfect place to cut loose in, and nearly everything worthwhile is close together. I know you would really enjoy it. It's a very pleasant thought at the present.

You know, Elnora, the more I look at your pictures, the lovelier you get. If I didn't know I were engaged to you, I'd be nuts by now. That close-up snapshot you sent me nearly finished the job. I know only too well you can smile that way. Please be careful who you aim it at. It's a mighty dangerous thing coupled with that red hair—I ought to know.

I've been wondering if Roger got away. I certainly hope so. If he has, I imagine he will really have a story to tell.

I'm going to have to do some laundry tomorrow or else. It isn't a very pleasant prospect as far as I'm concerned. I'm going to corner one of these native boys if possible and have him do it. See, you aren't the only one who has to work.

I must be closing this, darling, and head down the dark trail to bed. I've forgotten my flashlight to make things difficult. I hope all of my letters are coming through in fairly good time. I'm doing pretty well now as I've received letters in as little as two weeks.

I'm still not used to the idea of three people reading my letters, but actually I don't care how many people know

I love you. It's no secret. I should have told you often enough by now, but I'll keep on putting it in writing till I can tell you in person—I love you, my darling.
  Always, J.R.

Photo of natives washing clothes courtesy of the Lawrence J. Hickey Collection.

In 1941, President Franklin D. Roosevelt created the United Service Organization (USO) to provide emotional support to the troops, both at home and abroad.

WINGS AND A RING

Photo of Bob Hope courtesy of Marshall Riggan.

Photo of Bob Hope courtesy of the Lawrence J. Hickey Collection.

Wednesday, October 6, 1943

Dearest Elnora,

I received five more letters from you today—three of them V-mail. I feel like a pretty important guy receiving all that mail. It certainly is a change considering that two and one-half month period without a word.

What wouldn't I have given to have seen you dancing with the sailors at the canteen. They would probably have carried me out on a stretcher in convulsions. On the other hand, if I had been there, I'm not sure I would have turned you over to the Navy, not willingly anyhow.

I really saw a good show last night. It was Fred Astaire in *The Sky's the Limit*. We must get the films pretty quickly over here. The music wasn't as good as it usually is in his pictures, but the dances were better than ever. The ending looked rather familiar to me except for the fact you weren't there.

In those pictures I sent, did by any chance you spy my ex-crash bracelet? What did you do, rejuvenate it? It was in pretty sorry shape when last seen. At least you aren't leaving any doubt as to what your name is going to be sometime and that suits me just fine!

At least that church business is straightened out. I could have sworn that you said you were a Methodist, but this Episcopalian business had me stopped. You'll probably have to get married on a dead run without even looking around to see where it happened. I doubt it that will bother you very much—it shouldn't. It will really be a harem-scarem life for a few years, but think of the fun.

It's not long until Christmas, is it? That's the least of my worries at present. It's only a pleasant memory these days. Last year I had to report at Greenville Christmas Eve and the year before, well you know about that as well as I. If you had decided to spend that Christmas with some of your friends, I could have gladly shot you. On top of everything, you had to show up and surprise me with a hangover. What a night that was—The Ranch Club and *Wilhelmina, Queen of the Strippers*. Mary Lee was in bed with her new appendectomy scar, and she was irritated because she couldn't have gone along.

I don't see how we ever kept Mrs. Smith from getting wise when Roger and I both looked like we had been hit over the head, and after Daurice was included. It's a wonder Mrs. Smith didn't think I was a bad influence for her children. I never saw such a gal as Daurice. She'd have a fit if she couldn't go along with Roger and I. You missed out on many a good time then, but I suppose you were having plenty of fun on your own. Oh well, it all turned out for the best. It couldn't help but do that.

I must be closing, darling, as it's up before dawn for me. That's much too early for anything as far as I'm concerned. This has been quite a day as we had fresh eggs again. That's a big event here.

Tell everyone on the home front hello and have fun for both of us. I must be heading for my bed. Sleep is the best thing I do these days, other than think about you.

Good night darling—I hope your letters keep coming through as regularly as they have been. I'll write again soon.

Always—I love you, J.R.

Photo of J.R.'s crash bracelet courtesy of Lloyd Sullivan.

A FALLING BOMB DOESN'T WHISTLE: IT ROARS

MISSION FFO 284-AA: OCTOBER 12, 1943

Thirteen B-25s of the 501st Bomb Squadron were ordered to move to #12 strip in Dobodura with quarters at the 55th Troop Carrier Squadron. Eleven A/Ps took off under the direction of Major Fain, the Commanding Officer. The target for the day was Vanakanau Airdrome which was struck by the entire 345th Bomb Group under Lt. Col. True, with the 501st Squadron flying in number two position. Rendezvous was made at Oro Bay from where the Group flew in a north-northeast direction to the mouth of the Warangoi River on the east coast of the Gazelle Peninsula. The actual attack was made by flying abreast. Average distance between A/P was 100 ft. The practice of flying abreast over the target was found to be very effective. It calls for a rigid adherence of each pilot to stay on his course and not to be tempted by changing same in order to improve his own effective bombing. The mission was most successful with many large and small fires started. Two "Bettys" [Japanese airplane] and 2 SSFs were destroyed on the ground. There was no loss of plane or crew.

Thursday, October 14, 1943

Dearest Elnora,

I'm sorry I haven't written the past few days, but it has been rather impossible. I have been through a couple of hair-raising days, but I'll have to tell you about that some other time. I can tell you, however, that a falling bomb doesn't whistle—it roars. I make a very graceful picture dressed in underwear and helmet diving into a slit trench. Such is life—but I'll take vanilla.

I received several letters from you today—one as late as Sept. 28, others Sept. 4-8. I get variety, as you can see, and it takes me being on my toes figuring what is what. One of the letters contained that snapshot—pardon me, but is that your tongue hanging out? Also, I wish that was me with the arm around you. I guess one can't have everything, can they? Even with the tongue out, it's very nice of you darling. I can't tell you how much I appreciate it.

I was paid today, but Lord knows I don't need money very badly. I still get nearly $115, and $150 goes home every month. It probably won't take us long to spend it all once we get started, but think of the fun. (If you smell anything odd about this letter, it's probably brandy. It tastes good too.) Remember once I told you we'd have a great time talking in a bar, and we did in Montgomery. We must have talked for hours in the Drum Room. I know much better places, though, and I'll take you to them some day. Then however, there couldn't have been a better place in the world. In fact, we were rather oblivious of our surroundings.

I'm desperately in need of some clean clothes. If I can't find a native boy soon I'll be in a terrible fix. In fact, it will be so bad that I'll have to do it myself and that will be disastrous. I hate work like that—I would rather dig ditches. It's a hard job to keep clean around here too. If it isn't dust, it's mud. I've decided you can't win at all.

There are some kinds of bugs very definitely annoying me tonight. They go for the light I am writing by. Nothing but hardships—that's us. I'm really not complaining yet. Keep me about six more months however, and I'll really be crying on your shoulder. I guess I'll hold up though.

You said you had "Rhapsody in Blue" and "Love Walked In" by Kostelanetz. So have we, and you have nothing on us even in the sticks. You love your music, don't you, darling? Already you mention tunes I've never heard. You will be way ahead of me soon, dear. Think of how much you'll have to teach me when I get back. I hear the older songs and will continue to do so until the records wear out, and then heaven knows what I'll do. Just use my imagination I suppose.

Good night, darling—I'm heading for bed. I'll be back soon. I'll write as often as possible as you already know and you should already know too that I love you so much.

Always—I love you, J.R.

Photo of tent construction in New Guinea courtesy of Marshall Riggan.

Friday, October 15, 1943

Elnora darling,

Two more letters today. This has been quite a week. Four days out of a week, I get mail from you. I haven't received any from Mother lately though. Your last letter was a V-mail and quite exasperating too. In it you said you had much to tell me, and now I probably won't receive the letter for a few days now. You spoke of troubles. I hope you were kidding—such things don't sound pleasant to me these days.

I probably won't be able to write again for a few days, so there may be a short gap between letters. Not too long though, darling. It's rather hard to write when I have so much to tell and can say so little.

You must really run up a phone bill, my dear. I didn't know you were so gabby. Every time I called you on the phone, I had to talk like mad. I hate to think what our next conversation will be like, but it will be comforting to know that I'm close enough to make a call. When I get back, you'd better do your talking in the daytime and save the evenings for me.

I think I'll go off to a show in a little while. I feel wound up like a spring, and I don't know when I'm going to uncoil. I have no idea what the show's about, but it doesn't make much difference any more. Just something to do to relax.

I just got back from the show. It wasn't so good, but it helps to pass an evening. Just think—when we are together again we'll never have to wonder how to spend time. It will really whip by then.

I'm now writing this letter amidst utmost confusion. There is quite a party in progress in the club at present. All I wish is that you were here, but I don't imagine you would find this part of the world very fascinating.

I'm having a devil of a time finishing this letter between interruptions. We even have them out here.

I must close and skip as it is nearly midnight. Here the moon would really amaze you—however, to us it may mean having to wake up in the middle of the night.

Good night darling,—tell everyone hello and give them my love. Lord, but I'm in love with you and always will be.

Always my dear, J.R.

Photo of mission briefing courtesy of Marshall Riggan.

Wednesday, October 20, 1943

Dearest Elnora,

Another week is well on its way. I've received letters from you every day this week except today. Actually, I'm becoming very spoiled. I can see you are faltering now, but I can't blame you. You have been marvelous in the number of letters you have written to me. You must have a very fertile mind to be able to write so much. I've more to tell you these days than ever before, but they won't let me. As they say—that's life.

I told mother this evening that I have now been on five missions, and some of them have been killers. I've about seen everything now, and I didn't waste much time in doing it. I've really had my fingers crossed a couple of times. Every time it gets tough I take out that silver dollar you gave me and toss it for luck—saying to myself—come on, let's get back for Red.

Somehow that piece of silver means a great deal to me. I suppose it was because you gave it to me on the spur of the moment. I get rather amused when I think how I swindled you out of it. As I recall, I asked to borrow 15 cents at the same time. Just a gigolo, that's me.

As I said in the last letter, I haven't been able to write for a few days. I may be able to catch up somewhat now. I bought myself to a nice new uniform and a pair of shoes yesterday—both colored brown and GI, if you please. Latest style notes—if you could see the way we dress, you would give me up for lost.

You sound as if you are really having a wonderful time. Lord, but I envy you and those who are able to go out with you. Tell me, darling, hasn't a man ever crossed you up, or have you always had your own way? I rather imagine you have, and I can see why too. Have a good time for both of us and tell me about it.

How are all my friends in the Smith family? I do wish I had more time to see them when I was in Houston, but I had so much to talk to you about that it was impossible. I think Mrs. Smith was rather aware of that fact, however. She told me the next day that I was a pretty lucky boy, and I believe her. I have written to her, but I wonder if she has received it yet.

You speak of it getting cooler in Houston. That really sounds good to me. This weather is really getting to be something. It's even worse than Swamp Wallace [Camp Wallace, Hitchcock]. At the time, I thought nothing could be worse.

Something tells me I had better close this and get to bed as midnight is approaching. I guess you know that I love you don't you? You ought to—if you don't, you can't see your left hand.

Night darling—see you tomorrow.
Always—I love you, J.R.

Photo of J.R.'s good luck charm silver dollar courtesy of Lloyd Sullivan.

This is the coin that J.R. always carried on his person, given to him by Elnora as a good-luck charm.

The coin was originally given to Elnora by her father, which was a practice common at that time, being based upon the year of the person's birth. I actually have my mother's silver dollar.

Saturday, October 23, 1943

Dearest Elnora,

Another day, another letter. It's quite a pleasure I assure you. In your last letter, you finally became aware that I had received some mail. Now we can take it from there. It took quite a while to get everything straightened up, didn't it?

What I can't understand is how your friend recognized me at Hamilton Field when she didn't know me. I don't recall the name at least. Oh, I was there all right, as you know already. I would have liked to have stayed there too, but I wasn't around long.

I must get up early tomorrow and go to church. It's not a very pleasant reason, I assure you. I must also write the boy's mother. What does a man say at such times? I don't know—it's very difficult—I do know that.

We had a picture show this evening—*Edge of Darkness*—nothing like a good war picture, I always say. Personally, I prefer Donald Duck, but they can't please everyone. We also had one of those community sing jobs. I always especially enjoy the part where it says for the boys to sing one part and girls the other. It invariably brings down the house. See, we aren't hard to entertain. Betty Grable in a sweater is always good for a twenty-minute riot.

Did you say we danced that night we went to the Plantation? All I can remember is staring at you in amazement all evening and saying to myself, "No one can be that lovely and get away with it." You didn't get away with it, did you? As I recall, you're supposed to get married one of these days—any truth in that story? I know how you can get slugged by one U.S. aviator if you come up with the wrong answer.

I must be bringing this to an end, darling, and head for ye old sack. What in heaven's name do you put on your letters? Every time I open one in the mess hall to read in the evening, the boys eye me suspiciously, and I say, "Honestly, fellows, I haven't got a woman hidden anywhere." Don't stop it though, dear, for that fragrance brings me one step closer to someone I love. I can read and close my eyes, and you really aren't so far away. Have you ever been?

I love you—always, J.R.

Mission FFO 296-AA: October 24, 1943

Eleven B-25s of the 501st Bomb Squadron were ordered to proceed to Dobodura and be in readiness for a mission of 24 October 1943. The squadron was given orders by the FATF to conduct a strike on Vunakanau during the morning of 24 October 1943. Rendezvous with the fighter escort was made at Oro Bay, thence proceeded to the Bun's wreck for rendezvous with the Third Attack Group. The squadron's run over the target was executed excellently with all A/P being well spaced and covering the area thoroughly. The mission was very successful. All targets were left in smoke with seven Bettys, one SIKE [Japanese plane], and one U/I M/B definitely destroyed on the ground. Interception was weak and there was no loss of plane or crew.

Monday, October 25, 1943

Dearest Elnora,

Honestly, darling, it is so hot this evening that it is pitiful. These next months are really something to dread. I once thought Houston was hot in August, but that was nothing. Christmas should really be a killer. Dear, west Texas was never like this, and you may take my word for that.

So you'd like to have me for a roommate, eh? I can't say that I dislike the idea myself. It won't take long for us to arrange that legally some day. I'd like nothing more than to tell you where I am, but there are rules, my dear. Just read the papers for spectacular events around here, and you can guess. At least you should be able to. If not, you'll just have to wait.

I have imbibed in several Tom Collins this evening, and they were excellent. We have even had ice and that indeed is a rare treat.

I read by the papers where KU beat Nebraska in football. That hasn't happened since 1894, and I would have to miss it. It only took a second world war for us to do it. It's rather ironic.

Two months from tomorrow is Christmas. The time goes rapidly at that, still it seems a long time since June. You'll never really know how I worried about getting that leave then. If anything had prevented it, I would have torn my hair, and you'll never know how close it came to falling through. At last, luck came my way.

I'm so glad, my dear, that you think there is no mistake in our romance. I was convinced of that long ago. I couldn't help but be. You convince pretty well, my sweet.

When you see Mrs. Smith, give her a kiss for me. She was the closest to a second mother I ever hope to have. I would do anything for that family.

Have a good time, but when in doubt look at your left hand, and that is the most tangible proof that I—

Love you always, J.R.

Photo of mission briefing courtesy of the Lawrence J. Hickey Collection.

I GUESS IRVING BERLIN WAS RIGHT

Friday, October 29, 1943

Dearest Elnora,

This is the last of the paper, but I'll dig up some more; never fear. While I write this, I'm feeding the phonograph, so I'll break about every three minutes. You should know how that goes. Nothing new, just a few memories.

For my weather comment this evening—guess—it's raining. How did you do it? At least the weather is consistent even if it is bad, and it gives us something to talk about. It's still hot even with rain, and I'm sticking to the paper. I wish I could stick close enough to get back to you in this letter.

Speaking of letters, I haven't heard from you for four days. That's tough, isn't it? Especially since you have written me so much of late. I can't complain, my dear; you are the world's best correspondent. I once could knock out a pretty good letter in a short time, but now I always have to leave out so much.

I finally dug up another book to read. It is *Quietly My Captain Waits*. It's a novel about early French America. It's supposedly pretty good, but I'll read it whether it's good or not. God, I could complete my law studies in my spare time around here. Oh well, I didn't want to be a lawyer anyhow.

You really are getting around, darling. Perhaps it's a good thing you aren't married now. I think it would kill you to stay at home, wouldn't it? I like to know you are enjoying yourself—even though I do get a bit envious at times, but that's only natural. In fact, you'd probably be peeved if I didn't. It all goes around in circles, darling.

You should have been in Sacramento with me before I left. We really had a last fling. That is really some town. I hadn't been there for a long time, so I had to reacquaint myself. Donald Novis was singing in one of the nightclubs and we were there so much, we got to know everyone in the place. I amazed myself by doing a very funny rumba there one evening. I did it with the tap dance specialty in the floorshow, but it wasn't during the floorshow. Someone had a date with her, and I asked her to dance. The rumba usually comes out in me after the sixth drink.

I must be closing, dear. I miss you so much—so much more now that I know you're waiting. Good night, darling—I'll love you always. I'll write again soon.

Always, my love, J.R.

Saturday, October 30, 1943

Dearest Elnora,

Lovely paper isn't this, and I even had to pilfer it. I finally received a letter from you and, oddly enough, it was written on a Saturday evening. Three weeks old, to be exact. I'm not listening to the *Hit Parade*, however, as it is about Friday afternoon where you are. I am hearing J.

Strauss waltzes very beautifully played by Kostelanetz. Of course, it's on the phonograph and not the radio.

I saw a wonderful show last night. It was *This is the Army*. We really got that picture in short order. It was the best picture I have seen since I left the U.S. The music was lovely. You know the tunes—"I'm Getting Tired So I Can Sleep" and "I Left My Heart at a Stage Door Canteen." On the comic side was, "This Is the Army, Mr. Jones" and "Ladies of the Chorus." It was the kind of a show that you hate to see end. The music was very nostalgic, and it made one a trifle homesick. Nearly all numbers were sung by a large chorus, and somehow they gave the music a very definite appeal. I know you'll like it very much if you haven't already seen it by now.

I've done quite a bit of reading today. I began James Hilton's *Without Armor*, and I enjoyed so much that I had to finish it. As you can plainly see, I haven't been too busy today. It's a hard life I lead, darling.

So you don't like "Pistol Packin' Mama"? I've nearly been driven to murder after hearing it a few times myself. It was a great South Carolina favorite.

You shouldn't have bought me a Christmas present my dear. Heaven only knows when I'll receive it, but everything gets here eventually. Anyhow, darling, I thank you with all of my heart. I won't be able to reciprocate, I suppose you know. I could send you a bunch of bananas or a coconut, but I wouldn't guarantee their state of arrival. We really don't have a wide range of selection here. We are saving our largest presents for the Japs, and I sincerely hope they get a big *bang* out of them.

Believe it or not, it hasn't rained today. Anything can happen now. We'll probably have an air raid to pass the time. They don't bother us a good deal, but I've been at some other places where the b— kept me awake half the night. They don't like to come over in the daylight, because very few of them usually get home.

So you're in the mood for love—it says so in the letter. You think I'm not, maybe. It's been quite a while since I've even seen a white woman. All I have to do is look at your picture, and I'm quite ready to tear my hair out. After a year, little girl—look out. Perhaps you had better first greet me with a minister as your escort. See, I'm in a slightly devilish mood myself. You won't be the only one in the family.

Has Mrs. Smith heard any more from Roger? I truly hope so. Give the Smith family my regards. I shall have to write Mrs. Smith again shortly.

Good night, darling. I should hear from you tomorrow without fail. I hope you'll be doing the same. At least I'm trying and you already know—

I love you—always, J.R.

Photo of soldier relaxing courtesy of Marshall Riggan.

Monday, November 1, 1943

My dearest Elnora,

    I hit the jackpot today and received six letters from you. The last was dated Oct. 16, and that isn't too far away. Also I received a note from my grandmother, which rather surprised me. Mother usually does the writing for the entire family, and instead of my writing to everyone, they just read my letters. It really saves time anyhow. Grandmother says that it sounds as if I have a very fine girl—she doesn't know the half of it, but I'll make very sure that she does.

    I received the last snapshot too. Who is the shapely gal in the center? I could really go for her. Perhaps I should say I did go for her in a big way.

    We really threw a party in the club last night. One of the boys discovered that he was a father yesterday, and we all helped him celebrate. As a result, I've felt far from good all day. This climate is definitely not an aid to a hangover. We'll hold a party at the drop of a hat, and we don't have to strive very hard to dig up an occasion. Last night however was a super blast, and today I am repenting.

    Yesterday evening we had a rainstorm to end all rainstorms. It was faintly reminiscent of that night driving back from Ellington Field. The main difference is, however, that you weren't there this time. That small fact throws a different complexion on everything. The rainy season is just beginning, and oh what fun that is going to be. Many more showers like that one last night, and I'm going to transfer to the Navy.

    You must have seen that show with Fred Astaire within a few days of the time I did. Even a war can't keep me very far from you. I know all too well how it feels that last evening before you must leave your country. It's a great adventure, but it's rather sad to look at lights of home and wonder when you'll see them again.

Have you learned not to play with razor blades yet, darling? What made me think of that is that they have told us that the natives greatly value them. They are very useful in trading, in case the time ever comes. For my part, I hope it never does.

Tell me, my dear, how do you remember all the names of those places in Montgomery? You seem to have a very acute memory for such things. It's impossible to say how much fun we had then. I know I was the happiest then than I had been in a year and a half. Even in the knowledge that I had to leave in a short time. Oh well, it can't last forever I keep telling myself, but the memories of a few days with you do.

Good night, dear—what wouldn't I give to say that in person. I miss you so my darling and

I love you—always, J.R.

While visiting the National Air and Space Museum—Steven F. Udvar-Hazy Center at Dulles Airport, I saw an exhibit of items used to barter with natives if a crew was shot down in enemy territory in the SWPA. Items ranged from razor blades, as J.R. mentions in his letter above, to beads. There were many cannibal tribes in the area, but the majority of the natives were friendly toward crews and assisted them back to safer territory, even hiding them from the Japanese, which would have meant certain death for the natives had this been discovered.

November 2, 1943, was a very important day for the 345th in their efforts to advance the war toward Japan. Melvin Best shared a copy of a pamphlet that was sent to his mother by General H. H. Arnold, U.S. Army and Commanding General, Army Air Forces, which states the following:

Mrs. Grace A. Best
Dear Mrs. Best:

I know you will have a very personal interest in the accompanying book, which tells the story of the bold attack made on Japanese shipping in Simpson Harbor, Rabaul, on November 2, 1943. The book has been specially prepared as a tribute to the intrepid airmen who made this fine accomplishment possible, one of whom was your son, First Lieutenant Melvin L. Best.

The story and pictures reveal to you the scope and daring of this operation—how our aircraft attacked at below masthead height and, in only twelve minutes, destroyed or damaged 114,572 tons of enemy shipping and destroyed 85 Japanese aircraft.

This is a bright page in the history of the Army Air Forces, indeed in the history of our country. Aside from the importance of the raid for its destruction of enemy material, its morale value was incalculable: the aggressor was once again given a taste of barbed American steel, was once again shown how our determination, courage, and singleness of purpose have made us the great nation that we are.

What was done at Rabaul was done by individual Americans working together as a team for our common cause. The history of our nation contains the names of stirring battles, and Rabaul has now been added to this list. When its name is mentioned in time to come, and all our countrymen remember the glory of that day, you may contemplate with pride upon the part your son played in this historic event.

The foreword of this pamphlet states the following:

In the space of twelve minutes, a formidable Japanese sea and air armada, in the powerful, well-organized, well-defended stronghold of Rabaul, was attacked and decisively defeated.

Never in the long history of warfare has so much destruction been wrought upon the forces of a belligerent nation so swiftly and at such little cost to the victor.

Saturday, November 6, 1943

Dearest Elnora,

Hi, darling. Have you ever received a letter from a bartender? Well, you have now. I'm official Squadron barkeep this evening. Business is a little slack at present, so I'm standing behind the bar writing. Believe it or not, I'm not my own best customer this evening. I've had nothing but ice water, and that is a rare treat. I'm planning on drinking a can of tomato juice pretty soon, and that should relieve the monotony. Most of the boys are at the show now, so I'll be having a rush later on.

I looked in the mailbox this evening and what do you know, a letter from Elnora. It was dated Sept. 10. I don't know what happened to that poor letter, but it really has been around from the appearance of the envelope. I don't particularly care about the date of a letter just as long as it's from you.

One of the fellows heard the *Hit Parade* today, and it seems "Sunday, Monday, or Always" is number one. Of course the program was a rebroadcast, as it's Sunday in the U.S. I'm glad I finally heard that song so I know what you're talking about. I rather like it myself. I heard Red Skelton myself this evening and the Firestone Program with Richard Crooks.

I'll never forget when Crooks gave a recital at college. In the middle of "Kashmiri" song, a telephone began to ring backstage. After two rings, he was very exasperated and on the third ring he stopped completely and said, "Will someone pulleeze answer the phone?" His accompanist went scurrying offstage to see if he could get the annoyance stopped. Someone finally condescended to answer the phone, and so Mr. Crooks proceeded to sing the "Kashmiri" song all over again. It was all the audience could do to keep from laughing. He was such a pompous looking little duck. Lawrence Tibett made the best and most gracious male singer I've ever seen. Of course, the ladies always manage to be much more capable in winning their audiences.

I seem to be in the higher brackets this evening. I presume it's because I was playing highbrow music this afternoon—Wagner's "Love Music of Tristran and Isolde" and Schubert's "Unfinished Symphony." I like Tchaikovsky's "Romeo and Juliet" best. I suppose it is because it has a very recognizable theme. Larry Clinton made it very popular calling it "Our Love." Of course, I wound up the session with Harry James playing the "Mole." You might know that I couldn't hold out too long.

Well, Red my darling, the time is come for me to scram. I wonder if you were with me this Saturday night. Did you ever wonder what it will be like when we can spend all of our time together, and no more letters?

Good night, dear—I'll write again tomorrow, and I want you for Christmas.

I love you—always, J.R.

Sunday, November 7, 1943

Dearest Elnora,

I hit the jackpot today—seven letters from you and two from Mother, a whole week's supply. The last letter contained most welcomed news. So Mrs. Smith has finally received word from Roger. I guess that makes everyone feel better all the way around. I hope to God he isn't injured too badly. In Mrs. Smith's mind, the world must seem like a wonderful place again. I can see her point.

So you are going to take some more snapshots. That's music to my tired old ears. I can't think of anything I'd rather have from you—I mean, within reason. I think you know how that goes. I wish I could send you some pictures of me here, but I don't think I can manage it for a while. Besides, you'd be disappointed in the hair cut. I nearly have all my hair off again. It was really a dream in Hawaii.

You mentioned how much you liked Bettye's home. I hope you realize, my sweet, what you're getting into when you marry an Army officer. You may have to even live in a tree sometimes. Of course, even there you would look pretty, but it might be uncomfortable at times. It might be an apple tree though, and then you could keep an eye on me, and we could eat for nothing. No fooling though, dear. I've seen some pretty tough places.

I should have liked to have seen that fishing expedition. Did all the freckles jump out? I wouldn't be surprised. By the way, I was looking for something in the dictionary, and my eye caught the word *redhead*—a person with red hair; esp. with a quick temper. That's what Webster said, but I love you, dear, regardless.

You really came up with some beautiful color combinations in stationary in this last bunch. It took me ten minutes to get up nerve to take one out of the envelope. It was terrific. I sincerely sympathize in this stationary problem.

I'll try to write again tomorrow. It's very late, and I must rush. Good night, dear—I miss you so—and I love you with all my heart.

Always—my love, J.R.

Daily Log: November 11, 1943

2nd Lt. Jones from duty to sick hospital.

Sunday, November 14, 1943

Dearest Elnora,

Guess where I am—of all places in a hospital. Don't get excited, it's nothing serious, nothing more than good old dysentery. I'm all right now, and the reason I'm here is because they have me on a diet. I'm getting swell food, and I'm not the least bit hungry. I did spend two very miserable days, and I hope I've seen the last of this business.

This hospital isn't bad at all. Cool with a view of water—beautiful sheets. I haven't seen those in months. Breakfast in bed. It's quite a life, but confidentially, I'll be glad to get out. I should before long. This is a rather confining situation being sick.

I should have some mail from you in the squadron, and I wish I could get my hands on it. I'll be out of here shortly though, and I'll be able to satisfy my curiosity. It's the middle of November already. Lord if I don't get to work soon, I'll never get home. I have been far from busy lately.

Right at present, I wish you were an Army nurse, my dear Red. Of course, you would have trouble keeping a certain patient from trying to kiss you. How's your resistance? The days would certainly go much faster.

They're considering letting me out of the joint this afternoon, and that thought pleases me to no end. I hope I'm forgiven for this short lapse in writing, but darling, I just couldn't make it. I will catch up in the next few days, and I did write a good deal to you before I got sick.

I might think this very beautiful country if I didn't know I had to stay here. That spoils everything. I think the Fiji Islands are the most beautiful I've ever seen though. That is a true paradise. Then again, I've been on an island where they only had one tree, and that wasn't so nice. Frankly, I prefer my islands a little closer to the U.S.

There hasn't been much in the way of good shows lately. They have one at the hospital nearly every evening, but I didn't feel too much like going. I did see Red Skelton in *I Dood It*. I enjoyed the music in it very much, and I'll have to admit that Skelton was funny at times.

I think I'll close now darling and go eat and then prepare to go home. I'll write again this evening when I get back to the squadron and see if I have any mail from you. I certainly should by now.

Be back in a while, dear, so don't go far. Bye, sweet—you couldn't guess how much I love—

Always—my love, J.R.

Daily Log: November 14, 1943

2nd Lt. Jones from sick hospital to duty station.

In speaking with Melvin Best, 345th member, I learned that each morning the soldiers were given a large yellow pill, Atabrine, to help prevent malaria. He said that by the time they returned stateside, they had taken so many yellow pills that their skin had a yellow tinge. His wife, Gladys Best, confirmed that it took five or six months before his skin coloring lost the yellow glow.

Sunday, November 14, 1943, Evening

Dearest Elnora,

I had quite a surprise returning to the squadron. I had many, many letters from you. Beginning July 1 and a whole flock of them mailed July 22 when you first received my address. They were the letters that held so many answers to questions that had previously baffled me. Now much is very clear to me.

I have no idea what held these letters up so long, but I was very glad to see them. Most of them were written while you weren't hearing from me, and they show it. They were some of the sweetest letters I have ever received from you. Some of the things you said made me wish more than ever I was on my way to get you.

I also received two letters from Mrs. Smith that were originally mailed to Greenville. One of them contained a letter from Roger written to me. It seemed so strange to read it—like something from out of nowhere. Then later in the day when more mail came in, I received a note from you saying Mrs. Smith had received a letter from Roger. That made everything work out perfectly. I'm so glad Roger's letter didn't arrive till night, and I felt at ease once more about the whole thing. The Smiths mean as much to me as my own family, and their happiness is mine. You had such perfect faith, my darling, that he would be safe and he was. You must have been an immense help to them. I'm very proud of you for that. The letter in which you first told me he was missing, and what you said is something I never want to forget about you. With such an outlook you can't ever be unhappy, my dear. It erases all the doubts I ever had.

That four-month-old letter of Mrs. Smith's pleased me [to] no end. She said she would make you behave, and I believe it. She looks upon us as such small children, but beware my dear if anything should ever come between us. I think she would murder both of us.

Roger's letter was dated June 29, and even at that date, he was congratulating me on my engagement. He had pretty rapid news from someplace. See, my dear, you are surrounded.

As for your friend that saw me in California, I suspect that she was entirely correct. I was there at that time, and I didn't stay long. It's entirely possible that I was the kid. California is an excellent place to be. I'd certainly like being stationed there someday—I imagine you'd rather enjoy it yourself.

I also received several letters from you. The latest was a V-mail dated Oct. 31. In it you said I was to receive some more pictures that naturally I haven't received as yet, but I plainly have something to look forward to. That always irritates me to know I have something coming, and yet I haven't received it as yet. No patience, I guess.

Another surprise that I got upon returning to the squadron was that one of the boys had received two new albums of music. One of them was a Cole Porter tune as played by Eddy Duchin. The other was a familiar modern song by Kostelanetz. Such tunes as "Night and Day," "Time on My Mind," "Dancing in the Dark," and one of my favorites, "The Touch of Your Hand." Needless to say, I have played all of them many times. We do pretty well on records. It really amazes me. I see where the recording ban has been lifted, and I suppose all the new songs will go into action now. That shouldn't worry us too much.

So Mrs. Smith is going to tell me that you can hardly get through the door. I can readily see that gal is on my side. I hope she gives you hell regularly. She is my best ally.

You've gone and banged up a toe now. Actually, I don't know what I'm going to do with you. If you don't break your neck before I get back, I'll be surprised. I often wonder who is taking the bigger chance, you or me. I think I'll have to get your mother to keep you under lock and key. I can see that you are going to be a problem.

So you want to know my history. Well it's like this; in Wichita I attended High School East and in Kansas City it was Southwest High. That may sound like a lot of different directions, but that's the truth. Anyone who didn't go to Southwest in Kansas City will probably say, "oh," and let it go at that. It was that kind of a place. Everyone was rich in that district—generally speaking, and it doesn't include me, so no one else liked the place. I liked the place immensely, however, and had nearly as much fun as I did in college. Thus, another brief synopsis—more follows later.

Night, darling—I love you so much, and Lord how I miss you. Hope I get those pictures soon.

Always—I love you, J.R.

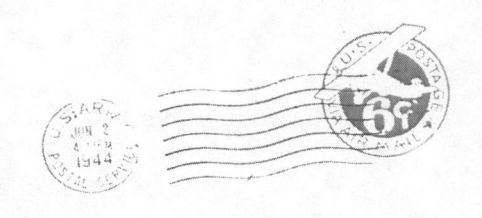

HOW ABOUT A DATE THIS EVENING?

MONDAY, NOVEMBER 15, 1943

Dearest Elnora,

Well here I am again, as you can plainly see. I'm not exactly crowded with news, but I have a good many of your letters to answer, both old and new.

How do you like this fancy paper? Some more of the Sydney Special, and it's pretty good stuff for letters. I hope you can read it when you receive it. I should get some violet colored paper and get even with you. White is hard enough to get, let alone something flashy. Paper is rationed in Australia, and that's the main reason we have trouble getting it. They will only sell us 50 sheets at a time. I'm lousy with paper now so I should do all right. Airmail does just as well, and besides, nothing can take the place of a letter. That's a slightly broad statement I'll admit, because I'll take my redheads in person any day.

I got into a swift game of volleyball today, and I'm in great condition. Under this blasted sun, even a game of marbles is too strenuous. It seems that no matter what you did before you got in the Air Force, you just naturally get lazy after a time and avoid all forms of exercise. All your talk about ice-skating though makes me wish I were in a position to try it again. I wouldn't go so far as to say that I wish I were in Alaska, but 15 degree less temperature would improve things immensely.

How's the banged up toe coming? I'm about even with you. I knocked a finger out of joint playing volleyball, but I can still hold a beer glass. Speaking of beer, we have a new supply in the club and now I can put back a little of that lost weight. When I go on leave, I'm going to drink beer by the gallon and eat steaks till I burst. I'm quite anxious to see this wonderful town of Sydney I've heard so much about.

I've just read the latest issue of *Life*—Sept. 16. In it was the latest fashions—leotards—in other words, long underwear with skirts. If that becomes an American vogue, I shall indeed throw up my hands. Women are truly nuts, but I love them. I'd best narrow that down before I get into trouble. Okay, so it's just one in particular.

How about a date this evening? We could go to dinner, a show and then someplace, for a dance and a beer. Afterwards we could neck in the parlor. There I go taking opium again. Oh well, I can tell you I love you even if I'm not with you this evening. Bye dear—I gotta go—

I love you—always, J.R.

Tuesday, November 16, 1943

Dearest Elnora,

What do you know—three letters today! Another old one turned up July 24th—then Oct. 29th and a really rapid-moving V-mail of Nov. 5. That last one really came through, eleven days and nearly 10,000 miles. That's nearly as fast as I got letters in Greenville.

I went to a show tonight and saw the *Constant Nymph*. I really didn't enjoy it very much. I suppose it was because I was too far back and I could neither see nor hear too well. I believe I could have liked it very much had I been able to see it in a decent place. Oh well, we can't have everything, can we?

In a couple of your old letters, you mentioned my getting promoted. That point rather tickled me. Rapid promotions depend upon the fact whether you get into a new unit or one that has room for promotion. To date I haven't, but I should in a couple of months. Promotion never is very rapid overseas for some reason. All the boys at home seem to get them, and they actually do less than anyone. As I was a new man in an old squadron here, I, as usual, got rocked again. The flying we do here is something that would curl your hair in a hurry. I know most of the other pilots don't envy us our jobs.

Good night, darling—I realize this hasn't been much of a letter, but I'll do better tomorrow. Perhaps I can dig up some fresh news. I can tell you some old news if you'd care to hear it. Of course, you wouldn't know that I happen to be in love with you. Anyhow, I am—very much so.

Always—my love, J.R.

Wednesday, November 17, 1943

Elnora darling,

High-ho—four letters from you today all dated November 4. Pretty big rush, isn't it? I still haven't received those pictures. I hope that letter didn't get lost in the shuffle, but I presume it will turn up sooner or later.

I did receive the letter from Shields. That was a pretty good picture. He makes a good-looking soldier, but you'd better not tell him so. I can't have you going around flattering other men. It's been nearly two and a half years since I've seen any of my good friends. I keep wondering when I'll run across the next one. I wish you knew more of my friends. You'll sure get a chance to meet some of them now. Also, I do wish you had met Jay. I've no doubt what he would think about you. I'd sure like to meet his wife too. I suppose all of that will come later.

Dear, I can think of nothing better I would like than a fruitcake. I most certainly do request. Also, we could use a few new records. Every time we get a new one we play it to death. I really go for those new albums by Kostelanetz and Duchin. That "Touch of Your Hand" is really a lovely bit of music. I think they could revive *Roberta* very easily as the music in it was a rare treat.

As usual I went to a show this evening. It was *Assignment in Brittany* and a nice evening's entertainment it was. It had a very good-looking young Frenchman in it. He should do quite well, but I believe he's joined the Army already. That reminds me—I see where the Army got Frank Sinatra—ain't we lucky? The war is nearly over now. Even that sort of stuff manages to crash the news over here.

So your roof has a leak. I can thoroughly sympathize with you there. My tent seems to have a nasty habit of leaking and just above my bed. I've found a way to beat that, however. I just throw my raincoat over me and go peacefully back to sleep. I'm getting so I can practically sleep any place these days—night too.

How is the future Mrs. J. these days? I'll be glad when I can call you that and no mistake about it. At least you find that people have very little difficulty in remembering your name. Combined with that red hair, they can't miss you.

The party seems to be getting rough again. It's late and I should be heading for the bed. I don't feel very sleepy though. I didn't that night in June when you didn't get home till 4:30 a.m. and I had to take off at eight the next morning. What a life! I'll certainly be glad when we can take our time for a change and not have to worry about whether there is going to be a tomorrow or not, and even when we find there is, I won't have to be going anyway.

Night, darling—I'll write again soon. Thank you for all of the lovely letters today, dear. I hope you received as many from me.

Always—I love you, J.R.

Don't ever forget it.

Thursday, November 18, 1943

Dearest Elnora,

Lord what a rainy day this has been. Nice way to begin a letter, isn't it? But all this water about me is a constant reminder. You should see our poor tent. The joint is nearly swamped, and my poor bed is a sight to behold. Thank God the mattress is rubber, and all I have to do is turn it over.

I received a V-mail from November 7 that contained the beautiful news that you now have a broken toe. Darling, I really don't know what I'm going to do with you if you persist in maiming yourself in such a fashion. I can readily see I'm going to have my hands full with you some day. I can't say that I mind either. I'll just take you to an Army doctor and then you'll wish that you had been more careful. I don't mean to joke too much about it, dear, but such things happen. Like the time I got running spikes in me at the Texas Relays. I do hope it isn't troubling you too much. I'm beginning to think you should marry a doctor and not a flier. Of course, I'm not really convinced of that. I'm not that dumb.

So you would like to know when I think about you most. That's a trifle difficult to answer, but I think it's in the evenings when I'm writing you. My thoughts are pretty much concerned with you just before I go to bed or around about five in the evening when the mail comes in. Actually, I'm liable to start thinking about you any time during the day when I sit back for a few minutes without anything to do.

It's a trifle later than I thought, my dear. I must go down and drain out my bed shortly.

I wonder at times if you really realize how much it means to me to know you are waiting for me back there. It makes all we do here seem to have some meaning. Anyhow, darling, it won't be so long. At least we know there is an end in sight.

I seem to be a trifle erratic about leaving out words, etc. this evening. I must have my thoughts slightly ahead of my pen.

I should break off and beat it at this point. They have a nasty habit of getting up early around here. When do I think of you dear—right now you're it. I love you so very much my darling. Good night—I'll be around tomorrow. I'm always around somewhere.

Always—my love, J.R.

Saturday, November 20, 1943

Dearest Elnora,

What a dead Saturday night this is—exactly nothing is taking place. I hope yours was more of a success than this, but I also hope you are missing me as much as I do you right now. It's something fierce.

I didn't write yesterday because I didn't have time during the day, and last night we threw another of our tremendous parties and I got slightly that way. It was some more of that lovely punch we make and what a kick it has. We used to call it *Purple Passion* in college. It could really put a lot of life in a picnic. Those picnics were really something, my dear. We used to build the biggest fire you ever saw, and everyone would gather round and have the time of their lives. After all this primitive life, however, I believe I'll settle for a city permanently.

I went to a show this evening, and it was a stinker; it isn't worth mentioning. I doubt if they ever dared to show that one in the states. I don't see why they should push it off on us either. I can't complain though for they manage to do pretty well most of the time. It's beginning to rain nearly every night now, and that rather puts a crimp in our entertainment activities.

I should be going on leave in a few days and am I ever looking forward to that. Just think, civilization again.

Perhaps I shall be able to get you a Christmas present after all. At least I hope so. I doubt though that you will receive it till after Christmas. You know me, always late, but I eventually come around. What I most want to see is a good meal. I'll probably eat myself to death. I know I am certainly going to try. I'm told Sydney is an excellent place for leave, and I'm plenty eager about the whole thing. I'm not sure if I'll be able to write while I'm gone. So if a lull comes you'll know the reason. I can't see why I shouldn't be able to though.

How is the broken toe these days? Much better, I hope. Do you have to hobble around? I thought you were going to break your neck once or twice, the last time we were together. I'll be more than glad when I'm around to keep an eye on you.

I'll write you again tomorrow, and if those pictures don't turn up soon I'm going to tear my hair. That reminds me I need to get a haircut tomorrow. I always forget to do that. Night, darling; it's a crime for anyone to miss someone as I do you.

Always—I love you, J.R.

The picture of the soldier on the latrine was added to give you a flavor of what an *advanced* camp's amenities were. The interesting thing to note here is that he is considered to be in uniform as he has his helmet on.

Photo of latrine courtesy of the Lawrence J. Hickey Collection.

Monday, November 22, 1943

Dearest Elnora,

Hi darling—I've been quite irritated all day and not feeling too cheerful, but this evening everything seems a good deal brighter. Perhaps the fact that I received three letters from you added to the bettering of my humor. Do you think you'll be able to cope with an occasional grouch, my dear?

I have been made airdrome officer again, which consists of taking care of anything that might turn up. I have answered the phone so much today I feel like a switchboard operator.

I have received both letters from Shields now. I don't know what I'd do without you, dear. You will make a very lovely secretary to sit on my lap some day. That is if you don't get too heavy. I'm really sorry, but I just couldn't resist that one. You should know by now, if you didn't have a really zoot figure, I wouldn't dare tease you.

I also had a letter from Mother Landes today. It seems my engagement was quite a surprise to her. I'd forgotten that I was so out of touch with everyone. If you ever meet some of my friends some day, they will look a little trifle surprised when they find I married a redhead. I don't think I'll introduce you to any single friends of mine, because if they are the wolves they used to be, look out. Mom isn't at the house any longer. She felt she needed a rest. I'll bet my bottom dollar she comes back some day though. She is definitely one of the people I want you to meet. She must have a terrific amount of correspondence keeping track of all her boys. It seems that none of them ever forget her.

I rather imagine that the inconsistency of Roger's addresses does worry Mrs. Smith, but if he was wounded, he more than likely has been moved from a hospital to a convalescent camp. Wounded are rather difficult to move and if he is unable to work, I'm quite sure he hasn't been sent to Germany, at least I certainly hope so. If Roger's outfit is home already, they certainly did make time. I'm afraid we just don't do it that way around here.

Are you a bridge fiend, dear? I can assure you that it isn't one of my vices. At college, they were constantly hounding me to play, but I usually escaped. I could always find something better to do, but over here, I can see its advantages. I suppose you will finally drive me to it. I think I'd like being your partner in anything.

The mosquitoes and I are beginning to have some terrific battles at night. No matter how hard you try—a few always manage to get inside the net with you. If you don't kill them before you go to sleep, they are so fat in the morning they can't fly. Also if you touch the net any place, they chew merrily away at you from the outside. You can't win.

Good night, darling. I'll write again shortly. What wouldn't I give to see that redhead tonight. Lord, but I miss you and I

Love you always, J.R.

René Palmer Armstrong

Wednesday, November 24, 1943

Dearest Elnora,

I received two letters from you today and in both of them, you seemed to be in quite high humor. Very sweet letters they were too, the kind that make you get that wild gleam in your eye and you say to yourself, "Just wait, oh boy."

I saw a very cute show last night. It was *Mister Big*. I really didn't expect much from it, as it was a B picture, but I was quite surprised, and I laughed till my sides ached. It was just a bunch of kids, but what a crazy outfit they were. The boy who played the lead [Donald O'Connor] will really put Mickey Rooney out in the cold if he isn't careful. See it if you get a chance, as I know you'll go for the jitterbugging.

I got a package from Mother yesterday, and she sent me a wonderful book. It is *The Robe* by Lloyd C. Douglas. I've heard a good deal about it, and I've been hoping to get my hands on it for quite a while. Everyone in the squadron will read it eventually. Good books are at a premium. Australian novels are a bit difficult to stomach. They can be nearly as stuffy as the English when they try.

Tomorrow is Thanksgiving—how nice. I've a good deal to be thankful for, but most of it too far away to suit me. It has been rumored that we will have turkey on that fine day, but seeing is believing. It will probably be C-ration with a feather in it. Lookout Australia, is all I have to say, because they will really have a hungry man on their hands then. That is really something pleasant to look forward to. Why don't you dash over and meet me there, just like Montgomery?

I also had a letter from Mother today, and she gave me my bank balance. God, I'm a rich man, at least compared to what I used to be.

Are the wolves still trying to lure you away from me? I shouldn't be surprised, but I'll fix them one of these days—wait and see.

I still haven't received those pictures as yet, but I have not despaired as yet. Nothing bothers me after two and half months without word from you.

It's getting quite late, dear, so the end of this epistle is near. I received mail from you with intervals of no longer than three days. You please me very much my darling. In fact, I'm very much in love with you or didn't you know. Just give me five minutes any time, and I can prove it. Night darling—

Always—I love you, J.R.

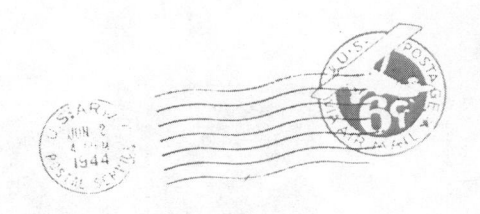

WINGS AND A RING: THE LONG-AWAITED PICTURE

Thursday, November 25, 1943

Thanksgiving Day

The Squadron enjoyed the traditional Thanksgiving Dinner. The Squadron as a whole enjoyed the day off.

Photo of soldiers enjoying Thanksgiving turkey courtesy of the Lawrence J. Hickey Collection.

RENÉ PALMER ARMSTRONG

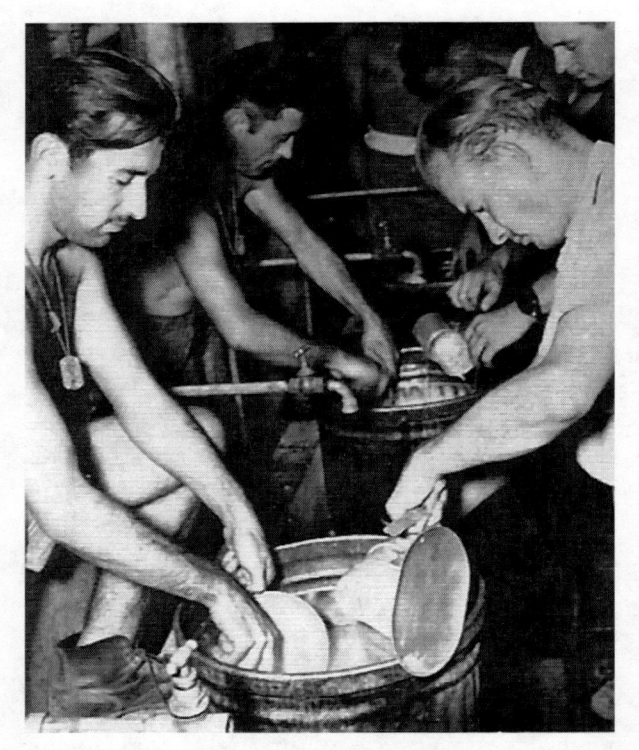

Photo of soldiers washing dishes courtesy of the Lawrence J. Hickey Collection.

THURSDAY, NOVEMBER 25, 1943

Dearest Elnora,

I just had to write you on this Thanksgiving Day. We did actually have turkey. It was quite a meal for these parts. Even with this, my mouth waters at the thought of a beautiful steak or a hamburger. I'm going to be terribly hard on a ration card some day. Oh well, you can always eat in the officer's mess when things get low. It's quite a system.

I really received a slug of mail today, and for some odd reason, I wasn't expecting any. Four wonderful letters from you—how do you do it darling? And guess what? One of them contained the pictures I have been sweating out for two weeks. They looked pretty good to me, darling—in fact, they looked wonderful to these tired old eyes. Lord knows what affect you'll have on me when I see you again. What wouldn't I give to get my hands on that gal draped on the radiator. That's an extremely nice looking suit you had on, dear. I wish I could see you in it. In fact, I wish I could see you period.

Also I noticed *wings and ring* appear very prominently. Needless to say it's one of those things that make me feel pretty good. It's time[s] like this evening when I could blow my brains out for not having married you. If I ever thought anything would turn up to prevent it, I believe I could swim all the way back to the U.S. You don't believe me—huh?

I also received three letters from Mother today, and that is quite a rare thing from her. I wonder why it takes her letters longer to get here than yours. If they are going to raise the price on airmail, it will break you up to write to me as you have. I'll have to send you an allowance so you can keep it up. Don't think I wouldn't either.

Mother sent me a subscription to *Time* magazine, which is gratefully appreciated. It's a miniature edition and is mailed in an envelope that rather facilitates its speedy arrival. Fancy talk, isn't it? Anyhow, it's good reading.

There is a plague of little bugs around here that are giving me no end of trouble this evening. Little white jobs with wings, and there are millions of them.

Hi, darling—this is the next day. The lights went out last night and stayed that way so I had to give up my letter writing.

How about this business of vamping naval commanders into catching a ride to work? I should have liked to have seen that bit of work. You aren't turning into a Mata Hare, are you, dear?

It's a good thing I wasn't with you at that football game. I would probably have died. I used to get into enough trouble at Rice [University, Houston] as it was. The boys there would glare at me and snarl, "Are you from A&M [Texas A&M, College Station, Texas]?" Then Roger, Mike, and Snelson would have to come to my aid, and explain I was just a poor soldier boy. I used to have a lot of fun out there though. Daurice used to get so irritated when Roger and I would go up in the dorm and leave her sitting in the car. It's too bad you weren't around during those screwy months.

If an interval should come between my letters, you'll know what I am doing so please don't get excited. I'll try to write if possible, but I can send a post card at least.

Hum—page four, quite voluminous, ain't it? If I used small pages as you do, I'd probably write a good-sized letter myself.

That was too bad about Mike's brother. That stuff is rather difficult to take, I know. My co-pilot was from Austin, and he used to kid me about beating me to Texas and looking you up. He wasn't flying with me at the time, however.

I had best wind up this letter and write home. Thank you again for the picture, darling—you looked pretty sweet in them to me. All they did was intensify the feeling of how much I miss you, and how lovely you are. Too bad they aren't in Technicolor. I'd really like to see that red hair again. Bye for now, darling.

Always—I love you, J.R.

Photo of Elnora's engagement ring and the wings given to her by J.R. courtesy of Lloyd Sullivan.

Daily Log: November 28, 1943

2nd Lt. J.R. Jones on leave.

Daily Log: December 9, 1943

2nd Lt. J.R. Jones returns to duty station.

Friday, December 10, 1943

Elnora, my darling,

I'm back, sweet, and I hope you aren't too perturbed with me, but I warned you, darling. I had one of the most wonderful times I could have without you. I mean by that that, the only thing that would have been better would have been being with you.

Really, my dear, you have never seen a place like this. It would quite startle you. I know I never suspected Australia of possessing such an amazing place. It is a large city and spreads for miles around the harbor and hills. San Francisco is the only place I can think of that resembles it.

The squadron rents a house there, and the boys live there while on leave. It is situated on top of a hill and from the front porch, you can see a great portion of the city. It certainly is a romantic sight at night looking down over the bay. Oh, I've so much to tell you about, I hardly know where to begin. I'll start at the beginning and work up.

Upon returning, I found quite a few letters from you, and lord, did my conscience hurt. The birthday card was the nicest. How lovely you are, darling. I can't see how I got you, but I'll never complain. Yep—in four days I'll be twenty-four. I hope the twenty-fifth birthday will be a much brighter occasion. In other words, you should be there.

I had a few dates while there, and the girls are very nice. Actually, quite like the girls at home, but there is a difference, and it only made me want to see you more than ever. Good lord, but I'm in love with you. You have a terrific hold on me so please don't ever let go. It becomes more apparent every day. The Australian girls really go for the Americans in a big way. I don't know what it is, but I think they would all marry Americans if they could. Maybe it's because most of the Australian men are in the army, but I think it is a little more than that. They really go for our cigarettes, and your life isn't safe if you pull out a package in public. It's very expensive there, and it's a good thing we don't go there very often. It really set me back, but I don't regret it in the slightest. It was great fun, and it doesn't happen very often.

I managed to get you a present in Sydney. I hope it gets through to you all right. It isn't much, but I thought you might enjoy it. I won't tell you what it is. Let it be a surprise.

You should have seen the way we ate while we were there. We even did our own cooking in the house—not very fancy, but plenty good. It's rather hard to eat too much in a restaurant as they have a price limit on meals and if you have an expensive entrée, that's about all you can get. Those girls can really eat, too. I've never seen anything like it. Oddly enough, they don't seem to suffer too much for it.

I have only begun to tell you my adventures, but it's quite late and I had best close for the evening. I'll be back tomorrow and every day thereafter.

Thank you for the birthday card, darling. Nice picture, in fact, you are quite beautiful. If you get conceited, I'll spank you. Night, darling, if there is some way to prove I love you over a distance of ten thousand miles, I hope I have been able to do so. I've tried, and I do

Love you always, J.R.

Saturday, December 11, 1943

My dearest Elnora,

Saturday night and here I sit at home, believe it or not. Where else could I go? I mailed a Christmas present to you earlier in the day, and I hope you receive it. One never knows. It was sent airmail, so it shouldn't take too long. Our regular mail is getting gummed up because of the Christmas packages. I've received quite a few, but none from you as yet, my sweet. I did receive a letter from you today, dated November 26, and that is doing pretty well again.

So you had a nice Thanksgiving. I've already told you we had turkey, but I never did like them. It's quite a change, however. I have to look up the boy you mentioned in headquarters. That was rather a coincidence. We have a boy in squadron from Houston. His name is Lt. Max Steck. I thought you might see his picture in the papers some day.

I've been tending bar again this evening, but I closed rather early. Business wasn't too rushing anyhow. The fact is that we are about out of anything to drink.

I should like to see this hat you are raving about. Probably all I would be able to notice would be you. That wouldn't disappoint me in the slightest.

That little private you keep staring at when you go to the Stage Door Canteen is probably going to think that you have a terrific crush on him. I probably wouldn't know what to think either if a strange beautiful girl kept starring at me—especially a redheaded one. What if he starts rushing you?

You should have seen me wandering around the zoo in Sydney. It is really a big place, and I walked till I nearly dropped. They have a small bear in Australia called a koala. It looks exactly like a teddy bear and is just about as harmless. They perch up in the top of the trees and eat the leaves. I would really like to send you one of these for Christmas, but I hear the Australians wouldn't like it.

It certainly felt odd to go to a nightclub again. They love to clip American officers, but we are usually too happy to care. Liquor only cost us $10 a quart and that really ran into money. I can see where I'm going to have to give up drinking. I wouldn't even think about it if you are around, but you aren't, needless to say.

I was just thinking this evening that I never wanted to do anything worse in my life than I wanted to get to Houston before I left. I was just about to give up hope when the phone rang one day and said get ready to go to De Ridder [Louisiana]. Lord only knows what would have happened if I hadn't been able to see you. Then another break right on top of that—five days leave. All that needs to be ever said is what a week! One thing about us is that it didn't take long to make up our minds. I guess they were made up long before that.

I wish I could really say what I think about you, Elnora, but I just can't find the words to do it. I've missed you the past few days. Knowing you has made these past months and the future months much easier for me. I have so much to look forward to when I come home. I have the love of a very beautiful girl, and I have the prospect of many happy days to come. What more could any man want? Nothing except for this blasted war to end.

I must close, darling—good night, sweet, and give my regards to all.

I love you—always, J.R.

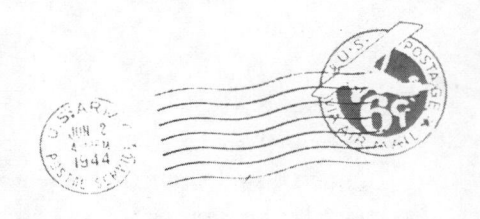

IF THIS IS SUNDAY, I'LL EAT MY HAT

SUNDAY, DECEMBER 12, 1943

My dearest Elnora,

If this is Sunday, I'll eat my hat, but that's what the calendar says. It has just been a day as far as I'm concerned. It has been terrifically warm the past few days, but I suppose I notice it so much now because I have just returned from a much cooler climate. It has even been quite warm during the nights, and that is quite unusual.

If you don't go to many shows, then once a year in Australia would be sufficient for you. In Sydney, to go to the show in the evening you must even reserve seats. Oddly enough, the balcony seats are considered the best in Australia. They have double features and between features, they have intermissions where you dash out for a smoke. An orchestra plays, as does the organ, two newsreels, innumerable shorts and, oh yes, some of the damndest advertising you ever saw in your life. They sell candy and ice cream just like at a baseball game. It's really a riot.

"Black Magic" is all the rage at the present time. The girls love to dance too. One date I had made me dance so much that I thought I was walking around on my knees before the evening was over. The Australian men must not believe in cultivating that fine art. Nearly every girl says it will be a sad day when the Americans go home. What the men have to say is a different story entirely.

These past months must not have been too much fun for you. I hope I'll be able to redeem all of that someday. You have been a very patient sweet little girl, my dear. The way I look at it is if that you held out for a year and half without so much as a proposal—then nothing can ever stop us now. It won't be so much longer if you look at the future the way you always have. I suppose that is just another of the million reasons why I am in love with you.

I remember your town quite vividly at this time of year. I think you'll find my name in the Smith's guest book at the ranch—Sunday, December 7, 1941. It was a nice quiet afternoon until I turned on the radio, and things haven't been the same since. At least I know I'm a long way from Texas.

How is everything with the Smith family? About this time—Sunday to be exact—Mrs. Smith herded us all off to church. She had a better time with me that evening. Anyhow, after it's all over she whips me up to the minister who asked if I had been around often. I didn't have a ready answer for that one.

Dear, it's quite late, and I must close—I'll write again tomorrow. Be a good girl, darling, and don't break any more toes. Gosh, but I love you. I want you for Christmas—you can say that again too.

Always—my love, J.R.

Mission FFO 346-F: December 13, 1943

Six A/P coordinated strike on Ring-Ring Plantation. The assigned targets in the area were gun installations, as well as bridges, supply and personnel areas. The squadron went over the target in two flights of three A/P each, in a shallow V-formation. Fires were started, and the area was well hit by bombs and thoroughly strafed. Antiaircraft fire encountered was of very light intensity; in all, about six to eight bursts were seen. The mission was 100 percent successful.

Tuesday, December 14, 1943

Dearest Elnora,

This seems to be my birthday, but actually I'm not sure. I'm wrong—today is only the 13th. Oh well, what's one more day. I'll still be 24, and I can't get around that fact.

I haven't seen any shows lately either. I really haven't had too much time. I did, however, read the book Mother sent me. I believe I mentioned it to you before. It is *The Robe* by Lloyd C. Douglas. I highly advise that you read it, darling, if you haven't already. You'll like it as no book you've ever read before. I know you are a pretty busy, little girl, but try it sometime.

Speaking of being busy, you really do manage to fill up your days. I imagine they go very quickly for you, don't they, dear? If you are like I am, the more quickly time passes, the better. How are you going to find time to squeeze me in among your doings when I get back?

We have received some more new records for our phonograph, but the blamed thing is still out of commission. I really miss it too, and I used to play it by the hour. It needs new tubes or something, and they are a trifle hard to pick up in this neck of the woods. Speaking of woods, I killed a spider yesterday that would really give you a nightmare. It was a great big hairy job.

The boy who lives with me was bitten by a black widow spider a few days ago, and it made him pretty sick for a time. They are common as flies around here, but they won't bite unless you disturb them. Their bite isn't deadly as is quite generally believed. Lovely part of the world we live in, isn't it? Even Camp Wallace has its points when you see this.

We have been having some very peachy night rains lately. They are usually accompanied by a high wind, and it gives the effect of raining sideways. As a result, it goes right through the tent and plays hell in general. I thought I was going to drown for a while, and the poor old tent was doing its best to fly off and leave us without any shelter whatsoever. Ah, the beauties of a house like in Sydney. They even had plumbing too. What a luxury!

The radio is really giving forth with some hot music. Most of the programs we hear are recordings of American broadcasts sent from Australian stations. Nice thing, radio; it gives one the impression of not being too far away.

Well, darling, it's getting late and I should be starting home before the rains begin. I'm wrong again, darling. It is my birthday. I'm nearly three years older than you are. I'm so mixed up on dates, I don't know what is what. All I remember is that June 9th was a very lucky day for me—one of the luckiest. I still have the mate to your ring, my dear. It will have traveled many miles before you see it again, but I'll be plenty glad to give it away. Just look what I get in return—all I could ever want or all I do want. Night darling—I'll write again soon. I hope I get your letters soon.

Always—I love you darling, J.R.

WINGS AND A RING

Photo of sick bay [medical tent] courtesy of the Lawrence J. Hickey Collection.

WEDNESDAY, DECEMBER 15, 1943, NEW GUINEA

Elnora darling,

Hello, dear—you seem to have gotten your wish. I received seven letters today, and the first one I read was the V-mail telling me your brother was all right even before I knew something was wrong. Of course, the other letters held the not-too-cheerful news that I read later on. I don't know what made me read that one first—fate or luck, I suppose.

I know you must have had a very trying time during that uncertain week, my dear. I'm very proud of you if your letters are any indication, and I know they are. You must have been a tremendous help to your Mother. Indeed she has a wonderful daughter. I'm glad you leaned on me even if I was on the other part of the world. I only wish I could have been there in person.

One remark you made had the profoundest affect on me of anything you've ever said to me. You said that you didn't know what you'd do if it wasn't for thoughts of me. That, my dear, told me all I ever need know. Nothing can ever be very wrong now. You have such a perfect faith, my sweet, that it increases my own a hundred times over. You are going to be the most wonderful thing in my life. You have been already. As I read that letter, it was one of those times that everything seems to stand still and I thought, my God, but I love that woman.

Now it's all over and we can laugh, and I pray to God, darling, that such an event never occurs again in your lifetime.

By the way dear, how did (I mean do) you like the heading on my letter? Yes, at last I can tell you where I am. Of course, I realize this is still rather indefinite as this is the second largest island in the world, but the Japs have half of it. Common sense should tell you where I am, however, and I believe you have a good deal of that.

We have been quite busy lately. Never a dull moment, and that will be all right with me. Of course the wear and tear on the nerves isn't much good, but it isn't too bad. I still haven't seen a show worthy of note. I hope things pick up soon.

I must close, dear, as I have to get up at five and it's nearly twelve now. I hope you and your parents have a wonderful Christmas, and especially you, darling, and tell your brother to look out where that boat is going.

Night, darling—I'll write again soon, probably tomorrow as usual.

I love you with all my heart—

Forever, J.R.

Thursday, December 16, 1943

Dearest Elnora,

I'm dead tired this evening so I don't think this letter will be very long. In fact, I think I'll go to bed as soon as I finish this. It's quite early, too.

I received two letters from you today that were of Nov. 11. This mail system is really screwy. I also received another Christmas card from you—pardon, birthday card. Only two days late—that's a miracle, dear. Two cards, too—you must have wanted to make sure I'd receive one. Very tender to make sure I'd receive one. Oh boy, send me home. You're really very sweet, but I don't want to spoil you with all this nice talk. I suppose I shall have to beat you once a week when I get home.

It's a good thing I didn't walk in and see you with that large diamond on your hand that you were telling me about. I probably would have dropped dead or I would have been demanding an explanation in loud tones, and then feel very foolish when all was explained. Speaking of large diamonds, they really have them in Australia—big enough to stagger the imagination. Next time I go down, I think, I will try to pick up some opals. They are very cheap and a very beautiful stone. Do you like them?

We were gathered around the piano a few minutes ago singing Christmas carols. "Silent Night" seems rather out of place in the tropics, but I think it would bring memories of Christmas past to any place. Anyhow, it's a good way to make yourself slightly homesick.

Something seems to have gone wrong with our water pump, and so we are now forced to take our baths in the river. I hope crocodiles are out of season, as I have no wish to mess with one of them. I hope it doesn't last too long.

Really, darling, I'm so tired I can hardly hold my eyes open. I don't know what's the matter with me this evening.

Maybe I'm getting sleeping sickness—I always did like to sleep anyway.

Night, darling—thanks for the sweet card, but what else could I expect from you?

Always—I love you, J.R.

Photo of men bathing in river courtesy of the Lawrence J. Hickey Collection.

Photo of man bathing in a box courtesy of Marshall Riggan.

Sunday, December 19, 1943

Dearest Elnora,

   These past two days have been the hottest since I came to this firetrap. I wonder what summer is like.

   Today, it was my painful duty to do my laundry. I had to do it, or else start wearing palm leaves. We don't have our native boys any longer, as the authorities ran them off. Lord how I hate to do it. I took my box of Lux (yes, I said Lux [a mild detergent typically used for washing ladies underwear]—dainty, ain't I?) and proceeded to boil them. I got all my khakis washed and was hanging them on the line, and as I hung up the last shirt, the clothesline broke and down all went in the dirt. I'll bet people could hear me swearing for miles around. I finally got them all done and put up to stay. It was a pretty good job if I do say so myself. Not even any tattletale black—well not much anyway. Now I have washday hands in a big way. Sherman was right—if the smell is gone, I'll feel greatly repaid. We haven't any way to iron our clothes so consequently our uniforms look as if we never take them off. I swear we do—honestly.

   I haven't received the presents you mentioned, but I'm sure they will turn up soon. I believe you said you sent them over two months ago. I hope you receive what I sent you. It isn't much, but at least it's from this part of the world.

   I got a Christmas card from Mrs. Smith, and she wrote all over it and thus it was a letter at the same time. It was a very sweet letter, and it echoed much of her grief about Roger. I do hope she hears from him soon so it will relieve her mind. God, but I hate to see such people suffer from all this. She also said that you had been over to see them and that you looked so pretty. That's one thing I needn't be told. Then she said you looked very thin, but not too thin. That sounds like a put up job to me. I thought I would split when I read that. I was also berated for calling Blackout an ornery pooch. Those Smith dogs always did give me a bad time. I nearly died last May when I came in so late and there she was, raising merry hell at the top of the steps and wanting to play.

Your Mother sent me a card, too, and she says you peeked. Can't you trust her? It was very thoughtful of her, dear; oh how I appreciated it. Give her my love and many thanks. I do wish I had been able to see her more while I was there, but I'll be able to some day. Wait and see.

I got San Francisco on the radio this evening, and they gave us all the latest music. It was a great feeling to hear the announcer say this is the United States of America. It's a wonderful place I'm told. They also gave us the latest news. I had just finished reading the same information word for word in a newspaper that is published on the island. Sometimes we see things happen, and the news is plenty stale by then.

Things have really been booming in this part of the world lately. Maybe this war won't be so long after all. We can always hope for the best anyhow.

Tokyo [Rose] is now pouring forth heart-rending tunes. The other night they said they would now play an old American operatic tune. They then gave us, "My Old Kentucky Home." They don't even know they paid us a compliment. They are playing "Careless" at the present time.

Night, darling—your letters have been so sweet, and I love you so. I wish you knew how much.

Always—my love, J.R.

WINGS AND A RING

Scan of cartoon from original "Warpath" courtesy of Lloyd Sullivan.

SUNDAY, DECEMBER 20, 1943

Dearest Elnora,

I'm still trying to catch up with the many letters I owe you. I don't suppose I'll ever be able to do that. I received that tremendous birthday card you sent me and by the time I finished reading it, it practically covered the whole tent. I got the general idea however, and it was very sweet of you dear.

I tried to go to a show this evening, but the blamed projector broke down so it was all in vain. It's very discouraging to say the least. This has been a very dull day, and I hope things pick up soon. Combat is really a very dull life most of the time. You'd be surprised if you actually knew.

Are you a ballet lover? Lord, they drive me wild. I can stand nearly anything but that. I get so impatient watching them jump around, and I frequently find myself hoping that one will eventually fall off the stage.

What do you mean by the crack that I was hard to get to know? I thought I outdid myself in your case in trying to make an impression. Of course, I will admit that you did sneak up on me. In fact, I'll admit that I was nearly floored. Awful lot of admitting going on here and those cute letters you wrote at school trying to find out something I had no intention of telling you, at least not then.

I suppose a lot of your friends do think we are crazy in the way we look at the future, but there is so much fun to be had and so much to see. There isn't any reason that I can't see why we shouldn't do it together, if you don't mind roaming around a bit. If it all turns out, it will be more fun than you can shake a stick at.

I must be closing this, dear, and heading for bed. I hope the mosquitoes are too tired to bother me this evening. Only five more days till Christmas—I have a quart of Scotch and that will be my celebration on Christmas Eve. Would you like to join me? Night, darling—see you later. Love you so much—as if you didn't know.

Always—I love you, J.R.

Wednesday, December 22, 1943

Dearest Elnora,

Good lord, dear, but I was nearly swamped with mail from you yesterday. I could hardly believe my eyes, but don't worry, dear, I'm not complaining. I was just amazed, and very pleasantly too.

This blasted hot weather is still giving us a bad time. I drink gallons of water, and yet I'm always thirsty. Right now, I wouldn't mind seeing a little of that rain that we had so much of recently.

Daurice really must be having a wonderful time flitting around the big city. That card she sent to you really brings fond visions to my mind. A nightclub is one thing Sydney hasn't progressed too far with. Oh, of course they have a few nice ones and the fliers really have taken them over. I imagine the food and drinks were much better before the war started. The Australia Hotel is the nicest one in town. It resembles an officer's club more than anything else. It's a beautiful place, and it has more dining rooms than any hotel I've ever seen in my life. In the bar, the boys all throw Australian pennies up into the chandeliers. The pennies are about the size of a fifty-cent piece, and no one likes to carry them. You should hear the noise when the place is crowded. Everyone talking at the top of his voice, and those damned pennies flying all over the place and landing on the marble floor. Oh well, it was great sport.

Yours truly had a very close one not so long ago. If they never come any closer, I'll be quite satisfied. Somehow I just can't get used to the idea of those Zeroes taking pot shots as me. I guess I just ain't the daring kind. I honestly thought one of those devils was going to come right through the cockpit. I'll have to tell you all about that some other day.

I saw a pretty fair show last night. It was *Above Suspicion* with Joan Crawford and Fred MacMurray. I like it, although we had to put up with spies, the Gestapo, etc. I hope we get some good musicals soon. I know they are appreciated the most.

So you are sending me *Life* and *Esquire* for Christmas. Those are my favorite magazines, along with *Time* and *Readers Digest* that Mother is sending. I certainly know a couple of wonderful girls. I only hope I'll be able to repay all you have been to me. It's a big job to take on, but just let me at it. I can't wait for the day. Thank you very, very much, my dear. I couldn't have asked for anything better. I never could, where you are concerned.

I suppose both you and Mother knew that I was in New Guinea before I told you so. Mother knew, so I suppose she passed the information along to you. I don't imagine it took too much deduction after you knew I had been in Australia.

What's this about having a draft dodger on your trail, sweet? I'll have to look into this. I know a good song you could sing to him that would shut him up, that is if you could keep from blushing. It ends with "Where the ack-ack [antiaircraft fire] is flying and comforts are few and good men are dying for b— like you." It's really quite effective.

Only two more shopping days till Christmas. I can hardly wait. I fear Christmas is just going to be another working day to us and, I'm afraid, a hard one. Oh well, they can't take our memories away from us. At least, I don't think they can. It will be just another day out of the way till I come back to you. That will be quite enough for me.

Thank you again for all the nice presents. I love you so, my dear, and here is to the day I'll be able to prove it by more than just a letter.

Always—I love you, J.R.

Photo of man bathing in drum courtesy of the Lawrence J. Hickey Collection.

MISSION FFO 355-G: DECEMBER 22, 1943

Nine A/P participated in a coordinated strike on Wewak and Boram. Our squadron was intercepted by 20 to 30 Zekes [official Allied name for a Japanese *Zero* airplane] and Haps [Japanese airplane] at the beginning of our bombing run, which was over the Wewak Missions area. These enemy A/P dove in from an altitude of 4000-6000 ft. from the sea, to the left of our squadron. They came in groups of four, making a split "X" during pass. There was a single pass made at our formation, from approx. 9 o'clock. The attacks were very aggressive, being pressed closely to within 50 ft. of our A/P. Our evasive action was speed and maintaining our low altitude, as well as dipping of the left wing, in order to give the turret gunners opportunity to fire at the incoming Zekes. Two of our planes were badly hit by A/A fire and were forced to land in the jungle. Capt. Kilroy and his crew were picked up on 26 Dec. 1943, by the Australian patrols. Lt. Bailey was picked up by the Australian patrols on 2 Jan. 1944, but his crew was still listed as missing in action. The bombing and strafing results of the strike are considered excellent.

Mission FFO 358-JJ: December 25, 1943

Six A/P participated on a strike to Silimati Point at Cape Gloucester with the mission successful. The 501st Squadron was the first over the target. The approach was made over the tip of New Britain with two passes made bombing and strafing. There was no damage sustained to any of our A/P or personnel as a result of enemy action. The Squadron's first Christmas overseas was celebrated with a turkey dinner, and the strike mentioned above on the enemy. Most of us are "Dreaming of a White Christmas."

While at the 345th reunion in 2009, I asked one of the veterans, Frank Dillard, what it was like to spend Christmas away from home. He told me they had watched *Holiday Inn* with Bing Crosby on Christmas Eve. Everyone was feeling quite down and started crying while they sang, "White Christmas." He recalled when he looked out over the white, crushed coral reef beaches and saw the moonlight shining down on the coral, it looked like it had snowed. For a brief moment, he saw the images of snow back home, and it seemed to make things better.

Photo of Season's Greeting card courtesy of the Lawrence J. Hickey Collection.

Scan of Christmas Wishes V-mail courtesy of Mrs. Nathan Etkins.

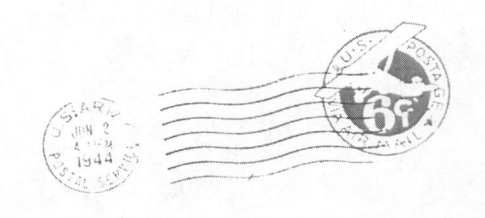

COMIN' IN ON A WING AND A PRAYER

Photo of 1st *Lt. Henry A. Kortemeyer in the* B-25 *Eager Beaver courtesy of the Lawrence J. Hickey Collection.*

Ten aircraft take off at dawn to Borger Bay to support landings of Allied Ground Troops at Cape Gloucester. The Target Area along the beach is well-strafed and covered with bombs on two passes; the mission was very successful, as was the landing. Fighter escort was provided by P-47s and none of our A/Ps or personnel received or sustained damage due to enemy action.

The second strike on this date, in which six of our planes participated, was to strike at the same place in support of our ground troops. The bombing and strafing were excellent. One Val [Japanese dive bomber] is probably destroyed. Flying in number 2 position, A/P 070 ("Outhouse Mouse") piloted by Lt. Kortemeyer with Lt. Jones, S/Sgt. Volpi, S/Sgt. Cohron and T/Sgt. Dean, was damaged by machine gun and ack-ack fire from our own landing barges over Yellow Beach. There was no actual interception by enemy A/Ps in this area, although Vals were in the area attacking our Ground Troops at Yellow Beach.

Photo of the B-25 Outhouse Mouse courtesy of the Lawrence J. Hickey Collection.

A/P 070 began to fall behind the squadron, but continued on in the same general run as was made by the rest of the squadron. The report of their run as given by the co-pilot, Lt. James R. Jones, is as follows:

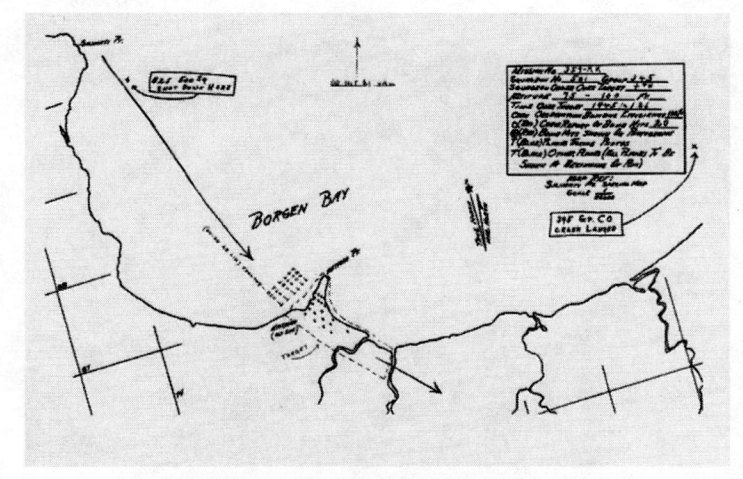

Photo of map of Mission 359-KK
courtesy of the Lawrence J. Hickey Collection.

When coming into Yellow Beach, we saw gun fire coming at us from the barges and from the woods behind the barges. This was machine gun fire, and it was very intense. There was also 20 mm fire coming at us. We were flying at 600 ft. altitude when a 20 mm shell hit in the nose of our plane right below my feet. At this time, we were directly over Silimati Pt. Our plane started to get out of control. A few seconds later, a bomb burst on the ground in front of us throwing mud up in the air, which splattered all over our windshield, completely blocking our visibility. [In a phone conversation in January, 2008, with retired Col. Kortemeyer, he said he simply reached his hand out of the cockpit and wiped the mud off so he could see, just continuing to fly.]

*Photo of landing strip control tower
courtesy of the Lawrence J. Hickey Collection.*

We immediately salvoed [dropped] all of our bombs. The right engine quit, and by the time we got the prop feathered, we were just about over our assigned target. We were losing altitude and were down to about 400 ft. when we started to fly south across the peninsula from Borgen Bay. Lt. Kortemeyer got the plane under control, and we slowly started to climb. Lt. Vogt, flying plane 082, saw we were in trouble, and even though there were many fighters in the immediate area—Zekes were directly ahead of us in our path of flight—circled back and gave us immediate cover. It was a good thing he did, because we learned later our gunners were injured, and could not have fought off an attack by themselves. At this time, I noticed that Lt.

Kortemeyer had been hit in the elbow and was bleeding visibly. He kept right on flying the plane and was doing a marvelous job at it. About this time, we were told that two men in the back of our plane had been injured badly and needed first aid, which we quickly sent back to them. When we reached the south coast of New Britain, the squadron had turned back for us and formed around us. On the way across the water to Finschhafen, we jettisoned all of our equipment and fired our guns dry of all our ammunition to reduce weight. We were climbing slowly and had gotten up to 5/600 ft. altitude at this time. When we reached Finschhafen, we were at 1000 ft. altitude.

Lt. Kortemeyer decided not to land at Finschhafen because it had a metal strip, and he was afraid the plane might catch fire in crash landing on the metal strip. Our plane was still climbing slowly, and we headed on to Lae for our landing. When we got to Lae, there were transports taking off the strip, and we had to make two circles while the rest of our squadron's planes buzzed the field to warn them that we had to make a crash landing. On our second circle around the strip, we tried to lower our wheels, but the hydraulic system was out, and our right wheel and nose wheel went down part way, and our left wheel wouldn't go down at all. At this time, we started losing altitude from sea to land, which was down wind, and we came in at about 150 miles per hour. We couldn't get any flaps at all. The transports on the field just barely got out of the way in time for us to come in. We hit on the left side of the runway, slid along the ground for about 200 yards, and then the plane spun violently to the right. Fortunately for us, the plane did not catch fire. I, the pilot, radioman, and cameraman all got out immediately. The crash truck was right there, and we had to chop out the tail to get the other two men out of the rear of our plane. It was after everybody was out of the plane that I first learned that Lt.

Kortemeyer had been hit in the back by shrapnel, when our plane was under ack-ack fire. He was given emergency treatment out there on the runway for the wounds in his back. I can truthfully say that all of us in that plane owe our lives to Lt. Kortemeyer for the skillful way in which he kept control of himself and his plane during this terrible ordeal he had gone through.

Photo of emergency response team courtesy of the Lawrence J. Hickey Collection.

The Aerial Engineer, S/Sgt. Henry E. Cohron was mortally wounded. Pilot 1st Lt. Henry A. Kortemeyer received wounds but continued to fly his crippled plane to Lae where he made an excellent crash landing. Armorer-Gunner S/Sgt. Leo E. Volpi received severe wounds in the legs and was later sent to Australia for hospitalization. Radio-Gunner T/Sgt. Guy I. Dean was wounded, as was Co-Pilot 2nd Lt. James R. Jones.

The Outhouse Mouse, A/P 070, was a complete loss. The plane in which Lt. Kortemeyer was supposed to fly on this mission was out for mechanical work. The Outhouse Mouse was usually flown by Lt. Robert "Bob" Larson. However, since Lt. Larson and his co-pilot were on leave in Australia, A/P 070 was assigned to Lt. Kortemeyer. The co-pilot who usually flew with Lt. Kortemeyer was also on leave, so Lt. J.R. Jones was assigned as his co-pilot for this ill-fated mission.

Photo the Outhouse Mouse after attack and crash landing courtesy of the Lawrence J. Hickey Collection.

Melvin Best explained that after each mission, the crewmembers were debriefed individually to collect information about what happened during the mission. He said that, due to the stress of a mission, each crewmember was given two ounces of whiskey to help calm his nerves and aid in the digestion of his food. I'm sure that each member of A/P 070, the Outhouse Mouse, would have liked to have consumed a fifth that day.

J.R. didn't want Elnora to know about the incident, so he merrily wrote along, telling her they had a busy day and that he had thoughts of Christmas past. However, the army air corps contacted J.R.'s mother, and she let Elnora know that he had been injured. You can only imagine what Elnora went through until she received a letter from J.R, finally confessing to her, but only after he received her panicked letter. Communication between people separated by different continents, with a lead-time of three to six weeks, is rough on relationships and emotions. Think about today's ability to text, e-mail, and video conference with our soldiers today. What would J.R. have given to be able to make only one phone call to Elnora?

Monday, December 27, 1943

Dearest Elnora,

If you are looking for a letter written on Christmas I'm afraid you are going to be disappointed. Due to circumstances beyond my control, I wasn't able to write to you, but you know I would have if possible. Even though we were quite busy, I still had time to stop and think of a good many pleasant past holidays.

We have been busier the past days than any since I have been up here. You probably can guess why when you read the news. Just mark Sunday in your calendar, and I'll tell you about it someday. Suffice it to say it was the roughest day in my life.

Christmas and Christmas Eve were just another day to me. The only way I recognized Christmas was the fact we had chicken for dinner. It was pretty good too. Christmas Eve, I went to a show and afterwards they had a recorded broadcast of *Command Performance*. It has as stars Bob Hope, Kay Kyser, and many others. It was quite an evening's entertainment for us.

I did receive several letters from you today, and I was tremendously happy to see them. It seems I hadn't heard from you for years. The latest letter I received from you today was dated Dec. 11, and it was odd that you should mention that silver dollar in it. No, I didn't spend it in Sydney and, in answer to your question, did it bring me luck? Darling, you'll never know how much. I have never been without it since you gave it to me. That's one piece of money I'll never spend.

Yes, Mother told me about the model plane that Dad has. When I was home to Indiana last year after receiving my wings, Dad had the time of his life dragging me around introducing me to his business acquaintances. When I started out to Grandmother's, and I said I wasn't going to wear my blouse [uniform jacket], he nearly had a fit. I had to get all dressed up to humor him.

I meant to answer a letter you wrote quite a few days ago. It was the one in which you said Mrs. Foster had written your Mother and told her how much in love we were. We must have seemed pretty far-gone to her, but it's pretty tough to live a year in five days and wonder all the time if your plans will ever have a chance to turn out. We've had pretty bad luck, but I know it will be all right. I've put all my faith in you, and I know I could never be wrong. Not about you anyway.

I'm not at home right now, but I'm not too far away. We are living right next to the most beautiful stream. It's a wonderful place to swim, swift and clear with many large boulders to sit on, so you can bathe and take in the sun. Ah, the lush tropics—I'd settle for a good shower, to be frank. It is nice, though, and it provides much good exercise. It is the most refreshing thing I've found in this hot box. We have a very nice breeze and no mosquitoes to speak of. Not bad, I calls it.

I must be closing, darling, as I'm dead for sleep. I'll write again very shortly. You know how much I love you, don't you? You should. I missed you so damned much Christmas it was awful. Thank God you are never very far from me.

Always, I love you, J.R.

RENÉ PALMER ARMSTRONG

Monthly Intelligence Summary No. 7, Period November 29 to December 28, 1943

Individual Cases:

There were no cases of suspicious or counter-subversive activities on the part of the individuals coming to the attention of the Intelligence Officer of this organization during the period of this report.

Rumors:

There were no important rumors circulating among the personnel of this organization. Only rumors coming to the attention of the intelligence officer were rumors to the effect that this unit is about to be moved to a more advanced base. This rumor is based on fact, since our heavy equipment is already being forwarded by boat. However, personnel have been instructed by the commanding officer to cease discussion and comment on the movement, and notices have been placed on all bulletin boards by this officer concerning loose talk of future operations.

Propaganda Activity:

Photo of soldiers dining in mess hall courtesy of the Lawrence J. Hickey Collection.

There were no enemy propaganda activities coming to the attention of the intelligence officer of this organization, other than the usual Jap radio broadcasts. It is the belief of this officer that these broadcasts are having very little, if any, detrimental effect upon our men.

Morale:
Morale of this organization continues to be high, due in part to the regularly scheduled leaves to the mainland for both combat crews and ground personnel, and also due to the improvement of the squadron mess.
Benjamin E. Green
1st Lt., Air Corps
Intelligence Officer

Wednesday, December 29, 1943

Dearest Elnora,
I'm still having a difficult time writing, but events have slacked off considerably for the present; at least, I think they have.
I did manage to sneak in a show this evening, but it was a stinker. Did I ever tell you about seeing *Princess O'Rourke*? That was really a funny picture, and I got such a bang out of it. You would really go for it. I haven't been doing much reading lately, as I haven't felt like it and I haven't had too much time for it.
The news tells us that one of our ships was sunk by enemy action and down with it went Christmas for many men in this area. I'm slightly afraid, darling, that is what happened to yours, as I haven't seen a sign of them. I certainly hope not though. That would be carrying things a bit too far.

Shades above—guess what. Our squadron now has its own laundry service, and I don't have to wash my own clothes any longer. That certainly is a relief to this boy. They would have to wait till I did that tremendous laundry job of last week. I was really hard up then, and something had to be done. I don't think I would look very well in one of those grass skirts.

Say, how about this getting silver from your mother? Pretty nice, I calls it! Now if we can only afford to buy food, we will be all set. All you have to do now is be able to cook. I don't know the first thing about silver and such, so I'll just have to take your word for it. I do know it was very sweet of your mother. I'm glad she likes her son-in-law, even though it isn't official yet.

That little masterpiece you sent me from the office was really something. It was pretty clever, whoever thought it up. The boys and I got quite a kick out of it. You are getting a little devilish in your old age, aren't you, dear? I like it though—it suits that red hair.

I got pretty tickled at your telling me all the trouble you have buying clothes. I can see I'm in for a rough time. I can hardly wait.

Night darling—oh how I miss you, and I

Love you always, J.R.

Thursday, December 30, 1943

Dearest Elnora,

This has been a day of complete rest. I have done a good deal of nothing. About the main thing was to drive to the hospital to see a friend. He was suffering from burns he received while burning the grass around his tent. He is quite all right now, I might add. Afterwards I sent to the quartermaster to buy some fatigue clothes. Then off for a few drinks of orange juice, and that was the end of that. Not very exciting is it, but we get our thrills bouncing along in a Jeep on these roads. Lord what a beating we take.

Those records you are sending me sound pretty good. I certainly hope they arrive in good shape. I heard "Paper Doll" the other evening, and it all came back to me. I've no idea where I heard it before though. On the same program, I heard Dinah Shore sing, "You'll Never Know," and it was the nicest arrangement I ever heard of it. That was on Christmas Eve and that didn't set me today dreaming much. They had all those speeches, and they would say, "to you men on the fighting fronts"—good Lord—that's me. At the time, it all seemed like a dream and a bad one at that.

Back to the original subject, though, thanks a lot for the records, dear. I seem to be constantly thanking you for something, don't I? Someday I'll be able to reciprocate in full measure. Your thoughtfulness means so much here, darling. Someday I wonder if I could ever repay that.

You say I should request some more records—okay, I want some records, a redhead, to go home, and few other minor things. How's that for requesting, while I'm at it?

All this talk about the fruitcake I'm going to receive some day is making me very hungry right now. As for dunking it in liquor, if I had any of that stuff I should be very tempted to drink it. Lovely thought, isn't it? Really, I'm not a confirmed souse—yet.

I received a Christmas card from Shields. Only a few days late, and that isn't bad. I would really like to see that bird, but I wouldn't wish this place on him. I hope it will be in the States to say the least.

I received that letter today with the fine, fat lipstick on it. Oh boy, would I like to be on the receiving end of that. It must be expensive to waste all of that on me.

I shall really miss that pink paper and the envelopes with the wallpaper on the inside. Where did you dig that up anyway? Sure smells pretty.

With all that fancy work you are doing, it's going to take a ten-roomed house to live in. I may as well warn you now that I'm the kind who usually manages to wipe his hands on the guest towels; just thought I'd warn you.

I take it you didn't think much of our island glamour girls. I'll admit there is room for improvement. One of the nurses gave a brassier to a native girl just to see what she would do with it, and she was later seen wearing it around her stomach and using it for a couple of spare pockets. You can't fool them.

I think I stood you up about two years ago right about now. That wasn't so good, was it? I also spent New Year's Eve on a troop train. Lord, I thought I was a long way off from you then. I have been missing you more every day since then. That really stacks up, you know.

Tomorrow is New Year's Eve, and I pray to heaven that before too many months in the New Year has passed, I'll be with you again. It's the main hope I've had for a long time.

Night, darling—I gotta go—I'll be home soon, and until then remember

I love you—always, J.R.

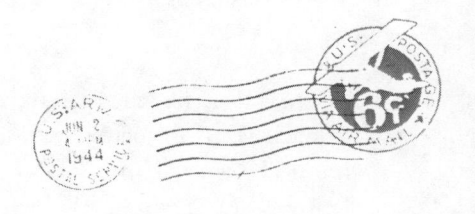

LOOK OUT: YANK DRIVING!

Friday, December 31, 1943

Elnora, my dearest,

So this is the beginning of a new year. I don't think it will start officially for me until you are around somewhere. The radio is giving forth sentimental ditties from San Francisco, and all in all it makes one wish he were somewhere else. Aha, I just heard Dinah Shore sing "How Sweet You Are"—first time, too. We aren't too much behind, darling.

Did I detect you saying "damn" in one of your letters? Good, good—I may teach you a few bad habits, but I feel rather uncomfortable around someone who doesn't swear at all. I've never heard any such thing from you, and it relieved me no end.

If you are going to have trouble with your bank balance, expect no help from me. I struggled all through college with that sort of thing. Money doesn't worry me a great deal, except what I carry around, and I never know what that is. You'll have to keep an eye on me yourself.

Your tale about the man in your office who has appointed himself your protector nearly threw me. I'm quite glad to know I have someone looking after my interests. Mrs. Smith is my best bet. Honestly dear, I think if you even looked cross-eyed at someone else, she would excommunicate you. It's all I can do to keep from exploding when I read her letters. When I think of such dear friends during my lifetime, I think I have been extremely fortunate.

Too bad I don't know more of your friends. They all sound extremely grand to me. I guess if you like them, I would too, as your recommendation is quite enough for me. You seem to like everyone though, dear. How I snuck in, I often wonder.

Now, what in heaven's name did Mother send you for Christmas? I'm awfully glad she was on hand because I wasn't very close at hand. She is a pretty good substitute for me as we are both pretty much alike.

The last letter I received from you was dated December 14. It was quite an eventful day for me. Of course, the fact that I was born on that date would have nothing to do with it!

I should be closing, darling, as it's nearly the time. The party here is getting pretty loud, and I can't think straight. Your New Years is some eighteen hours hence as yet. I hope you had fun on this night. I would have given all to have been with you. That's one of those things we have to dream about for the present. Goodnight, darling, and may the good Lord keep you for the time that follows.

Goodnight, darling—or should it be good morning? It makes no difference; it's bound to be a happy new year, for your love can make it so.

I love you so much—always, J.R.

Sunday, January 2, 1944

Dearest Elnora,

First of all, I must tell you to notice the change of APO—it's 503 now. This moving is really a pain. The new place is just alike, however, and as far as I'm concerned, it all looks the same.

I got paid today, and it was a nice, healthy feeling. It was about time too. I missed last month, as I was on leave at the time. Oh well, I haven't much need for money these days. I never thought I would have occasion to say that during my life, but I've been wrong more than once.

I saw a very good show this evening. It was *Top Man* with that kid Donald O'Connor again. He is about the funniest thing I have ever seen on the screen. He should go great guns, till he's old enough for the Army to reach him.

Last night the radio was really on the track. Good music by the carload. It was all the best bands playing a New Year's program for the men overseas. Of course, they had to sneak in, "Pistol Packin' Momma." I could have done without that very well.

I received a letter from you dated Dec. 17 today. So, you still remember me telling you your knees were baggy. I'd better watch what I say if you persist in having a memory like an elephant. I didn't recall that other remark. It all goes to prove that even I don't know what I'm going to say next.

I think I'll close, dear, as the lights are flickering so badly this evening, they are about to drive me nuts. I'll write again tomorrow. What all did you get for Christmas? Did Santa fill your stocking like a good boy? As far as I'm concerned, you've got enough in those stockings already and Santa couldn't make any improvement. There I go again.

Night, darling—I love you and miss you. May this year be good to both of us.

Always—my love, J.R.

Saturday, January 15, 1944

Elnora dearest,

Methinks you are tearing your hair out again, but the truth of the matter is that I have been in Sydney for another week. I may sound like a lucky man, but the truth is, I was sent there. I didn't ask to go.

I suppose I may as well tell you why, as you probably will find out sooner or later. You've heard that song "Comin' in on a Wing and a Prayer"? Well that's me, and oh how I prayed. We really had it bad, but I was extremely fortunate and only got a few small scratches on the back of my legs. Some weren't so fortunate. We crash-landed and some fun. Oh well, I'm all right—I was in the first place, but they said, "You need a rest." Who am I to argue?

I had a great time as usual, but not so much money. The weather reminded me very much of Houston, and the mosquitoes were tough there too. We rented a car and dashed wildly all over town. We were really good driving down the left side of the road and the steering wheel and gearshift on the wrong side of the car. We would sail down the street and if anyone got in our way we would yell, "Look out—Yank driving." One taxi cab driver really gave me a laugh. He gave me one of the wildest rides I've ever had, and when I asked where he had learned to drive like that, he answered in a very Aussie accent, "Oh, I'm from Texas." I knew you would have really appreciated that.

I wanted to go swimming while I was there, but the beaches were having an epidemic of sharks and they don't really appeal to me. They are man-eaters, and they come right onto the shore. They are only about fifteen feet long. Not exactly goldfish.

I did see a very good show while I was there. It was *Best Foot Forward* with Lucille Ball. I suppose you have already seen it, and I hope you enjoyed it as much as I did. I also was able to see Bing Crosby in *Dixie*. I'm not much behind, am I?

An odd thing happened to me while I was there. When I was in California, I met another boy in the Air Corps and a Lt. in the Navy. We used to have a good time together in the bar of the Senator Hotel in Sacramento. That was before I left the West Coast. Believe it or not, I was in the Australia Hotel in Sydney, and I saw both of them coming over to meet me. Small world, isn't it? I really didn't do a great deal while I was there. Just drink beer and eat to my heart's content. It's wonderful.

What I'd like to know is where you have been. I haven't had many letters from you at all. I suppose moving had something to do with it. Good Lord, but I've missed you, Elnora. Even in the big city, I couldn't get my mind off of you for an instant. You can imagine how much I think about you up here. Every time I look at your picture, I could slug myself for not having married you before I left.

My pretty, how could you make me fall so in love with you? Of course, I'll have to admit it was my own free will. Anyhow it's done, even if it took a war to do it.

I think I'll close, dear, as it's very late. I have so much to tell you—mainly how much I love you and how lovely you are. I'll write again tomorrow and more too. Night, darling. I love you with all my heart—

Always, J.R.

René Palmer Armstrong

Photo of one of J.R.'s friends surrounded by Australian beauties in Sydney, Australia, courtesy of Lloyd Sullivan.

Tuesday, January 18, 1944

Dearest Elnora,

Ah, the mail finally came through today, and I really scored. I might have known you were there; you always are. I feel very guilty when I haven't written for a few days, but you know that I write whenever I can. You're much too sweet to me, dear, but please don't ever stop being that way.

I really like our new home. It's much cooler and not so many mosquitoes. Our new club is right on the edge of a river, and it is rather a pretty sight. We do most of our bathing in the river these days. All in all, it could be worse.

I suppose you will be perturbed by this latest lull in my letters, but if you knew how close you came to getting a telegram instead of letters, you wouldn't kick. I'll try to make it up though, darling.

I still haven't received those packages, but I suppose they will turn up sooner or later. You haven't missed yet.

What is all this about Sigma Chi's in Honduras at the age of sixteen? He must have really been eager proposing then. Perhaps I missed something not knowing you in your younger days. Perhaps I might have been too infantile for you then. You sound like the village vamp or something. I feel like the victim of a plot or something. I like to flatter myself that I thought up the idea all by my lonesome. Frankly, I must admit that you're the only girl I ever proposed to. I guess that means you're the only girl. I never even gave it thought before. See what you did to me? Something tells me that you rather enjoy it, too. You'd better.

"Pistol Packin' Momma" seems to have wound its way to New Guinea and, much to my dismay, they insist on playing it before the start of every picture show I go to see. You can't escape it, even here.

I was quite happy to know that Roger is well, and I know his mother is. I'm sure he will be home before too long. That shrapnel isn't much fun, but such is life. I haven't received his address that you say you sent, but I presume it will turn up soon. Give Mrs. Smith my love and tell her everything is jake with me. Also tell her to keep on being my bodyguard for you.

I imagine Roger is getting good treatment. That is one consolation we don't have around here. I'd rather be dead than have it happen to me. It's much easier that way. [Roger Smith had been captured and was a prisoner of war in the European Theater.]

The snapshot of our family in Montgomery really tickled me. Suzan looks like a doll. They certainly multiply fast, don't they? That bench does seem bare though without us sitting on it. When you start thinking about those days, it's hard to believe that anything could have been so nice.

You nearly floored me when you started going to a CAP [Civil Air Patrol] class. You haven't mentioned it since. Are you still going, dear? I know it interests you very much, but I shouldn't start it unless you have joining the WAFS in mind. If you ever did that, it would really complicate the situation. We'd both have to get leaves to get married then, and I'd have to chase you all over the country. As you say it's very expensive, but some day it will be much cheaper, and perhaps I can be your teacher. Don't think, however, that I'm trying to discourage you, because I'm not. I'd like very much for you to become interested in it and know more about it. I just don't think it opportune. There, I've said my piece, and I hope you do as you darned well please. I love you more that way.

Well, I seem to have meandered through quite a few pages this evening. I have many other letters to write, but I really don't feel like it. You're the only one that matters anyhow, except Mother and that's understandable.

I started thinking again this evening about the first night I flew into Houston. Especially when I was driving you home. You had the smuggest, contented look on your face. I like to think of the way you looked then. If I could make you that happy the rest of your life, how pleased I'd be. I'm certainly going to try at any rate.

I must be closing, darling. I have reams more to write you, but I'll continue tomorrow. It isn't necessary to tell you how much I love you, but I'll never cease trying.

Always—I love you, J.R.

THAT PINK PAPER IS BEGINNING TO GET TO ME

Daily Log: January 19, 1944

Regular routine duties were carried out, with a ball game in the afternoon between the officers and enlisted Men.

Wednesday, January 19, 1944

My dearest Elnora,

Here I am back again. I still marvel at the number of letters I received from you yesterday. I can easily see I found the right woman to fall in love with.

Nothing out of the ordinary seems to have happened today—just another warm day. I'm beginning to wonder about clean clothes again. I suppose I'll be down on the edge of the river like the natives. They should have the laundry set up soon, but I don't know if I'll be able to wait.

From what Mother tells me, she isn't having much better luck with the laundry.

I shouldn't worry too much about the Australian beauties, if I were you. Some I met were very nice, but everyone I know wouldn't take the whole town for an American girl. You have to be careful what you say to them. If you say "thank you for a lovely evening," they are ready to get married. They are too eager for their own good. I never saw such a town.

That pink paper is beginning to get to me. Right now I'd be thankful if I had some myself. I'm beginning to run short again, and I wasn't able to pick any up in Sydney this time. They really have a paper shortage there. Oh well, I can always start writing on those small squares that I mentioned once before.

It sounds as if you and Doodle really had a talkfest. I think I have heard you mention her name more than any other person, with the exception of Daurice. I rather imagine the gossip was terrific. I hope I shall be able to meet her some day. Your friends will probably be as widely scattered as mine by then.

Ah, so you like to remember our last night in Montgomery—frankly, so do I. Those days were a short frantic grab for happiness, but we made it. I've never been more content in all my life. Odd how one can be so completely happy just wandering about aimlessly as we did. I could just have looked at you for five days, and asked nothing more. It's not difficult to imagine what the next time will be like.

I'm glad you had a nice Christmas Eve and day. I certainly envy the Lieutenant who had the pleasure of being with you, and he certainly must have been the envy of any place you went to. I know I always felt that way.

What is the love affair you're building up between Shields and your friend? You make her sound something slightly less than terrific. No wonder that boy is all ears. It will probably take quite a few years to get over the kick in the teeth he got before. I certainly hope not, however.

I must be closing as the boys are heckling me to come and play cards. We don't have our lighting system up yet, and so we have to go to the mess hall where there are lights.

Night, darling—I'll be back tomorrow. I have many more letters to answer, and they are mostly from you. Try and guess how much I love you and if you do, you get me for free.

Always—I love you, J.R.

Thursday, January 20, 1944

Elnora dearest,

I started gazing at your picture awhile ago, and I couldn't resist writing. I seem to be borrowing your habit of writing at lunchtime, although I doubt if you are having lunch at this precise time.

You must have received quite a few nice presents for Christmas. I couldn't understand how you received a present from me until you explained more fully. At least I was represented. So Mother gave you stationary. And that holds forth the prospect of more letters. That was a pretty bright trick on her part. I must congratulate her.

How about this picture? It was taken a while ago, but it gives you an idea how we live and the fellows I live with. From the look on my face, I guess the meal didn't appeal a great deal to me, but you can disregard that fact. I also appear to have had rather short hair at the time. That box you see in the upper right-hand corner is where the mail was when we came in to eat supper. Many times, I have been engrossed in reading your letters in such a picture.

I received that letter that you wrote a long time ago and didn't mail. The odd part is that I read it without noting the date and, before I read your explanation of it, I thought *good God, what have I done now?* It really didn't sound like you, and I couldn't understand it. I'm glad you received a letter from me before you mailed it. I don't think I would have enjoyed it. It gives me rather a start when I read it yesterday. You certainly must have been burned up. I hope I never get you in such a mood again. If you ever get that way when I come home, I'll turn you over my knee.

I'm awfully glad that you received the bracelet I sent. I was a little afraid that it might not go through because of the manner I sent it. That little bird that you couldn't fathom is called the Kookaburra. It's the Australian national emblem, and the bird itself is as common in Australia as the English sparrow is at home. It is also sometimes called the *Laughing Jackass* bird, because of its unholy cry. They really make a hell of a racket early in the morning.

Love you always, J.R.

Photo of bracelet J.R. bought for Elnora while he was on leave in Sydney courtesy of Lloyd Sullivan.

Mission 22-L-1: January 22, 1944

Shipping in the Seeadler Harbor was the object of today's raid. This Jap-held base in the Admiralty Islands received a thorough going-over by our squadron and on flight from the 499th. The approach was made from across Manus Island, swing east over Lorengau. A direct hit on a patrol boat was scored with 1000 lb. bombs. Three barges offshore from the west side of Salani Plantation were heavily strafed. Supply dumps on Los Negros Island and in the Lorengau-Lombrum Bay area were bombed and strafed. There are estimated 5,000 to 10,000 troops in this area, which is also loaded with supplies. The Momote A/D is in excellent shape, and this area offers an excellent target for aerial attacks. There was no interception by enemy A/Ps. This squadron suffered no injury to personnel nor damage to our A/P.

Saturday, January 22, 1944

Dearest Elnora,

I just received a letter from you and one from Mrs. Smith, saying that Mother had sent you a telegram saying that I was slightly wounded. I can't figure out how she found out about it. I did get slightly cut-up—ack-ack in the back of my legs and on my left elbow. I didn't even go to a hospital except to be X-rayed and bandaged. I did get out several small pieces about the size of a needlepoint. It's amazing how such a little piece can dig such a hole. I don't want to see any big ones.

I was the luckiest on the plane. Guy next to me got some pretty big pieces. One was killed, one badly injured. We got home on one engine and crash landed because the hydraulic system was shot out. I guess strain was the worst effect on me as they shipped me off on leave immediately.

I'm flying again, so you know I'm quite all right, and you shouldn't have heard anything about it in the first place.

Believe it or not, I received your Christmas present yesterday. It was the leather jewelry box. I've been needing something like that. At last I have a decent place to keep your ring and my wristwatch that is in very bad need of a jeweler. I guess that will have to wait. And, oh yes, those silver bars—they are going to come in handy, quite soon I think. The papers are in, but please don't say anything to anyone till it's a sure thing. Anything can happen you know. You are the only one I've told, so bear with me awhile. I was really happy to receive that package, as I was rather afraid it had been lost.

Did I tell you that I have received a Christmas card saying that Miss Elnora Bartlett was sending a year's subscription to *Esquire*? I don't remember whether I mentioned it or not. It had a rather classy *Varga* girl [scantily-clad drawing of a shapely young lady] on it too. Rather risky sending something like that, isn't it, dear? Or do you like them because they aren't real? Oh well, I know where I can find a real one that looks even better than Varga's creations, but I'll confess I've never seen her under such circumstances. Getting rather fresh, ain't I?

I received a letter from Mrs. Smith in much the same tone as yours, so please put her right on the matter as soon as possible. I wish all this fuss hadn't come up, and I can't understand why it did. I'll write her a letter tomorrow.

Today I had to take a detail of men into the jungle to cut saplings for construction work and what a job that was. It's really terrific working in these surroundings. Oh boy does it ever wear you down. You can't see ten feet ahead of you, and it's near impossible to walk with any speed. The silence in there is ear splitting. I can't see for the life of me how men fight in there, and live at the same time. You can go fifty yards off the road and get lost. It's almost impossible to describe. I hope to heaven I never have to come down in it. I also had to lay some pipe for the showers today, and I got a nice blister for my pains. As you can plainly see, I haven't been loafing today.

I'd best be closing, dear, as I can't get many of these sheets in an envelope. Your silver dollar still hasn't failed me yet, and I know that you must be somewhere around. I was really thinking hard about you. It couldn't convince me any more than I already knew that.

I love you—always, J.R.

Photo of Elnora's wedding band courtesy of Lloyd Sullivan.

Monday, January 24, 1944

Dearest Elnora,

I received three letters from you today—Dec. 20, 21, and Jan. 10. Ain't I popular though? In your last letter, you mentioned receiving letters from me that were written the day after the fireworks. I hope they convinced you that everything is all right. I ran off without your silver dollar today, and I really regretted it before all was said and done.

I thought I had it, but it seems I was mistaken. I won't forget again.

They finally have the lights installed, and the guy next door has a radio. Very nice of him, I calls it. Frank S. is now singing "Night and Day." I suppose it is a recorded program from Australia. We can get San Francisco every once in a while, but it's a rare occasion. Oh well, why worry?

I can't write very well with your picture sitting in front of me. I just sit and stare at you and wish. It's quite an occupation these days. You say six months have already passed. Well six or less and perhaps I'll be able to start home again. Let's hope for the best anyhow, darling.

I think I'll close, dear, as I have a headache, and I'm not doing such a wonderful job on this letter. I'll write again tomorrow, and I promise to do better. Night, sweet—

Always—I love you, J.R.

Wednesday, January 26, 1944

Dearest Elnora,

I received a letter from Mother Landes today, and she says you wrote her telling that I had been wounded. You certainly must have gone into action, dear, when you first found out about it. I suppose the news did come as a shock to you, even though it wasn't too bad. She appreciated your writing though; it was very plain to see.

I was delighted to hear from her again as she usually gives me news of some of the fellows I have lost track of. You remember me telling you of a Captain Ed McComas that turned up as my commanding officer when I was at gunnery school in Florida? Mom tells me that he is now a major and overseas. I know that will make him happy, as he is a fighter pilot and they get a kick out of this racket. I wish to God I were at times. This bomber driving gets pretty rough at times, especially at low level and that's where we work.

She also told me of a friend of mine in Kansas City who had returned from Alaska, and now he has to go back. I imagine that he really enjoys that. Mom also said she didn't blame me for loving you as you seemed to be a very sweet girl. Too bad you don't know her, as she has more boys devoted to her than Betty Grable. It sure would be nice to see her again, especially if you were along.

We are supposed to have a party at the club tonight, and I presume we are going to have that death-dealing punch again—more accurately termed Jungle Juice. I think I'll go light on it this evening as it invariably gives me a bang-up hangover. This climate is definitely not made for wild parties.

You ought to see it rain around here. As sure as night falls, it starts in. I haven't seen the finish of a show yet. One thing that I'm thankful for is that the soil is sandy, and we aren't always wading around in mud up to my knees. Now, shall we talk about the weather?

Talk about a noisy tent, this is it. One of the fellows in here used to play drums in a dance band at school, and by some strange method, he managed to dig up a drum over here. Needless to say, he is the most popular man in the squadron. On top of that, a fellow from next door with a tin flute comes to join him in a concert. I'm often tempted to mayhem, and I think everyone would congratulate me.

We also have a show this evening, but it appears that the storm clouds are gathering, so that is out. The radio next door is pouring forth some very good music. Gosh, but I would like to go out to a dance with you this evening, as doing anything, for that matter, as long as it was with you. Has it occurred to you lately that I love you very much? It had better.

I must be a closing as the time for the party is drawing near—and I must go see what is up. Night darling—hope to hear from you tomorrow.

Always—my love, J.R.

Photo of Lt. Col. E.O. McComas courtesy of Photo Section 118th TRS via Robert Boulier.

Information provided by Robert Boulier: This brand new P-51D "Mustang" was presented to Lt. Col. McComas on Dec. 25, 1944, by the 14th Air Force commander, Maj. Gen. Claire Chennault. At this time, Lt. Col. McComas was the highest scoring fighter ace in the 14th Air Force with fourteen aerial victories, including four Japanese airplanes destroyed on the ground and one Japanese destroyer sunk in Victoria Harbor, Hong Kong.

Daily Log: January 27, 1944

Movies have been shown for the third time in the area, with T/Sgt. Davis and Cpl. Hogan of the Photo Section in charge. We are still receiving Christmas packages, which are much better late than never.

Thursday, January 27, 1944

Dearest Elnora,

How about this fancy paper that I was able to borrow? I wish I had more of it, though. Still no letters from you, but I bet you turn up tomorrow with a couple. That's the nice part of it. I always know you have written whether I get any letters or not. It's a great feeling, and I hope you feel the same. I'm sure you do.

I didn't keep my good intentions very long last night. One of the boys invited me in for a few drinks before the party, and then at the party the punch was stronger than I thought. It hit me like a hammer. Lord, but I got looped. Afterwards, I found out that they weren't sure whether they put rubbing alcohol or grain alcohol in the drink. Frankly I think it was the former. As I predicted I woke up with the granddaddy of all headaches. It was really a wild party, and I wonder that anyone survived.

I have written quite a few letters today—one of them to Mother Landes. I imagine she has a terrific time keeping up with her correspondence. It has been threatening to rain all day, but it hasn't quite gotten around to it yet. It has been cool though, and that is something. Now that I have finished my daily weather report, what shall we do?

I'm sure hungry right now, and it's already nine o'clock. When I get home you will probably find me eating at all sorts of odd hours, anything I take a fancy to. I intend to gorge myself on hamburgers the first thing. All this talk is just making me hungrier, so I had best shut up.

Some of the older fellows in the outfit will be going home soon. Gosh, but those words sound good to me. Heaven only knows when the day will come, but it will be one of the happiest. I can just imagine how I would feel when I see the lights of San Francisco again; then, the day I'll see you again. It will be like the first night I flew into Houston. It was hard to believe that it was really happening. But it must be true because the gal said she would marry me. I really sneaked up on her.

I think I'll close, dear, and go over to the mess hall to see if I can dig up a cup of coffee. I'm eagerly awaiting that letter tomorrow to find out how badly I was hurt. I hope that news didn't frighten you and Mother too badly. Bye for now, darling—and remember that I love you so.

My love always—J.R.

Photo of the 499th Bats Outa' Hell club courtesy of the Lawrence J. Hickey Collection.

Friday, January 28, 1944

Dearest Elnora,

I was right, I received two letters today. I'm still pretty much in the dark as to explanations, but I suppose that will clear up sooner or later. I haven't heard from Mother lately, and I imagine she will tell me what it's all about.

We have a very good show this evening and I hope we don't get rained out of it, and it looks very possible at the moment. It's *Watch on the Rhine* with Bette Davis, and I've been told it's quite good. We have been having lousy shows of late and they are old too, which doesn't help a great deal.

I should write Shields by all means. I've been intending to for some time, but I'm quite prone to put things off. He really is getting around in the state of Illinois. I'd write to quite a few of the fellows if I could keep track of their address. It seems odd, but I've never found any friends as good as those at school. You would think we were all crazy if you knew them. It's drawing close to three years since I have seen some of them. Time has really run by since 1941.

For some reason, I feel very blue this evening. Thinking too much again, I suppose. It's not too good for one I guess—at least not around here.

No, I wasn't worried about you reproving me when I cut loose swearing. After I get away from here, I should be a master of the art. Those Aussie Diggers can let loose like no one I've ever heard. After what some of them have been through, I can't blame them. They are terrific soldiers, and the job they do is amazing.

Quite a few of the fellows have been getting clippings from their hometown newspapers in which our squadron has been mentioned. We are known as the Black Panthers, and our club was called the Panther room. Officially our squadron insignia is a picture of José Carioca toting a bomb, but quite a few use the panther. You've probably seen us in Newsreel and never known the difference. I know I've seen pictures of us in Australia.

I know what you mean when you find yourself saying to yourself a million times a day, "I love you, darling." It's not

too hard to do when you have plenty of spare time. Night, dear—with all my heart I love you—
Always, J.R.

Photo of the 501st's Black Panther emblem courtesy of the Lawrence J. Hickey Collection.

Monthly Intelligence Summary No. 8, Period December 29, 1943 to January 28, 1944

Morale:

The recently announced program of sending the ground personnel back to the States on the basis of a point system has had a strong effect of keeping our squadron's morale at a high level.

Benjamin E. Green
Captain, Air Corps
Intelligence Officer

Sunday, January 30, 1944

Dearest Elnora,

If I haven't been receiving much mail of late, I certainly made up for it yesterday. Six letters from you and four from Mother. The rest of the boys in the tent were certainly irritated at the smug look on my face. It's not my fault they weren't lucky enough to find someone like you. At last I found out it was the War Department that notified Mother. I guess they really keep track of us.

The radio was really going strong last night. It was the best reception I have heard here. I just sat and listened without attempting to read or write. It was quite a treat. I heard several tunes I had never heard before. I guess I must be getting behind the times.

I'm glad you had a nice time New Year's Eve, but it's plain to see that Mrs. Smith doesn't approve. When I told her to keep an eye on you, I can see that she is taking her duty seriously. I guess she can't see that I wouldn't want you staying home all the time. It does one good to go out and laugh these days.

Hello again, sweet. This is evening and my mood has greatly changed—only as it can by events present around here. I tried to go to church awhile ago, but services were held this morning and so I came back. I haven't felt moved to go to church in a long time. Somehow through all that has happened, I have begun to realize what it is all about. I have found that a time does come when His faith is our sole support.

My thoughts are pretty confused at present, and yet many things are a good deal clearer to me. You have proven a great many to me. One is your love for me. Before I knew you, I wondered if such a thing really existed. It does—of course we know that few things are perfect, but our relationship has been closer to it in the past two years than anything I've known. It is very gratifying to be aware that life can hold such joys in troubled times such as these. Although much of the time has been spent apart, I have and can always feel that I'm with you somehow. I do love you so very much. Every day it becomes more apparent.

Perhaps I should turn to a lighter vein. Jack Benny is blaring over the radio, and it may be mixed up with what I'm trying to say. This evening I have been reading *G-String Murders*. Quite a high piece of literature, but it's amusing and highly diversionary. It's really funny, but use your own judgment as to reading it—perhaps at the office in your spare time. I know you'd enjoy it hugely.

This is rather a hodgepodge letter isn't it, but I ran out of the other stuff and didn't feel like stopping.

I got a small clipping Mother sent me that stated I had been wounded. Highly informative bit. No wonder people get frantic. Mother seemed to take it well as my letters came in soon afterwards—thank heavens for that. Luckily you heard from me so soon too. I hope my not writing while in Sydney didn't worry you. Such a thought never occurred to me at the time. I had no idea that Mother would be notified.

I think I'll close, darling, and write Mother, and then listen to the music for a while before going to bed. Good night, my dear. These next months must run by rapidly. I'll pray that each day will bring me closer to you.

Always—I love you, J.R.

Unit History for Month of January 1944

The month of January 1944 opened with our Flight Echelon in Dobodura, near the historic settlement of Buna Mission. The Ground Echelon and official Squadron Headquarters were still in Port Moresby at our original camp near Schwimmer Drome (Fourteen Mile Strip) and were preparing to move over the

Owen Stanley Range—locally known as "The Hump"—and join the Flight Echelon at Dobodura. Ten combat crews, plus skeleton Intelligence, Operations, Engineering, Armament, and Ordnance Sections, under the command of Major Fain, had moved over to Dobodura around the middle of December 1943 and were busy flying daily missions to New Britain in support of the American invasions of Arawe and Cape Gloucester.

This was to prove an unusual move for the 501st Squadron as this time they moved into an area that was already built up and ready and waiting for the Black Panthers to move in and start operations. The 22nd Bomb Group had occupied this area at Dobodura prior to our arrival, and they had left everything in readiness for us—mess hall, Orderly Room, Intelligence Briefing Room, showers, latrines—even wooden floors and frames for practically all of our enlisted men and officers. Our camp was on the bank of a fair sized river, and about two miles due north of the big Number Four Strip at Dobodura. Our line and hardstands were adjacent to our camp area, and ground crews and air crews alike could easily walk to and from their planes.

There was no club or day room of any kind for the enlisted men, so the mess hall was made available for their use in the evenings, with Mess Sgt. Mason providing coffee and bread and jam sandwiches in the evenings. Needless to say, this was greatly appreciated by everyone. The 22nd Bomb Group had left us a partially finished Officers Club building on the bank of the river, which our officers used for a few "informal" parties. No effort was made to build or to improve things very much, as we were all confident that Dobodura was to be merely a temporary stay for us and we would be moving north in a short while.

The last days of January dealt this squadron a very hard and bitter blow, when Captain John "Mandy" Manders and his crew were killed in a raid on Hansa Bay. Mandy was one of the original Flight Leaders of the 501st Squadron; as a pilot, Flight

Leader, and later as Operations Officer, he had given a very great deal to this organization and was greatly respected and admired by all officers and men.

   Benjamin E. Green
   Captain, Air Corps
   Intelligence Officer

A MOVIE, AN AIR RAID, MORE RAIN, AND A GAME OF GOLF

Tuesday, February 1, 1944

Dearest Elnora,

Another month, and another pay day. I drew my usual $100 and, as usual, I have no place to spend it. Never did I think that I could be in a position like that, but I have been for quite a while. I do manage to get rid of it quite easily in Sydney—spent two months pay in a week. Quite a system, isn't it?

The mail has really been messed up the past few days. No one seems to be getting any, and I can't say that it pleases us. I should receive quite a batch in the near future.

We had quite a time at the picture show the other night. The film broke several times, and the sound gave out once or twice. Just when things were going smoothly, the air raid alert sounded and we had to black out. It lasted about thirty minutes, but no planes came over. By the time the show was over it was nearly midnight. Oh yes, I forgot to mention it rained intermittently during the proceedings. Some fun.

This has really been one exciting day. The morning consisted of finishing a book I began several days ago, and during the afternoon I played volleyball and cards. Took a shower, ate supper, and here I am. Next thing I know I'll be talking to myself. Don't know what I'll do this evening. I guess I'll have to dig up something to read.

If you are worrying about your income tax, think about me. I think I have a pretty good-sized exemption because I am overseas, but I'm not too sure. I should have married you and used you for an exemption. Now that's a cold-blooded thing to say isn't it?

I'm at a loss for anything to write this evening. I'm more prone just to sit and daydream. I was thinking just now about how lonely I used to feel some evenings in Greenville. I don't know why I detested that town so. I'll never forget that New Year's Eve there. I've never felt so lost in my life. Perhaps I should have been better off drunk, but for some peculiar reason I was sober. Then after a day's flying, we go to eat supper and the club would be filled with officers' wives. It was really a very pleasant place just before I left. I'm through with all that, and how well I realize it now. All I want is to look forward to seeing you at the end of the day. Come a Saturday night, and we'll go to the dance together. You'll get to know many other girls just like yourself, and the days won't be long either. We won't have to make so many wishes, and just have a beautiful time. Pretty good daydream isn't it, but it isn't beyond the realm of possibility. That's why I like it.

There is quite a golf game going on outside. They have one left-handed club and all the boys are right-handed except one. They have fun anyhow as the game consists mainly of arguments.

I guess I'll close, darling, and start my search for something to read. I'll probably have to canvass every tent in the area. Night, darling, I'll write more later on, or didn't you know?

Always—my love, J.R.

Melvin Best informed me that because of the heavy amount of rain they experienced while on New Guinea, Japanese nighttime air raids were rare. With mountains rising higher than the Rockies, it was difficult enough to maneuver the airplanes in and out of the airdrome without the triple challenges of night, rain, and cloud cover. I'm sure the soldiers were thankful for not having too many nighttime raids, but at the same time, they cursed the rain since it created mud everywhere. I have heard that their shoes grew several times heavier than their original weight due to the multiple layers of mud. When possible, tents were constructed with wooden floors and elevated on oil drums in order to keep them dry and out of the way of torrents of rainwater and mud slides.

Daily Log: Wednesday, February 2, 1944

Promotions were in order today with the following coming out: 2nd Lts. Jones, and Kirmil to 1st Lts.

Wednesday, February 2, 1944

Elnora dearest,

You are now engaged to a First Lieutenant, if you didn't already notice on the envelope. It took a pretty long time, but promotions aren't as rapid as they used to be—especially overseas. Those bars you sent to me did come in very handy, as Lord knows where I could get them around here. It means a pay increase of over forty dollars.

We certainly can't kick about the pay in the Air Force. A married man makes plenty—that's a nice thought, isn't it?

Still no letters today—the mail is really on the Fritz [something is wrong with it]. Here I am impatient after five days, and I had to wait over two months once. I guess I'm never satisfied.

I got involved in a baseball game today, and I was slightly rusty as I hadn't played since I left Greenville. I was in pretty fast company, and the enlisted men defeated the officers 4-0. That can't go on.

It started to rain after the game and has been at it ever since. I mean, it really poured for a while—quite a tropical downpour. You should have seen me out taking a shower with the rain streaming down. Oh well, I was doubly sure of getting clean. As you might suppose, the show was rained out, but it was a stinker so I didn't mind so much. I haven't seen a good picture in a long time, and *Watch on the Rhine* disappointed me very much. I think the best films are sent to forward areas. I certainly hope so.

It's quite late now, as I have been listening to the radio and shooting the breeze. We talk for hours and usually about the same things. I'll bet you'll feel like slugging me someday when the fliers began to recount old experiences. It seems an endless subject.

How did you like this picture of the local kids? I think the lady in the background could use an uplift of some sort. Send this picture on to Mother when you finish with it, as it is the only one I have.

I think I'll close, darling, and get some sleep, as they have some nasty idea about getting up early. Night, sweet—know I love you very much—you should.

Always my love, J.R.

Mission FFO 34-C-1: February 3, 1944

Photo of February 3, 1944 Mission on Dagua courtesy of Paul Van Valkenburg, www.345thBombGroup.org

The enemy base of Dagua was the object of today's strike, and the mission was particularly successful. The approach to the target was made around the row of hills to the southeast of the strip and the run was made along the strip. The lead flight of the squadron covered the center of the runway, the wings flights took the right and left dispersal areas respectively, and in this manner the strip as well as the revetments areas [sloped structures formed to secure an area from artillery, bombing, or stored explosives] were well covered with bombing and strafing. It was estimated that there were forty fighters and twelve to fifteen bombers caught on the strip and the majority of these were destroyed by the group attack. One crew reported a direct hit on the Betty Bomber with a parafrag bomb [fragmentation bomb equipped with a parachute to slow down the bombs descent], and a large fire to the east end of the strip in a gasoline dump was started. Ack-ack was heavy in intensity and moderately accurate.

Fighter protection was provided by P-40s and two squadrons of P-38s. These were seen to have encountered enemy planes over the strip. There was nil damage sustained to our planes and no injury to personnel. There were individual actions on this mission that deserve awards and citations, and recommendations will be submitted.

Thursday, February 3, 1944

Dearest Elnora,

This probably won't be such a long letter tonight as I really earned my money today, even if I did get a raise.

The mail came through today, and it contained four letters from you and three from Mother. Not bad after nearly a week's wait. One picture of you came today, and I was delighted with it. I won't flatter you too much because I didn't like the expression on your face, and your hair didn't look natural to me. However I can say that you did have on a very pretty suit. I can see I am going to have lots of nice surprises some day. As for your gaining weight, all I can say is that everything looks perfect to me and in the right places too. I knew it all the time, darling, but I have to pick on you about something—however I wouldn't be kidding if you did gain. I'd hound you to death. Just like you'd do to me when I need a haircut, and I usually do.

I received another surprise today. I was informed that I have been awarded the Purple Heart. I thought I probably would get it, but I wasn't sure. I'm told it is a very pretty medal, but I haven't received it as yet. It won't come for some time yet, but the citation came through today. Two days and two surprises, not bad, eh?

So you think Mother (Landes) has great expectations of you? Well, she knew every girl I went with in college, and I think she has some pretty good opinions formed. All the girls I ever introduced to her immediately fell in love with her, and I often found myself without a date because she was such a charming person to talk to. You took the same pride in introducing your date to her as you would to your own mother.

Good night, darling. I'll write again as soon as I have a few spare minutes. Thanks for all the nice letters, and I did appreciate the picture very, very much. I guess that's why I'm so in love with you.

My love, J.R.

Mission FFO 37-C-1: February 6, 1944

The objective assigned on today's mission was a strike covering the coastline from Bogia Harbor to Cape Croisilles, with intent to destroy any barges, supply dumps or enemy personnel in this area. Our squadron was to form with the 500th Squadron over Dobodura, then proceed to Finschhafen with one squadron of P-38s and one squadron of P-47s which proved to be very good. The 500th Squadron led the attack and there were no interceptions by enemy A/Ps. The mission was considered a success. There was no action on the part of individuals that seemed to warrant citations. There was nil damage sustained by our planes and no injury to personnel. The planes were loaded with 5 X 500-pound demolitions each.

Sunday, February 6, 1944

Dearest Elnora,

Today may have been Sunday, but it wasn't very quiet or a day of rest. It passed quickly though, and I like that. I'm tired, and it won't be long till I hit the hay.

I have quite a few letters of yours to answer, and my dear tent mate is beating that damned drum. A lot of peace I have. Ah, he has stopped, and I can continue.

I received the letter you wrote January 6th, and you must have been rather disturbed. Lord knows you have received enough such news. I just hope it never happens again. I don't want any part of it.

There isn't much news around here—same heat, same rain. One bright note is the fact that we have had eggs and fresh meat the past two days. That is the best thing I know of around here.

I certainly like that crack, "Why did I let you go home at nine o'clock?" If I had had anything to do with it, you never would have done it. I felt like wringing your neck as it was. Nice trick to play on a stranger in town. I got even, though, when me and the Army stood you up for the dance. I didn't exactly appreciate that myself, but it was just one of those things.

I doubt it if I'll be able to look up that friend of Rosemary's for a while at least. As a result of moving, I haven't the faintest idea where anyone is. It's really very confusing. I don't think I could even find myself on a map.

I think I'll toddle off to a show this evening. It doesn't look too much like rain either.

Night dear—I think of you constantly and I

Love you always—J.R.

Tuesday, February 8, 1944

Dearest Elnora,

My letter writing seems to have slipped lately. You must think my last letters pretty dull, but I feel blank as the devil. I have several unanswered letters from you so I'll try to pep up a bit. I have good enough music as Martha Tilton is giving out with the latest music. In fact it's "No Love—No Nothing" and it sounds like a pretty good idea to me.

This has been quite a day—I haven't been asleep once, very unusual for me. Flew this morning and played baseball in the afternoon. I'm really in good shape—I don't think I could run fifty yards without falling in a dead faint. I get lazier every day too. I wonder if I'll ever be able to hold a job. You'll probably have to take in washing.

I'm glad you liked the charm bracelet. I thought it would be quite a novelty if nothing else. There really isn't a great deal to buy in Australia, and I always have had an abhorrence of useless souvenirs. Guess I bought too many of them when I was little.

I have heard a very dirty rumor to the effect that they are going to stop airmail letters overseas so people will use more V-mail. I'll tear my hair if they do that. I hate those things with a passion. It doesn't seem like getting a letter at all. I don't think most of the men appreciate them.

No, dear, that's not a boat I sleep on. It's a mattress the size of our cots, and we pump them up with air. They are really very comfortable—much more so than a regular mattress. I think Air Force combat crews are the only ones that possess them, much to the envy of the other branches of the service. Of course, the Navy gets the good food. One officer from a ship came in here and complained of having ice cream every day, and we nearly mobbed him. We proceeded to take him to our mess and feed him Spam. I think he wished he had stayed home.

Valentine's Day had completely slipped my mind till I received your card. A very sweet little number—where did you dig it up? It fairly gushed. I'm afraid our local drug store is out of Valentines. I guess you'll just have to dig up the one I sent you last year. That was quite an item, wasn't it? Anyhow, I still mean it—more than ever, in fact!

As you might guess, I went to a show last night. Some day I'm going to see a good one again. I've read several good books lately. One was John Marquand's *So Little Time*. His writing has always fascinated me. He seems to portray accurately the way I have felt many times. Also I'm now reading *C/O Postmaster*. It is a G.I.'s view of Australia and New Guinea. It's very amusing, and the situations are quite familiar to me. I should be a well-read man by the time I get home. I wish I could see *Dick Tracy* and *Blondie* more often.

Thank you for the sweet valentine, dear. I think you're mine too. Know how much I love you? Try guessing, for I do with all my heart. It's been a long time darling, but the day will finally come, and I can kiss you and say—

I love you always, J.R.

Friday, February 11, 1944

Dearest Elnora,

I haven't written for a couple of days because I haven't been around to do so. We have really been busy of late. I'm certainly doing enough flying. I know that for a fact. It makes the days go a good deal faster, and that makes me plenty happy.

Not a great deal has happened in the last few days, at least that I can tell you about. I'll sure be glad when I don't have to have any reservations on my writing. I never had any trouble digging up letter material at Greenville, or while I was in flying school. Now everything is a military secret and you have to read it in the newspapers. Confidentially, after two and a half years I'm ready to do my talking and wooing in person. How about you, dear?

I saw a show last night, and I really liked it. It was about four years old, but it was still good. It was the *Tuttles of Tahiti* with Charles Laughton. Of course it concerned the lush tropical isles and beautiful Polynesian maidens. I'm still not greatly impressed with either as yet. I have been told however that the maids of Tahiti are quite pretty. Me, I'll take a redhead.

Some of the older men in the squadron are now ready to go home. I know how happy they must feel. I know how I would feel in their shoes. The word *home* certainly covers a lot of territory now. Any place in the U.S. would be home now. It would be waking up in the morning without wondering if you're going to see the end of another day. It will be a happiness we've never known before in our lives. You can't imagine what wonderful daydreams we have here. Of course knowing you are on the other end waiting makes things a great deal more pleasant.

With all your activities, darling, it looks as if you are going to keep me healthy with bowling, ice skating, etc. I'd like to ice skate again. In fact I'd like to see some ice period, even in a Tom Collins. It will be fun though if we do it together.

I think I'll dash over to the mess hall and get a cup of coffee before retiring. Nothing like a late snack. The food has been wonderful lately.

I have to get up at five tomorrow, and the day promises to be a long one. Night, my dear. I'll try to write again tomorrow. Until then and ever after,

I love you always, J.R.

DAILY LOG: FEBRUARY 12, 1944

The orders came through today to send most of the personnel and equipment to Nadzab, only the Combat Crews and a few ground personnel were to remain behind, everyone expected this move, as Capt. Gallagher and some advance echelon men have been there for several weeks cleaning and setting up our new area, but it was a bit sudden, another move means a lot of work for all, but it's a move that much nearer home.

Sunday, February 13, 1944

Dearest Elnora,

Another Sunday, and it's February. It seems a long time ago since I sent you a telegram and said I'm off to Maxwell Field. Tonight it seems like the longest event I can remember. These Sundays just naturally get me down. Also coupled with the fact that I haven't heard from you since last Sunday, this has been a slow moving week. Wonder where all the mail is. Everyone is in the same boat, so at least I'm not alone. I guess I'm just tired and that's why I'm so blue this evening. I hope you are hearing from me regularly as I know that would make you happy too.

Someone finally got a record player going again, and we get a few request tunes periodically. Of course we have "Pistol Packin' Mama" by Bing Crosby and the Andrews Sisters. It's actually pretty cute the way they do it. Then we have "Paper Doll" by the Mills Brothers. Outside of that we haven't many new ones. I'm hearing "You Can't Get Stuff in Your Cuff," and that is quite a ditty.

Did you know that I haven't received my luggage from Greenville yet? I can't even remember what I packed in it now. I do know I had a new pair of shoes I'd never had on. I'd sure like to have them, as the shoes you buy in Australia aren't exactly what you might call a dream model. We have Australian flying boots that are really something. They are sheepskin lined, and it is very soft leather. I hope I can get home with a pair of them. I like to have on boots when I go wandering around in this high grass. You can run into anything in this joint.

We have been having trouble with mice in the tent lately. I wouldn't mind so much if they didn't make so much noise after I go to bed. We set a trap, but so far no results. They just eat around it and go on their merry way.

Has Mrs. Smith heard any more from Roger lately? I often think of him. Time must seem interminable to him. We don't realize how fortunate we are at times, do we? Have you heard any more from Shields lately? You are certainly trying to fix up the love life of a lot of people.

Ah! Over the radio comes "Where or When." I haven't heard it since that night in Houston. That was a beautiful evening, wasn't it? Everything went along as if I had seen you every Saturday night for a year. No awkward moments. Just as if it was meant to be that way. It must have been or it wouldn't have happened. Anyhow, it didn't take me long until I got said what I had been thinking for a long time, and what's best it took you even less time to answer. It doesn't take long to figure out what you want at such times, does it, dear?

I guess I'd better sign off. I've been daydreaming for the past hour, and it's hard to come back to earth. I've missed you so this week, and I love you more than you know.

Always—my love, J.R.

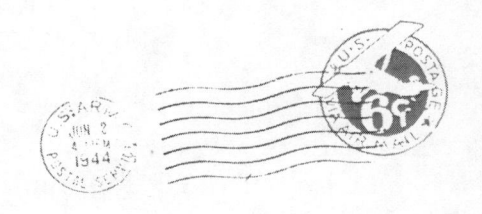

LORD, I MUST BE THE ONLY ONE OF THE BUNCH NOT MARRIED

MISSION FFO 46-C-1: FEBRUARY 15, 1944

The assigned target was a strike against stores, personnel, A/A positions, and shipping in the Kavieng Township area of New Ireland. The 500th Squadron led our group with the 38th group leading the attack. Two squadrons of P-38s made the fighter cover and rendezvous was made at Sand Island. The mission was highly successful and was carried out as ordered. One large building in Chinatown was blown up by a direct hit, forty-two of the forty-five bombs dropped hit in the assigned target area, and the entire area was also strafed, leaving large fires visible for miles. One A/P, 074 flown by Lt. Tunze, was hit by A/A and damaged to the extent that it had to land at Finschhafen where it was turned into a service squadron. Our crews reported two B-25s went down near the target area. A late report was made and confirmed that these crews were picked up by PBY [Catalina multi-role aircraft] rescue service. Our crew returned with no injuries.

Lt. Jones flew A/P 437—Little Thumper.

Tuesday, February 15, 1944

My dearest,

Still no mail today, so I dug out some old ones to read. They are good no matter what the date. I can console myself with the thought—look how much I'll have when they all do arrive. It's very helpful to know that even if I don't get a letter, you have written anyway and it just hasn't arrived. That must prove I'm loved or something.

I did get a letter today and heaven knows how it arrived. Of all things, it was a wedding announcement dated December 15th. It was a fraternity brother of mine who, much to my surprise, is a Lt. in the Air Force. He is several years younger than me. I knew the girl too, as she lived in Lawrence. Lord, I must be the only one of the bunch who isn't married. God, but you get to feeling old over here. Oh well, I'm certain that I have the nicest girl of all waiting, and when the day arrives, I'll find that I haven't minded the wait at all.

I just read in this evening's paper where they are having much snow in the north at home. I didn't know the word snow could look so good to me. The days here have been horrible lately. No rain, and the sun nearly knocks you down. I can be thankful though that it's nearly always cool at night, and you can sleep well.

I am plenty pooped tonight, darling. In fact, I have been nearly every night this month. It's getting so I can hardly stay awake long enough to even go to the show. I'm really shot at this moment, and I feel so dull I can't think straight. Oh well, the harder I work the sooner I'll be home.

I hope the radio is working well this evening. I feel like just relaxing and listening for a while. I hope you'll enjoy doing something like that, because after a full day's flying you don't feel like chasing around so much. It's the most exhausting work I know of, but it's such nice work.

It's beginning to grow dark, and I've just discovered that we haven't any light this evening. That's a very pleasant thing. Frankly, I can write better with some light.

I think I'll close anyhow, darling, as I'm so tired I can't see straight.

Always love, J.R.

P.S. Give me Shield's address again as I can't find the other one you sent me.

Love again, same guy

Photo of Jerry and Glee Smith by René Armstrong.

This is a picture of Jerry and Glee Smith, the couple J.R. writes about in the above letter. René and Glenna flew to Lawrence, Kansas, in May of 2008 to visit with Glee and hear some of the delightful stories that he and J.R. experienced during their time in the Delta Tau Delta Fraternity at Kansas University.

Wednesday, February 16, 1944

The objective assigned today was a convey [transport] strike believed to be bound for Kavieng with alternate target being Garove Island that was struck, as the convey was not sighted. A message from FATF while in route to the target was received and our planes were instructed to sweep around New Hanover in search of the convey, which was still not sighted. Garove Island was hit, several buildings in Ndoll Village were destroyed. Slight and inaccurate M/G [machine gun] fire was received causing no damage to our A/Ps nor injury to crew. Capt. Neuenschwander led our Squadron.

Lt. Jones flew A/P 064—The Wild Indian.

Thursday, February 17, 1944

Dearest Elnora,

Hello, darling—how is the Texas terror today? How do you like this stationary? I got a ton of it from Mother, and it should last me till I get home. It's not so heavy either.

I finally got some mail today. Three letters from you and two from Mother. They were a month old, but ever so welcome. You'll never know how pleased I was. It brightens the whole outlook.

I didn't have to fly today either, and the rest was really needed. We have been in strange territory of late, and the flying is plenty long. It has been cloudy all day and thus very cool. The letters from you made the day complete.

Mother sent me a clipping of some Mitchell bombers and on the side she wrote 'this might be you.' Sure enough it was our group, but not our squadron. I was around very close, but not in the picture. Incidentally it was taken the day I had a slight misfortune. [Dec. 26, 1943] She doesn't know how close she came.

So, you are going to get a raise too. You are quite the worker, aren't you? I rather imagine that money doesn't go too far in the states these days. I usually have fifty pounds on me, and it's a bit difficult to realize that's over $150.00. All that money and no place to go! I guess if I had some place I wouldn't have that much. That's life, and oh how I'd like to live it that way. I don't know if I would appreciate your working at the Municipal Airport, especially with all those wolf pilots coming in there. Believe me, I know how they operate. I used to see lots of pretty girls working in operations offices, and the boys really gave them a fit. Of course, I only watched. There used to be a girl in Macon who looked remarkably like you, and she must have thought I was crazy the way I stared at her.

You certainly are getting classy going to the Empire Room. It's funny I never did go there while I was in Houston. I guess Roger and I liked the Ranch Club too well, and of course you always had your favorite dive.

I told you that you might as well get used to hangar flying. It's a subject that I can go on forever, and usually do. I can see you saying very discretely, "let's dance," while trying to pull me out of a discussion. It's funny, but no matter how long you fly, you look overhead when a plane flies by.

So Mrs. Smith heard from Roger again. She is getting word pretty regularly now, isn't she? It's too bad they can't send his clothes to him. I don't imagine they give them much if anything. Perhaps he'll be able to get home one of these days.

I'll close this, dear, and write again tomorrow night. It was so nice hearing from you again. I hope I'll get some more tomorrow. I don't want very much, do I? Just you, that's all.

Night, dear. I've thought about you so much the past week that I feel I'm gypping the Army out of their time. Be back soon.

Always—I love you, J.R.

Friday, February 18, 1944

Dearest Elnora,

How goes it, Red? I got another letter today from you. I'm doing all right these days. I hope I don't have any more slack seasons.

I got a package also and guess what it was. The records, no fooling! I immediately dashed out to give them a try. I liked "People Will Say We're In Love," and "Oh What a Wonderful Morning" best. Of course I always like Eddy Duchin. They arrived in very good shape. Only one of them was cracked, and it didn't hurt its playing quality any. I have enjoyed them very much already and so will all the other fellows. We are getting quite a collection now, and the phonograph is in good shape so we will be able to reminisce again.

I'm eagerly looking forward to that fruit cake now. I could use a little something to eat right now. I hope it arrives intact as I'd hate to see anything happen to it. Every time you do get a package all the vultures gather around, and you have to work fast to salvage anything yourself.

This has been an exceptionally cool day for New Guinea. You can guess what I did to make the most of it. Yes, that's right—sleep and read. Ah, it's wonderful.

We had chicken for dinner today, and I nearly dropped dead when I saw it. I think it was Christmas dinner arriving a bit late. Everything else does. What I would like now is some good Mexican food or some fresh shrimp. I can dream, can't I? That's always free.

I must drop the newlyweds a note when I finish this. I can't imagine kids like that being married. I guess I'm older than I think. The years have run by pretty rapidly since 1941. I met the girl when I was 21, and I'll be close to 25 when I see her again. Not too close, I hope. Maybe in four months, who knows? It's not too impossible.

I got a kick out of Mother's letter yesterday. She said she had seen a show with Frank Sinatra in it. She said she guessed she was one of his fans as she liked it very much. Can you beat that? I can't see anything wrong with him. Just too much publicity and some of it bad. Anyone who can make a pile of money, I say go for it.

I still haven't received any of the magazines you are sending to me. They probably will start coming through about the time I get ready to go home. I'll just have to will them to someone.

You know, darling, it's difficult to believe I have been out of the states over six months. At times though it seems like sixty, especially when I start thinking about you. When I do get back we may have to make the most of our time. It's very likely that I may have to return again at some future date. Of course I wouldn't be so actively engaged in combat, but I wouldn't be with you. They can't retire the whole Air Force just because you've been to combat. We needn't worry, however, about making the most of our time though. That will be the easiest thing we ever have done, and also the best.

Must close, dear, as I have some more correspondence to bat out. Thanks again for the records. It was a wonderful present. Night, darling.

Love you always, J.R.

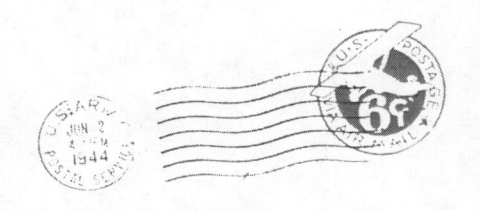

FINALLY A PILOT: BOMBING, MORE BOMBING, A DRINK, AND DEBRIEFING

MISSION FFO 53-K-1: FEBRUARY 22, 1944

The primary target assigned for today's mission was the Monote A/D on the Admiralty Islands. Due to a heavy front, the secondary target was attacked, which was Iboki Plantation at Rein Bay, New Britain. The target area was well bombed, with 30 out of 40 bombs dropped hitting the assigned area. All Squadrons of the Group participated in this mission with one Squadron of the 38th Group. Major Fain who was to lead our squadron did not take off due to a leak in his fuel line. Lt. Barth led the squadron. There was no enemy A/A [ack-ack or antiaircraft fire] and nil damage to our A/P; no injury was sustained by personnel. Lt. Jones was in the third flight with A/P 335.

Photo of Major Fain's B-25 Mitchell
courtesy of the Lawrence J. Hickey Collection.

Tuesday, February 22, 1944

Elnora dearest,

I cleaned up today—eight letters from you. Overwhelming and did I go for it. This won't be such a good answer as I'm dead tired.

First of all, I want you to note my change of address: APO 713 Unit 1. Here I go again. This is getting rather tiresome, but this is war, they tell me. At least we keep moving forward, and the Japs aren't having that much fun.

The fact that we are still going in high gear and moving on top of everything doesn't help a good deal. I really feel beat down at the end of a day. It makes you sleep good, as if I couldn't anyway.

I'm glad you received some mail from me at last. Two weeks is a long time, and I know you didn't appreciate it. I'm sorry, dear, but it won't happen again soon. From all the good times you have been having I'd say it was a good thing I got back. I'm glad you are enjoying yourself, dear. If you work hard you deserve to play, and I'm sure you do—work hard, I mean.

So your date said you looked beautiful—I agree, but I don't know if I appreciate him working on that angle. That is strictly my game. I can't afford to be shoved out.

I'm glad you like the picture. It wasn't too much, but it gives you a small idea of the comforts of combat. We always console ourselves with the thought that it could be worse, and it actually could be. I suppose we will be roughing it again for the next few weeks. Never a dull moment for us. I hope this is my last move before I start home. This kicking around is beginning to get me down. I could use some peace and quiet.

Good night, darling—I miss you like hell, and I love you with all my heart.

Always, J.R.

Thursday, February 24, 1944

The new Squadron area at Nadzab is set up along with the other Squadrons of the 345th Group. The Officers' tents are some half-mile away on a hill overlooking the valley, and the line at present is about five miles from this area. All sections are busy getting ready to operate, most of the tents have already been put up in rows, and the communications section is stringing wire for lights, new tables are being built in the mess hall which is supposed to be the best one we have ever had.

Photo of camp layout at Nadzab courtesy of the Lawrence J. Hickey Collection.

Mission FFO 56-B-2: February 25, 1944

The mission today was a strike against Boram (A/D) and dispersal areas, our particular target being the ack-ack positions south of the central part of the strip. Three flights of the three planes each of the 498th, 499th, and 501st took off from strip 4-B and made rendezvous with the 38th Group and fighters that were two squadrons of P-40s.

Lt. Jones was in the third flight in A/P 074—Tin Liz.

Friday, February 25, 1944

Dearest Elnora,

Hi—I'm back, and my tail is dragging. We are moved now and what a joint this is. We live on top of a mountain that overlooks a plain. It's quite a sight at night—you might think you're on Knob Hill in San Francisco, but the illusion doesn't last long.

We are roughing it again as our facilities aren't all they could be. Perhaps in three or four weeks everything will be okay again. I certainly hope this is our last move. It's very tiring, and we keep right on flying combat missions. No rest for the wicked.

I suppose our mail will goof up again, because of this move. It had just started to come through at the last place. I'm certainly glad that I received quite a few letters before I left. Nice ones too.

I see a very nasty rain headed this way. I hope our tent stands the onslaught. We haven't had time to put up our permanent home. I have blisters all over my hands now from sawing lumber to build the place. I also acquired a pretty good sunburn, but this has gone away now.

One nice thing about this place is that there is a constant breeze, and we are up high enough to keep from burning up during the day. There are very few mosquitoes, but we have grasshoppers big as frogs. They are really fierce.

We have really been having some wild rides lately. In a week or so I should be ready to go to Sydney again. If I do get down there, I'm going to sleep and eat and little else. I'd give plenty for a full day's rest right now, but the days certainly whiz by this way.

I was glad you decided not to take a job that might take you to parts other than Houston. I would certainly hate to chase you all over the country. Besides, you may not be working too much longer. At least I hope not. I have another job in mind for you, and I hope you accept. In fact, you already have. You just need to sign the contract.

I should like to see you lugging a thermos bottle all over town. You must resemble the working girl deluxe. I can see what you mean about keeping coffee, however. I thrive on the stuff. Mother and I would sit talking and drinking it by the hour when I'm home.

It seems that I have been away for centuries, and I'm so eager to get back. Perhaps the day isn't too far away—then to make up for a year of lost time!

Night, my darling—I'll write again soon. Very soon.

Always—I love you, J.R.

Photo of Nadzab camp layout on hill courtesy of the Lawrence J. Hickey Collection.

Mission FFO 57-G-2: February 26, 1944

Lorengau area—Targets 13, 14, 15, and 16—was the objective assigned today, but due to a heavy front, the target attacked was at Madang. Targets being 59-B, 63-D, and 60-D, nine A/P of this Squadron formed over strip 4-B at Nadzab, proceeded up the valley, over the Bogadjim Road area and out to sea, but due to the above mentioned frontal area, turned back and made a landfall north of Alexishafen, strafed that area, and area between there and Madang. The assigned targets were well covered with bomb hits, a fire was started as a result of a direct hit on target 63-D, and smoke was seen to rise 300 feet. No enemy A/Ps were destroyed nor was there any interception by enemy A/P, there were nil ack-ack, no fighter cover, no damage sustained by our A/Ps and no injury to crews. Capt. Neuenschwander led the Squadrons.

Lt. Jones was in the number two position in the third flight flying A/P 082—Meany—and put three bombs in Target 63-D and two in Target 60-D.

Note: The middle plane in the picture is the Meany; however, I cannot confirm that this was the mission mentioned nor the fact that J.R. was flying the Meany in this specific picture.

Photo of B-25 *Mitchell bombing run courtesy of the Lawrence J. Hickey Collection.*

Sunday, February 27, 1944

Dearest Elnora,

Well here I am again writing from my new home. It's funny, but when I first arrived in New Guinea, the Japs owned this place. I must say, they didn't do a great deal toward improving it.

I didn't get to build today, so you can guess what I've been doing. I got up at 4:30 this morning, and I don't have to tell you I'm dead. I figure on going to sleep darn soon.

I received another letter from you today. One of those violent pink jobs. You were in great spirits when you wrote that one. I now have so much mail to answer I don't know which way to turn. Perhaps I'll get caught up soon, but until then, I'll just be able to take care of you and Mother.

Lord was it ever raining when I got up this morning, and pitch dark too. I skated all the way down the hill in the mud. I was really unhappy with combat about that time. It's all in a lifetime.

Of all things, I'm reading a history of the Civil War. I want to be able to hold my own when I get back among you rebels. That Corpus [Mary Lou Byers] really gave me a bad time the first night I was in Houston.

So you are now known as *Legs* Bartlett. I can see there is plenty that I don't know about. You'll probably give me a good surprise from time to time. Especially if your old boyfriends turn up. I hate to disappoint the boys, but I intend to take up a great deal of your time—to be specific, all of it.

I went to a show last night because of the light shortage and was it ever a stinker. I regretted the walk more than I can say. It was Judy Canova in something or other, and you could smell it for miles. I haven't seen a decent film in ages. The other night it was Roy Rogers, and I'm happy I missed it.

What do you mean by saying I was wearing a zoot suit the night I had a date with you? It was perfectly good 1941 fashion. God, but those clothes seem remote. I don't think I even remember how to put on tails now. I have lived in un-pressed khaki so long that I can't remember how it feels to look decent. I'm afraid I will have to buy all new uniforms when I do get home. Ah, hardships. I didn't get to wear my pretty uniform much either.

This is my last page for the night, sweet. Four seems to be my limit these days. I have plenty to say, but I get tired and forget what it is.

I have plenty of your letters to answer as yet. I'll get on the ball some night and write one of those good California jobs. I really went to town in those days. It was certainly a long time from then till last May. Old Jones always comes through.

Well, darling, the time has come, and I am going to give up. A letter from you at the end of a day like this always seems to make things come out right. I'll always be fortunate that it had to be you. Night, dear, I certainly miss my redhead, and I love her.

Always and forever, J.R.

Mission FFO 59-E: February 28, 1944

The objectives assigned was a strike against stores and personnel areas at Targets 13-D, 14-D, 15-D, and 16-D in the Lorengau area which were to be strafed and bombed at minimum altitude with 5 X 500 lb. 8/11 second delay bombs per airplane. The secondary objective was to obtain complete photo coverage with low oblique photographs of the Lorengau area. There was no secondary target assigned.

Lt. Jones was in the number two position in the second flight flying A/P 074—Tin Liz. He strafed Target 14-D, 15-D, 16-D, and dropped two bombs in Target 15-D and three bombs in Target 16-D on his first pass. One of the two bombs dropped in Target 15-D fell 100 yards south of the jetty, and the other one hit on shore at the jetty. On the second pass, he strafed the entire length of Target 14-D.

Monthly Intelligence Summary No. 9, Period January 29 to February 28, 1944

Rumors:

There were no important rumors circulating among the personnel of this organization. The only rumor coming to the attention of the Intelligence Officer was the one to the effect that the Japs had landed paratroops and captured an airfield only 15 miles from Nadzab. A careful investigation revealed that this was based upon a misinterpretation of facts. A notice was posted on all squadron bulletin boards stating the rumor as it was circulated and presenting alongside of the rumor the following correct facts:

> On 8th February a small party of Japs were reported as being seen near [unreadable in log], which is about 25 miles south of Saidor, and 45 to 50 miles northeast of Nadzab. This group are undoubtedly refugees from Lae or Sio. Our ground force patrols are investigating and have not yet found any Japs in this area. There definitely has *not* been an aircraft captured by paratroopers or any other Japs.

Results were immediate. This was another illustration of the fact that the best way to stop a rumor is to present the facts.

Morale:

Morale of this organization continues to be high, due to the regularity of leaves to the mainland for both combat crews and ground personnel. Another big boost in our squadron's morale is the fact that officers and enlisted men have begun to return to the States after completion of regularly scheduled combat service in this area.

    Benjamin E. Green
    Captain, Air Corps
    Intelligence Officer

UNIT HISTORY FOR MONTH OF FEBRUARY 1944

Because of the apparent lack of training of replacement crews, this squadron has adopted the policy of training to insure a maximum degree of safety and efficiency on combat missions. Pilots and co-pilots are first sent on at least eight missions as co-pilot to an experienced pilot before steps are taken to check them out as first pilot. They are then sent on practice strafing and bombing missions as first pilots both in single ship and three to six ship flights. All pilots and co-pilots are checked on instrument flying ability as well as knowledge of the emergency procedures of the B-25 type airplane.

Upon arrival to the squadron, engineer-gunners are turned over to the line chief for training. Aerial engineers work as personnel of the engineering section until they are thoroughly familiar with the mechanics, emergency systems, pre-flight, fuel system, etc., of the B-25 type.

Armorer-gunners are assigned to the armament section to increase their proficiency and knowledge of the guns of the B-25-D and D-1 type airplanes. They are then sent on the number of practice gunnery missions that are necessary to qualify them as combat crew members. During these training flights, they are under the instruction and guidance of an instructor gunner. The number of practice missions is determined by the ability and the collectiveness of the gunner.

Engineer-gunners and radio-operators are also instructed by the armament sections.

Radio-operator-gunners are assigned to the communications section until capable of participating in flights. They are then sent on all local flights with special instructions on what messages to send to the ground station. This aerial training continues until these operators are capable of handling all problems that might arise while on a combat mission.

All crews are familiarized by the Intelligence Officer with the current and past activities in this theater of war. Bombardiers and Navigators are made acquainted with the areas in which we fly, from maps and as Navigators on the second or third flight of a squadron strike.

February was a rather busy month for the Squadron, with missions executed and a move to a new base included. Our rear crew arrived in Dobodua from Port Moresby on the 2nd, while an advanced echelon had already gone to Nadzab to establish our new *home* there.

The event that looms longest, however, was that of our combat personnel starting to go back to the States, as they had completed their 50 missions. The first to leave was S/Sgt. Joseph Seale, who returned to the U.S.A. with two Zeros and 1 probable to his credit, and numerous pounds in his pocket, proving he was as good a shot at dice as he was at enemy planes.

On the 15th, the *big* strikes of the month took place—a surprise was achieved, and the resulting devastation was equally thorough. Our pilots reported that never had they seen such heavy fires and such destruction—ships and float planes in the harbor were destroyed, fuel dumps were set afire, and buildings blown to bits.

On the 17th, 19th, and 21st, our squadron went after enemy shipping in this same area, and the three day totals put a decided crimp in the Nips's [Japanese] supplies to their stranded forces in the Solomons and at Rabaul. In addition to these two blows, a third on the 3rd of February dealt the Japs another walloping against another of his weaknesses. This time our strafers swept Dagua Airdrome, and the entire group picked up sixty-one enemy planes in their sweepings.

On the 23rd, the flight echelon left Dobodura for Nadzab; the ground boys having gone on the 12th. This is a beautiful valley, and we were all pleased to see the excellent progress that had been made in setting up our new area by our advanced echelon under Captain Gallagher. The officers were not quite so happy with their tent area perched atop a steep hill which is rather inaccessible in wet weather, but they have built several *mansions* up there and are now used to the climb, and awaiting eagerly the opening of the Officers Club and Mess that should soon be finished.

Benjamin E. Green
Captain, Air Corps
Intelligence Officer

Mission FFO 62-1: March 2, 1944

The objective assigned was ground support for our troops in the Momote area in the Admiralties. The primary target was to be assigned by the 12th Air Liaison Party when our planes reached the target area.

Six A/P of this Squadron were to take off from Nadzab and form with the other three Squadrons of the Group over the strip at 2,000 ft. The Squadron carried out the mission as ordered. Capt. Neuenschwander, Group Leader, was unable to contact directly by radio with the Ground Forces Control Station. He did finally make contact and they in turn relayed him through the right channels. The order was to attack "both sides of the river on thousand feet SW of the strip on a heading of SE to NW." Crews reported all bombs falling into the assigned target areas. Shortly after releasing our bombs, a voice was heard saying that our bombs were falling among friendly troops and to cease attack and return to base. It is considered likely that this was an attempt by the enemy to upset the attack by false radio orders, as Intelligence reports from the Blue Landing Force after the attack reported bombing excellent. Our Squadron was not intercepted, but about forty-five miles out from the target, seven to ten unidentified SSF were seen off of the right of our Squadron. After we passed them they jumped the last Squadron in the group. We flew a very tight formation and dove down from 2,000 ft. to sea level, the results of the attack on the straggling squadron was unobserved. There was nil ack-ack and fighter cover, which was reported as good, was provided by P-47s. There was no damage sustained by our A/Ps and nil injury to crew members. The 501st led the Group. As usual, and in our customary manner, we blasted the hell out of the target and all planes returned safe and sound.

Lt. J.R. Jones was on the 2nd flight and flew A/P 076—The Jaded Saint.

Daily Log: March 3, 1944

A new order came out today rescinding the old one that we dig Fox Holes [holes dug in the earth to provide protection]. They are to be as uniform in alignment as our tents are now.

Saturday, March 4, 1944

Dearest Elnora,

How's my redhead today? I'm feeling pretty good myself. Can't figure why. It must have been that steak we had for dinner.

If you think you have been busy you should be around some time when the Army moves. Boy, what a job. Thank the Lord that I always go by air.

I'm beginning to get that old yearning for a Coke or a beer and a hamburger. I wonder what my first act will be when I get home. Probably wire you and Mother, and then get stinko. I'll most likely be so dead that I'll go to bed for two days though.

So you want to know how my Rumba is? Well, I'm plenty out of shape at the present moment. You'll have to begin teaching me all over again when I get home. I'm even beginning to forget how the hula girls did it in Hawaii. Honolulu was the darndest place. It was just one big Coney Island as far as I was concerned. It must be wonderful in peacetime though. Even in wartime they certainly have some nights you can't forget. I spent a very lovely three weeks there.

Vacation with pay—I never thought I'd see the day. I've really enjoyed my service in the Air Force. How else could I have had all these experiences? Perhaps they will never come again in a lifetime. I hope that someday I can take you to all those places, but the future remains to be seen. It looks bright though—at home or abroad.

I have been informed that I must arise at a very early hour tomorrow. Also, I'm O.D. [Officer of the Day] and that means censoring the mail again. That's one of the roughest jobs I've seen.

So you see, my sweet, that I can't stay up much longer. I hope May will be my last month in New Guinea. Already I'm dreaming of what you and I will be doing by June or July. It will be summer again, and we can just forget the year that has passed, but you can remember that I

Love you always, J.R.

MISSION FFO 65-I: MARCH 5, 1944

The objective assigned was ground support for our troops in the Manus area in the Admiralty Islands. The particular target was Target #14, as shown on the Air Alert Target Map sheets #1 and #2. This target was to be bombed and strafed at minimum altitude, each A/P being loaded with 5 X 500 lb. 8/11 sec. delay bombs. Lt. Jones dropped all of his bombs on the second pass, strafing on the first and second passes.

Lt. J.R. Jones flew in position #2 on the 2nd flight in A/P 518—Quitch.

Sunday, March 5, 1944

Dearest Elnora,

Hello darling, and how's it with you? I had to get up at 5:30 this morning, but I didn't stay up long. Just long enough to eat and finish censoring the mail. I get more discouraged every time I get that job. It seems that everyone wants to get home. I can't understand it. Most of them are pretty cheerful, but you must have the usual percentage of bellyachers.

Pardon, but we now have a slight change of ink. I started to tell you once how many missions we need before we can go home. You must fly fifty missions, and have 200 hours of combat time. I now have 25 missions and 122 hours. Halfway through, but don't start thinking that I'll have to stay over here as long as I've already been. I've flown fifteen of those missions since the first of February. Those months I was sick and when I was hurt, held me back. It won't take much longer at the rate we are going. I figure June at the latest. How does that sound to you, darling? Every mission is one closer to home and to you. Think you can hold out that long? That will have made it a full year. God, what a long time to be away from you. I don't see how I did it. I hope I won't have to do it again for a while, but I think I won't have seen the end of service yet. Any time we do spend together, I shall be more than grateful for.

What do you know, I finally saw a good show last night. It was *Government Girl* with Olivia De Havilland. I laughed at it till I was nearly sick. She is about as cute a girl as I have seen on the screen. I know you'd get a huge bang out of it, especially the way she runs around with no shoes on. A good picture like that always gives a boost to your spirits. I think we should be getting more good ones from now on.

The mail has given up again for the past few days. I'll really be a happy man when my letter writing days are over. I don't want to write any more letters to you. I want to do my talking and wooing in person. It's much better that way, I'm told.

You know, darling, if I hadn't decided to fly I probably would still be sitting in Hawaii and I never would have seen you again. In fact it was through flying that I finally did get back. What a happy day that was. I felt like parachuting out over Houston so I wouldn't have to waste so much time.

Well, darling, it's drawing near closing time for me. The closer the time gets for me to come home the more I miss you. Good night, dear—I love you with all my heart. Future events will easily prove that.

Always—my love, J.R.

Photo of Apache Playhouse courtesy of the Lawrence J. Hickey Collection.

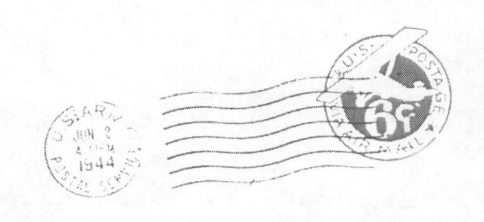

FLYING, BUT AT WHAT PRICE: THE FATE OF THE TREE TOP TERRORS

DAILY LOG: MARCH 7, 1944

T/Sgt. H.R. Bartlett, a Radio Gunner of this Squadron, gave the Group its new name *The Tree Top Terrors* and was rewarded with a quart of *gin* by Col. True, the Commanding Officer of the 345th Group, at the G.I. movies last night. We were told that its permissible to refer now to our group in letters back home as *The Tree Top Terrors*. We have been doing this for some time with our squadron name the Black Panthers, and several have received some nice publicity. There was no mission today, and Regular Routine Duties were carried out in the squadron.

DAILY LOG: MARCH 10, 1944

T/Sgts. Jimmy Johnston, F.D. Nielsen and S/Stg. Jimmy Immenkus, left today for the U.S. via Port Moresby. We learned today that Capt. Cather, upon arriving at Port Moresby, jumped in a jeep and was on a C-54 in route home all within 40 minutes, which we believe sets an all time record. It's good to see these men get back, and it will be a happy day when the word comes through for the ground personnel to get back, we all wonder when? The mission today was incomplete due to very bad weather; three of our A/P landing at Port Moresby and one at Dobodura due to heavy overcast.

Note: Melvin Best said the B-25s flew just above the land or treetops, about fifteen to twenty feet. He indicated it was not uncommon to have to pick tree leaves out of the bottom of the plane because of their low altitude. In this manner, they were able to evade radar detection and surprise their target. I recall at one of the reunions of hearing one pilot of the 345th say they were instructed not to fire until they saw the whites of the enemy's eyes. The B-25 was a very noisy airplane, and they could be heard before they were seen. When the planes flew in at such a low altitude, the enemy would hear them coming and begin to run for cover. As they ran, they would instinctively look back over their shoulders to see where the planes were. When the pilot could see the *whites of their eyes*, he would engage the .50 caliber machine gun button on his yoke [airplane steering wheel] and fire away. Pilots who flew the non-converted B-25 would normally not have to deal with the images of seeing their targets blown to pieces. Such was not the case of a B-25 strafer in the S.W.P.T.O. I also have noticed that just about everyone of the crew members I have had the privilege of meeting had hearing aid, with many having hearing aids in both ears. I understand the B-25 was one of the loudest planes in WWII.

Saturday, March 11, 1944

Dearest Elnora,

Well here I am back, and it didn't take too long. As I had predicted, the show last night was putrid. It didn't get started until ten o'clock, and that irked me no end.

We have a Victrola in our tent, and now we can have continuous music. That is if we can keep someone winding it. That takes up a lot of spare effort. The blamed thing eats up needles faster than we can put them in. I still like the records by Kostelanetz best.

This is certainly a hot day. It is rumored that the temperature hits 150 degrees down in the valley, but I won't vouch for the truthfulness of that statement. I do know it is warm though. The dust is getting fierce too. You take a ride, and you don't recognize yourself when you get home. I hope we get a little rain this evening.

I got a letter from you today, and it was really in sad shape. It looked as if it had spent a week under water. You could just barely read the address, and ink was all over the place. I finally managed to decipher it all though. It was the letter that you enclosed Shields letter in. Thanks for sending it on, dear. He didn't sound too happy, but he'll get over it.

About those moron jokes—there were several among them that were new to me. I often wonder where they all come from. I got quite a bang out of some of them. I must always pass the latest on to my tent mates.

Yes, Red, I know I've never seen you in a formal. I'll get around to it though. Just give me time. I've sort of had my hands full these days.

I'm getting in desperate straits for laundry again. I really haven't time to do it these days. I guess I'll just have to go dirty. Sure is smelly too.

In one of your letters, you speak of the fact that your friend Rosie and Lock have only been together six months out of two years of married life. Well, darling, the same thing may happen to you. Perhaps you had best think it over. You also said that you were glad we had waited to marry because the advantages outweigh the disadvantages. Life isn't all fun. I've had damn little of it in the past months. In the events to come, both of us will be required to give more than we ever have. My work is only beginning. I want you to be more than the girl I left behind. We've tried that once—remember? What I want you to realize is that when I come back our life together will be hectic and wonderful, and probably brief. You'd be married then, and the party would be over. You'd be waiting again, and not free. Have you thought about all that, darling? I presume you have, as you're no fool. I hope you are trying to see what I mean. I do love you so very much, my dear. It won't be too long until I'm back, and then look out for me.

I don't know if you fully realize how much I think of you. I sincerely hope so. I haven't had too much opportunity to show you, but I've tried. Good night, my dear.

Always—I love you, J.R.

Thursday, March 16, 1944

Elnora darling,

Well, sweet, by the time you receive this my vacation will be over. My last leave without you I hope. I wish I could get leaves this easily in the states. I'll have 20 days due when I get home, and that will be something. It won't be much of a rest, but who wants to sleep at such times?

I think this leave will be a very quiet one for me. My only ambitions are food and sleep. I think you would be quite proud of me. I hope there are some good shows on as I wouldn't mind seeing a few. I guess you must get all the hell out of your system on the first trip down. I know I don't feel a bit wild.

Ah, what a life of leisure I am leading—four meals a day. Plenty of eggs, milk, meat, etc. Honest, darling, I'll be getting fat the first thing you know. I could eat till doomsday if I stay this hungry. The New Guinea food has been horrible, and I surely need a respite from it. I hope it improves soon.

Thanks a lot for the calendars, dear. I rarely know what month it is, let alone the day. I prefer to judge my time by your letters, and then I don't feel so far behind. Because of you I always think it's February instead of March. I'll have to catch up on those two weeks soon.

If you don't mind, I'll drink a beer while I write. I'll have to start giving you lessons again when I get back. I didn't have quite enough time in Montgomery.

I'm afraid this leave will be indeed lonesome without you. You've been constantly on my mind, but that's nothing new really. I couldn't get you out if I tried, and I'm sure I won't.

So, you didn't make the officers dance? What's the matter—feet hurt? Mine sure as hell do. These Aussie shoes kill me. I prefer the old G.I.'s to them. I need to hire a little man to break them in for me.

Well, darling, it's nearly lunch time, and I think I'll dash. It's been wonderful seeing you these past few minutes. We've still got that date for Sunday afternoon, and I intend to keep it. Bye for now—and it's

Always—I love you, J.R.

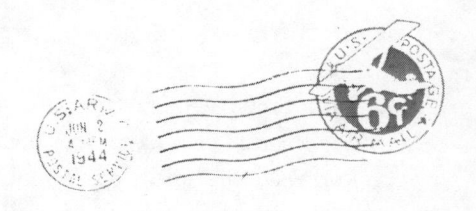

THE FRUITCAKE WILL PROBABLY PASS ON THIS EVENING

Sunday, March 19, 1944

My dearest,

Just started wondering where you are and what you are doing and that certainly gives me enough incentive to write. Good old Sunday—it's the same the world over. Nothing to do, and you don't feel like doing it anyhow. It is also, I might add, one less Sunday I'll have to be away from you.

Ah, the radio is really putting out this evening. Best music I've heard in a long time. Not so new, but very pleasant. Been wondering a lot about you lately. Did you go dancing last night? I did. Did you think of me as I did about you? As usual I got involved in a rumba again. I'll learn to handle that one yet. Perhaps I won't tread on your feet with a little more practice that I doubt seriously that I'll get. I did have fun though, even though I was slightly hampered by the fact that my life is slightly mixed up with a redhead. I also happen to be in love with her, if you didn't know. Madly, and I wish I could do something about it.

I should have plenty of mail from you by the time I get back. That is really something to look forward to. I still can't see how you put out all that private correspondence. At times I privately suspect you of having a secretary or else an abnormally large right arm. How about it, are you developing a big bicep?

I haven't seen that good show as yet. I missed *Madame Curie*, and that irked me greatly, as I particularly wanted to see that one. [J.R. believed that Elnora looked like Greer Garson.] I wonder why. I also missed *Du Barry Was A Lady*. All the good shows are beginning to come through again, and it's about time. Perhaps I'll catch up with the above mentioned numbers at some future date.

How is the Smith family these days? Is Mrs. Smith still such a Marine supporter? I've had more than one argument with those guys about flying. We usually go after it hot and heavy. It's a good thing we don't fly together, or it would be murder. But to get back to the Smiths, I hope my adopted family is well. I often wonder about Roger, and if they have heard from him lately. He must have plenty of company now from what I see in the papers. It must be plenty tough. I've seen all I want to.

Good night, darling. I'll write again soon. Until then—

Always—I love you, J.R.

Monday, March 27, 1944

Dearest Elnora,

Well, darling, here I am back from Sydney again—back in dear old New Guinea. I certainly spent a quiet time down there. I ate till I nearly popped, drank beer, saw a few shows, and that was all. I must be getting old or more probably a little bored with it all. I did enjoy it though, and I certainly needed the rest. I rested for a change too. I have 20 missions to go, and I hope to get through without too much trouble.

The mailman certainly had some surprises for me when I got back—reams of letters from you. I was really in all my glory. Three *Life* magazines came through, and that really stopped me—all January issues. Not bad, then to top it all off I found the records you sent and a fruitcake. Really a holiday! Only one record was broken, and that's not a bad average. We've been playing them all evening, and I certainly go for that Dinah Shore. Nice going, darling—we all thank you. We were in a bad way for needles too, and those you sent certainly saved the day.

The fruitcake will probably pass on this evening, but you can bet it will be enjoyed. We've been brewing up a little coffee before bedtime around here, and it should be particularly good this evening. It wasn't spoiled a bit.

The situation is still about the same around here. The food is still lousy, but living conditions are quite a bit better. Moving is certainly a job, as you will find out one of these beautiful days. Maybe it won't be so bad with you around to boss.

I did finally manage to find a decent pair of shoes in Sydney, and Lord how I needed them. Shopping in that town is an indescribable job. There isn't much in the first place, and what they have got is difficult to locate. I suppose it's getting that way in the states too however.

What an Easter card that you sent. It certainly had me fooled for a minute. Quite a gushy job, darling—where did you dig it up? Sweet thought anyhow, and I love you.

Damn, my leg just went to sleep. Pardon me while I stomp around the tent much to everyone's annoyance. Ah! That's much better—now I can continue in comfort.

I suppose I'll be getting up at the crack of dawn tomorrow; that I can't say I appreciate either. Maybe I'd best say night, darling. Thank you for all those lovely letters, and the records, and fruit cake. I think you're pretty sweet, you know. I don't know what I'd have done without you all these months. In fact, I don't know how I did do without you. I must be sounding a bit nuts about this point.

Bye for the moment, dear, and even that would be too long if you were near.

Always—I love you, J.R.

Tuesday, March 28, 1944

Dearest Elnora,

Well, more mail today—how things have changed. They were even dated Mar. 13 so perhaps they are finally getting the situation under control. I hope you are receiving my letters as quickly.

My tent mate is now playing all the new records and everything else he can lay his hands on. We are beginning to get a pretty good collection of them again. We have lost a good many of them in our various moves, and then of course the usual number always get broken. We have one of the hand-cranked jobs in the tent, and it keeps you plenty busy. I'm glad Sy is supplying the music while I write.

They finally dug up some fresh meat for the meals today, and that makes us feel that life is not quite so in vain. I never knew I could grow to dislike anything as much as I do bully beef [canned corned beef]. God, what a meal that makes. C-rations aren't a good deal better either.

It's getting pretty close to May again isn't it, darling? I'm afraid I won't be dropping into Houston this time, but I hope I'll be pointed in that direction by then. Perhaps in June we can take up where we left off.

It hasn't really been such a long year, has it darling? Maybe it's because we've had so much to look forward to. Of course I've missed you like sin, but that's only to be expected. You couldn't give that red hair much credit if I didn't.

It's been a long year in some aspects too. It's much too long a time to have been away from you. We didn't have a great deal to go on, but thank heavens we made the most of it.

I think I'll close, darling, and go to bed as I'm tired. If I go to sleep I'll dream of you, and if I lie awake I'll think of you. Either way I can't lose for I—

Love you always, J.R.

Mission FFO 89-F: March 29, 1944

The objective assigned on today's mission was the personnel area at Dagua, Targets 6, 7 and 8-D. The secondary target was Target 2-D at Hansa Bay, the target was to be bombed at an altitude of 6,000 ft. by six A/P each carrying six 500 lb. inst. demo. bombs. Lt. Jones dropped his bombs with the same excellent results—all six in Target 8-D. Lt. Jones' crew reported the possible sugar charlie [inter-island cargo vessel] at Wewak.

Lt. J.R. Jones flew in position #3 on the 2nd flight in A/P 084—Hung Lo.

Monthly Intelligence Summary No. 10, Period February 29 to March 29, 1944

Individual Cases:

Suspected Sabotage: During the month, one of our B-25-D-1 airplanes was damaged as a result of a truck being backed into the wing while the airplane was on the hardstand during the night. As this was the third instance of damage to our airplanes since we have been operating in New Guinea, a thorough investigation was made to determine the possibility of sabotage. After checking carefully and exhaustively into this latest case, as well as the two earlier cases, it is the opinion of this Officer that this plane was damaged unintentionally and that there was no deliberate intent involved. CASE CLOSED.

Information has been received from members of this organization that they have noticed a light burning at night halfway up the mountains in back of our squadron area. On two occasions, this light was seen between the hours of 2300-2400/L, 24/25 and 25/26 March 1944, and turned on in such a manner as to suggest the possibility of signal. The following two nights, 27/28 March, 1944, the light was observed burning steadily around 0300-0400/K, but was not seen burning at any other time during the early evening or night. An unconfirmed source reports that personnel of the 500th Squadron, when tramping through this area on a daytime hike, found what was apparently a cache of tinned food and supplies, in the approximately same locations as the light. It is possible that this may be a friendly ack-ack or searchlight installation post. The area is being kept under surveillance and any further activities will be reported.

Rumors:

The principal rumors coming to our attention seems to be those based upon the latest dope on how the system for sending the ground personnel back to the States is working. As this is a subject of which all of our ground personnel are keenly interested, it is easy to understand such rumors can circulate freely and rapidly.

The other type of rumors coming to our attention has been of possible greater significance. These have been reports or statements made by persons in responsible positions who would be expected to be accurately informed, and who on at least one occasion made incorrect statements as to the latest landings made by American Forces in the Pacific campaign. One officer stated that American Forces had landed on Truk. Our policy in counteracting these rumors has been to present as completely as possible, in compliance with necessary security, the full and correct facts regarding Allied operations.

Propaganda Activity:

This officer was informed by reliable sources that during the past month the radio Tokyo station broadcasted their version of a briefing of a combat mission by the 90th Bombardment Group, giving intimate details about the Group, and its officers and personnel. It is felt that they may prove to have been a boon to us, as it certainly should be an excellent example for all of our men of the necessity for strict security discipline.

Morale:

Morale of this organization continues to be high, but it is being subjected to severe strain from two sources, which if not corrected, may result in a marked lowering of our unit's morale. These sources of strain are: (1) Apparently inadequate source of food supplies, particularly meat, vegetables, sugar, etc. It is understood that the Quartermaster in the Nadzab area is issuing all available foodstuffs, but that his source of supply seems to be inadequate. Needless to say, good food is vital to the morale of any Army unit, particularly Air Corps organization that has to continually combat the problem of boredom on the part of its ground personnel. (2) Any system that results in enlisted men going a year or more without one day's leave is obviously inadequate. The necessity of rest for men stationed in this area has been recognized by all parties concerned. However, at present there are inadequate facilities for getting men to the Mainland. At the present rate, there will be men in our unit who will not be able to go on furlough for many months to come. It is suggested that every possible step be taken to provide additional facilities for furlough for Air Corps personnel, as existing authorized quotas are decidedly inadequate.

Unit History for Month of March, 1944

To: Commanding General, Army Air Forces, Washington, D.C.

There was no change in our training policy during the month. All new men are thoroughly checked and *broken in* by experienced men, giving them full benefit of our combat experience in this theater.

Narrative Report for Month of March, 1944

Our squadron started this month with a strike against Nubia-Awar areas at Hansa Bay. As usual, and in our customary manner, blasted hell out of the target, and all planes returned safe and sound.

For the next several days, we ran almost daily missions to the Admiralty Islands in support of ground troop operations there bombing the Nips out of their holes around the Momote area and around Lorengau. As usual, all planes and all crews returned safe and sound.

On the 17th, we hit the old Jap standby—Wewak. Fighter cover was provided for us by one squadron of P-40s and was excellent, and included an elaborate display of aerial gymnastics by the P-40s on the way home after the bombing attack. This was obviously the beginning of the end for Wewak, as the light ack-ack encountered definitely showed results of the terrific pouncing we have been giving it. There was no damage to any of our planes and no injuries to any of our crews on the mission. On the 19th, we went back and hit Wewak again, just in case they might think our earlier strike was an accident. Again, our bombing was devastating and Nip defenses were weak. This day was a double header. The afternoon game was a contest between our boys and the Jap convoy north of Wewak. We carried out the mission as ordered, but before our planes could get to the ships, the A-20's had completely obliterated them, sinking 2 P/C boats and a FOX TALE UNCLE. Our planes stayed in the area until 1655/L strafing the few remaining Nips, who were clinging to the wreckage in the sea, and then turned toward home bringing back their full bomb load.

On the 22nd, we went out again to hunt Jap shipping this time around KAIRIRU-Muschu Islands north of Wewak. Again it was a hard job to find a target that had not already been blasted to bits, as the A-20s were also working the area, and our boys were only able to get 3 barges and blow up numerous huts and houses in Kairiru Village.

On the 25th, we went back to Wewak for a return engagement, which was not very successful, due to very bad weather, 7/10 cloud coverage, over the target.

On the 26th, we hit Dagua very effectively, with Lt. Col. Fridge, Deputy Group Commander, leading our squadron.

On the 27th, our Squadron Medical Officer, Captain Oscar W. Still was transferred to V Bomber Command. We were all sorry to see him go, and wish him well in his new position. Capt. Donald Marcus joined us as our new Flight Surgeon.

On the 29th, we went back to the Wewak area this time hitting targets 6-D, 7-D, and 8-D at Dagua. Col. Fridge again led our squadron, with Major Fain, Squadron Commander, leading our second flight. The target was hit hard and heavy, and all our planes and crews returned safe and sound.

We closed up the month with a practice run of possible future things to come. All squadrons loaded their frag racks and went up to Kairiru Island to give them a test run. Again, our armament boys showed us that they are on the ball, because ours were one of the very few squadrons in which the new racks worked well.

In all, a total of 18 bombing missions were carried out during this month. The main targets being ground support in Momote and Lorengau, bombing of Wewak and Dagua, and barge and shipping attacks in the Wewak area. Our group was congratulated by General Kreuger and Colonel Crabb for our excellent work in the Admiralty Islands operations which did much in contributing to the capture of these important bases.

Lt. Bailey became the first officer in our squadron to be awarded the Silver Star and was also promoted to Captain during the month. In all, this was a typical month's operations. All the targets were hit hard and heavy with absolutely minimum damage sustained.

Benjamin E. Green
Captain, Air Corps
Intelligence Officer

Daily Log: April 2, 1944

Church Services were held for the first time today in the new Group Chapel adjacent to our Squadron area. Regular routine duties in the Squadron.

Monday, April 3, 1944

Elnora, my dearest,

I've been slightly off the ball the past couple of days on this letter writing. I don't know what's wrong with me. I'm still grounded, but my cold has improved to some extent and my sense of smell isn't too sharp yet. It seems to be my sinus acting up, but it never bothered me before.

Just while I think of it, dear—if you ever pull out a can of tuna or salmon on me I'll brain you. Lord, but I hate the stuff, and the Army seems to have plenty of it. Merely a word of warning, sweet!

The main reason I didn't write yesterday was that I was O.D. and I had to censor mail. It was the most I've ever seen, and I was heartily sick of letters by the time I had finished. You have no idea what a dull job that is. Most of them sound alike, and if I thought I sounded like that I'd quit here and now. I've been able to hold on to you for over two years by means of letters, so I feel that I haven't done too badly. It's a good thing that job doesn't come around too often, or I'd be a roaring maniac.

I'm even passing up a good show to write you tonight darling, so you can see that you really rate. I'd rather be with you in this letter any time though. Besides, I know you'd be fit to be tied if I didn't start in writing soon. Who am I to talk? I feel neglected if I don't get a letter on every mail. You rather spoil me, dear, but still don't keep you from being the sweetest girl in sight.

I'm still getting an occasional *Life* magazine. The latest is February 7 which isn't bad for that sort of thing. I hope they keep coming. I really had rapid service on a letter today. It was dated March 22 and the ink was barely dry. I wonder if you are doing so well. In it you said that you had just received three letters from me so it doesn't sound too bad. Perhaps we won't have to keep this up too much longer.

What's this talk about a dangerous gleam in your eye—the kind when your father makes you stay home? I'm not quite certain that I like that with me this far away. I've seen it several times myself, and it's disastrous to those who get in the way. Just look at me—a hopeless case and all because of a gal named Bartlett looked too good to be true. I'll say one thing, she knew all the right answers and didn't hesitate giving them, much to my joy. I was pretty smug myself that night, only I guess you didn't notice.

The little poem about the wolf was pretty cute. I'll be strictly that way about you when I turn up, so be on guard!

Shucks, it will be all legal though. Can't say that I would mind that either.

The Gulf picnic you mentioned in your letter sounds strictly peace time, but O.K. I'll take you up on that someday. I'll bet you are a pain in the neck when it comes to swimming. You and your lily-white skin. If you can put up with it, I can too. The only trouble is that if you get sunburned, I wouldn't be able to put my arms around you, and I wouldn't go for that at all. Gee, I bet you make a peachy blister. Do the freckles come out all over then? I can easily see you will take a beating from me on such days, but I love you. We have one consolation, darling—just look at all the things we can do together that we have never done before. Every day will be a new day and a new adventure. It's a life that I eagerly look forward to.

Well, darling, it's been a lovely evening seeing you again, at least your picture. I've taken the best of care of that item. Every day you look prettier to me in that picture. I don't know what I would have done without them. I'm certainly glad I received it before I left. Just imagine waiting for it in this mail system.

I seem to have rambled on at considerable length this evening, and if it isn't pretty obvious by this time that what I meant most to say is I

Love you, always, J.R.

Melvin Best commented that he didn't like censoring the mail either. He told of an intense conversation he had with one soldier about writing his mother about being under Japanese attack at night. Melvin said that they never once were threatened with Japanese ground troops at their camp sites. He cautioned the soldier not to write a letter like that to his mother and have her worry as she had enough to deal with without having to worry about something that didn't happen.

I find it very interesting that J.R. censored most of his mail and wonder if he told more or told less of what actually happened based upon the fact that he could censor his mail. As I previously stated, he had only one letter where the censor cut out portions of that letter, and it was his first letter from the warfront. Either he stuck to the rules, or he was very lucky.

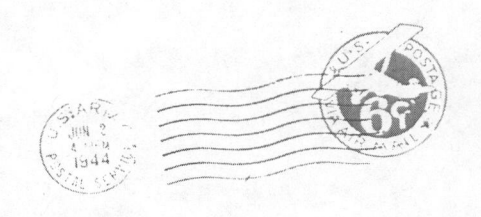

THEY CHANGED THE RULES: HOPES OF HOME SEEM SO FAR AWAY

DAILY LOG

Change of rules to rotate home:
　　March 5, 1944
　　Must have 50 missions and 200 hours; J.R. thinks he will be home June 1944.
　　April 7, 1944
　　We must spend a year in the theatre before we get a break.

FRIDAY, APRIL 7, 1944

Dearest Elnora,

　　Well here I am again and with none too cheerful news. It seems I made a slight error in my estimate of coming home. Yep, they changed the rules, and as usual I got caught in the midst of it. Now we must spend a year in this theater before we get a break. That makes it the middle of August for me, my dear. Missions and hours don't mean a thing, and Lord how we'll stack them up. I hope this doesn't come as too much of a blow, dear, but I well imagine you are used to it. Even in your last letter you said even if it was longer than I thought it would be, the worst part is over. That, my darling, is a very commendable attitude, and it quite relieved my mind to be aware of it before hand. It won't be too much longer. Two months over a year since we had to say so long.

This way I have an excellent chance of coming home a captain. You don't need to say anything about this, however. I'd be mighty glad to become a First Lieutenant, but it doesn't hurt to get all you can. Leave it to me to get stuck, but you don't get much choice these days.

Saw a wonderful show last night, *Sweet Rosie O'Grady*, with Betty Grable. It's not hard to see why she is the soldiers' favorite—sex and more sex. It goes a long way around here. I still thought it was a good show, and enjoyed it hugely. Pretty colors and good music—what more could you ask? Don't say it. We are doing plenty O.K. as far as the cinemas are concerned. I hope it keeps up as it's the best form of relaxation that I know of.

I finally got up enough courage to begin another book. It's *A Tree Grows In Brooklyn* by Betty Smith. I haven't heard too much comment on it pro or con, although quite a few fellows have read it. I've only gotten past the first pages so I haven't had time to form an opinion.

We really have some good records going this evening. T.D. in "It Started All Over Again." Plenty good—"In the Blue of Evening" too—all the latest. Oh well, we like it. Guess what I just heard—"Where Or When." It's been a long time, but it brings back the night much too clearly. In fact I've been thinking instead of writing for the last thirty minutes. Guess what about? Oh, just how you looked, what you said, and how you said it.

Well, darling, it's time for me to be on my way. Kinda late it is. Night, dear –

Always—I love you, J.R.

Mission FFO 100-G: April 9, 1944

Nine B-25-D-1A/P of this Squadron took part in a raid on the Tadji area, the primary objective being an open place or patch south of the south runway at Tadji. The purpose was to burn kunai grass in this patch. After forming with two other squadrons of the group, we proceeded to the Leron River to form with the 38th Group and one squadron of P-47's. The first and second flights bombed the assigned target but the third flight did not, the results were not observed other than small fires. This flight misjudged the target when coming in for their bombing and overshot the assigned area, dropping their bombs in a very similar shaped Kunai patch 2500 yards west of the Tadji runway. Several small fires were started that were visible 15-20 minutes out from the target.

Lt. J.R. Jones flew in position #2 on the 3rd flight in A/P 518—Quitch—taking off at 5:05 a.m.

Crew members were: Lt. C.A. Lorenzen, S/Sgt. J.A. Liparela, S/Sgt. H.C. Aslin, and S/Sgt. M.R.W. Adams

Sunday, April 9, 1944

Dearest Elnora,

Happy Easter and stuff. Did you know that I didn't go to church? Of course I wasn't able to for the usual reason. The fact is that I didn't even know it was Sunday, let alone Easter, till the day was half over. I'm really on my toes. Did you have a nice day and go to church like a good girl, or were you out tearing around Saturday? It would have been a great pleasure for me to be your escort on one of my infrequent trips to church on this day. Such is not luck as yet.

Let's see—two years ago I was at Maxwell Field. I went to church then. That's not so bad. Lord, that seems a long way from New Guinea and fighting a war. I guess we didn't know what we were in for.

Little did I think at the time either that we would be seeing the city of Montgomery together. I always did have the ambition to take you to that Officer's Club, but I never thought it would be a reality. It looks as if anything can happen and usually does.

We really had a red-hot show last night, *The Leopard Man*, and what a stinker. Everyone gets killed—very cheerful little piece. Myself, I prefer Betty Grable, but you can't please us all. What I'd really settle for is that redhead of mine. That's asking more than ever.

I received a letter from you today, and you really gave me a blast. Okay, you don't have to convince me. I did get kind of tickled when you reminded me of that ring ultimatum. You were really emphatic about that. It was kind of funny. I really let you bluff me that time, but I didn't mind in the least. I'll never let you forget that one. Particularly when you started telling me about all the proposals during my absence. I think you were getting even with me for that 'going to see my girlfriend' line. Boy, what a pair we're going to make. It looks like fun from where I sit though. I really deserved it, but when I think how you said, "No! Now," I still have to chuckle to myself. I thought oh, oh, this lady isn't to be put off. She wasn't either—hot dawg!

Darling, I'm going to bed before my eyes drop out. I'm plenty tired this evening. I'll continue this in another letter—many of them, and they'll all say I

Love you always, J.R.

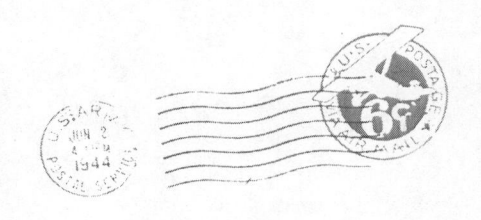

ENOUGH OF THE HARDSHIPS OF THE WAR

MISSION FFO 102-D: APRIL 11, 1944

The primary objective was Target 27-D at Wewak. There was no secondary objective assigned. The target was to be bombed from medium altitude with twelve A/P, eleven of which carried 12 X 100 lb. white smoke bombs and one A/P carried 6 X 100 lb. white smoke bombs. We formed with the 500th and the 38th Group over the Leron River at 1500 ft. and then proceeded to Annenberg for rendezvous with one squadron of P-47s at 3,000 ft., and on directly to the target. The mission was carried out as ordered, with bombing excellent—a total of 102 bombs were dropped in the area covering it with smoke. Lt. Col. Fridge, Group Deputy Commander, led our Squadron. The entire flight's bombs hit in the target stringing directly across the center. Col. Fridge took K-21 photos and Lt. Jones took K-17 photos of bombing results.

Lt. J.R. Jones flew in the #3 position on the 1st flight in A/P 082—Meany—taking off at 3:45 a.m.

Crew members were: Lt. W.E. Henley, Sgt. J.O. Coskrey, S/Sgt. H.D. Aslin, S/Sgt. H.R.W. Adams, and T/Sgt. E. Davis.

Tuesday, April 11, 1944

Dearest Elnora,

Another day and what do you know—a package turns up and what is it but blessed cigarettes. They really come in handy now. All four of us thank you. We have a very difficult time getting them these days. I just got them in the nick of time as I was nearly out. Thanks so much, darling. They were a little late for Christmas, but actually they were appreciated more at the present time.

We really had a red-hot show last night. Hedy Lamar and William Powell in *Heavenly Body*—very appropriate title! It was good though and quite enjoyable. We have a slick theater now and that helps. Also we aren't bothered by rain, and you have no idea how much better a show is when you aren't sitting in a puddle. I must not be as hardy as I used to be.

I also finished a *Tree Grows in Brooklyn*. It really gave me a bang, and I think you'd like it too if you have time to read it. It's very well written, and it's easy to see why it was a best seller. That leaves me short of reading material, but I'm kind of busy now so I don't worry. Days are really buzzing by again now. It seems I'm going to be getting up a trifle early in the morning, and I can't say that I'm pleased in the slightest. Such is life.

It must be getting quite warm in Houston by now. That should curtail your ice-skating before long. I hardly remember what a piece of ice looks like. If I could get back in August that would make it three years even. That's a lot of time when I stop and think about it. How would you like to be getting up at three in the morning! That's exactly what I think.

Night, darling—I certainly would much rather be staying up late with you than getting up early. I'd be telling you there that I love you personally instead of at the end of a letter.

Love you always, J.R.

Mission FFO 103-K: April 12, 1944

This mission was a Weather/Recco [reconnaissance] Lt. J.R. Jones flew in A/P 437—Little Thumper—taking off at 4:00 a.m.

Crew members were: Lt. A. Osborne, Lt. E. Davis, Capt. T.W. Lacey, T/Sgt. C.A. Krauss, S/Sgt. F.E. Faulkner, S/Sgt. O.D. Spencer.

Wednesday, April 12, 1944

Dearest Elnora,

Here it is the next day, and I'm back. I can't leave you alone for very long, can I? I'm plenty dead too. Lord, but I dread flying night in these parts. It's the worst place in the world for that sort of thing. I certainly hope I don't have to do much more of it. You grow old too fast that way.

Did I ever receive two fat letters today. One of them carried the weekly installment of the funnies and the other was a short note about eighteen pages long. You are really on it, dear. It must break you up to buy stamps for those little items. You must have really been in the mood. The guy who brought it in to me came in staggering under the load.

I ought to really sleep tonight and whee, I don't have to fly tomorrow. That is really a break. I intend to sleep until it gets so hot that I can't stay in bed any longer. I'm not very lazy, oh no.

One of the boys is certainly giving the Victrola a work out this evening. It provides nice inspiration, except that I listen more than I write. Have my letters been dull lately, dear? Somehow I don't feel I'm doing as well as I used to.

You haven't mentioned [Mary Lou] Byers in your letters lately until this one. What is she up to these days, and how did she finally make out with the Captain? Did it turn out to be another dead-end street? It's going to take a good man to tie her down. She certainly is a character, and I like her a lot. I guess they only grow them in Texas.

It looks to me as if there is going to be a party in this tent tonight. The boys are beginning to gather, and the bottles are beginning to appear. The flying will most likely begin soon too.

I'd best be closing shortly before the uproar starts. Night, darling—I enjoyed that big letter so much. I wouldn't mind a few more of those. It's evident that you already know,

I love you very much, J.R.

Daily Log: April 15, 1944

Pay day was today which does not mean very much over here. The Officers and Enlisted Men's Soft Ball teams were organized as of today.

Saturday, April 15, 1944

Dearest Elnora,

I've only received nine letters from you in the past three days. You must be slipping, darling. Last night I received another package from you too. It was the fruitcake in the coffee can and did it hit the spot. It didn't last long though as you might imagine. The boys accused me of being engaged to a boozehound because there was so much brandy in it. It was pretty potent, dear. Danny even claims he got a slight buzz on it. It was swell though. I could use one of those every day. All the boys thank you too. It's a good thing this bunch of wolves have never seen you or they probably would give me a bad time.

You should see the records we have now. They are issued by the special service division, and there are four pieces on each side of them. They are played at the low speed, and each one lasts about thirteen minutes. That certainly saves us a lot of winding. We have such good numbers as "Manhattan Serenade," "I've Heard That Song Before," "Strictly Instrumental," and "Moonlight Becomes You" by Harry James. "In the Blue of Evening," and "Chicago" by Tommy Dorsey. Several good numbers by Benny Goodman, Kay Kyser, Fred Waring, and many others too numerous to mention. We sit around and knock ourselves out by the hour and wish to hell we were home. My favorite is "You'll Never Know" by Dinah Shore. I give that one particularly hard wear. We have the only Victrola that will handle these records, so we have a monopoly on them in our tent. I'll tell you more concerning them as I write again.

As for my daily report on the cinema, it was Kay Kyser in *Swing Fever*. Nothing terrific, but nice entertainment. I can always enjoy the music if nothing else. Don't know what is showing this evening, but it doesn't make much difference as we always go anyhow.

The screen broke down last time and proceedings were held up while some guy climbed up the pole to fix things—always an added attraction at our shows.

Not much has been happening to me for the past couple of days. It has rained the last two nights, and I mean *rain*. It nearly washed the joint away the first night. As a result, we are now surrounded by a fine sea of mud. Walking becomes rather difficult after about ten steps. Your feet get about three times their natural size and plenty heavy.

But enough of the hardships of war, let's talk about my more pleasant side of life—meaning you, naturally. I'm in the mood to take you out for a good meal of Mexican food. Of course if I ignore you while I'm busy feeding my face, don't get worried. I've been more or less hungry for the past year, and I hope to get over it someday. I can always smell of garlic afterwards. Damn I get hungry when I start thinking of such things.

What made you think that I wasn't very sure of you at times, darling? You're pretty much wrong there. I've never had any reason to believe otherwise, and I'm not looking for any. At times I almost wonder if I'm too sure, but I hardly think so. We've always played fair so I don't worry. I just love you, and that's all there is to it.

Thanks again for the fruitcake. There I go getting hungry again. Bye for now, darling.

Always—my love, J.R.

Mission FFO 107-E: April 16, 1944

The primary objective was supplies and personnel in Target 6-X at Humboldt Bay in the Hollandia area. Nine A/P of the Squadron carried 10 C 260 lb. frag. bombs, dropping 86 bombs in the target assigned. The 499th and 500th Squadrons formed with our squadron over strip #4 at Nadzab and made rendezvous with one squadron of P-38's for fighter cover over Buriu and from there proceeded direct to the target. Bombing weather over the target and in route back as far as Atemble was good. This flight dropped all of their bombs in the target, hitting the approximate center. At the point where very bad weather was observed ahead, our squadron changed their course and crossed over to Bogadjim, and from then on the flight proceeded on instrument. Due to the exceptional flying ability of our pilots, all of our A/P's returned without damage to crew or A/P.

It is the opinion of this Officer that all our pilots flying on this mission, particularly Lt. Kortemeyer, Squadron Leader, are to be highly commended for excellent airmanship and pilot's skill in maintaining a tight squadron formation on instrument flying through such bad weather. The proof of this splendid work lies in the fact that all crew members in this squadron returned safely, and that there was very minor damage to two airplanes.

Lt. J.R. Jones flew in the #2 position on the 1st flight in A/P 089—The Gay Mare—taking off at 7:10 a.m.

Crew members were: Lt. R.L. Welch, S/Sgt. W.D. Helvey, S/Sgt. H.C. Aslin, and S/Sgt. M.R.W. Adams.

Daily Log: April 17, 1944

Flew local leaving at 1:00 p.m.

Lt. J.R. Jones flew in A/P 033—Sandblasters.

Crew members were: Lt. M.H. Symens, S/Sgt. H.C. Aslin, S/Sgt. M.R.W. Adams, Lt. H.A. Geer.

Monday, April 17, 1944

Dearest Elnora,

Well, darling, the little blue envelopes have really been pouring in the last two days. It was a veritable deluge. I hardly know where to begin answering them. I spent a good part of the evening reading them.

Yesterday was another of those rugged jobs, and I couldn't have written if I had wanted to. The less said about that, the better. Didn't even feel like going to the show tonight. Think I'll hit the sack early and get some slumber.

Honestly dear, the number and size of these letters amaze me. I've got enough ammunition for a week. The boys froth at the mouth when they see me with so many letters.

I've been drinking coffee all day, and I'm just about saturated. I hope it doesn't affect my sleep—anything but that.

We have a record of Martha Raye singing "Once In Awhile" and it's terrific. I could listen to it by the hour. I always did go for that number.

Listen love, I'm about to offer my first and only piece of advice to you. In one of your letters you were quite in a lather because your boss and this gal you call Martha had been stepping out on the side. It's none of your business and perhaps too much, but at least you know what I think.

We received our big cigarette ration today. Two packages to last God knows how long. I guess they must be expecting us all to cut down. I smoke enough during a mission to kill me normally. I'll certainly have to slow down one of these days.

What I could go for is a can of that good American beer. There is a rumor to the effect that we are to be issued some—oh well, nice rumor. We did get a bar of U.S. candy at the P.X. It wasn't standing up too well in this climate though. Messy, but good!

You sound as if you have been beating your brains out on that job of yours. See nothing and hear nothing, and you'll be out of it. That guy's wife would probably hold you accountable as much as anyone concerned, even though you had nothing to do with it. You'll find out that your own life and affairs will be complicated enough at times without getting mixed up in other people's. I don't know much about this Martha, but sounds as if she hasn't much damned sense, and she surely doesn't sound like the ideal playmate. I don't think she would score very high with me, and you find out that I make no bones about it to the person concerned. If I were you, I'd forget it, and stay out of it. I've said about enough—

[No ending to his letter was found, or the last page had been removed from the envelope.]

Mission FFO 141-D: April 20, 1944

Six A/P of this squadron were ordered to bomb Dagus, but at an altitude of 4000 feet and later strafe on a second run. Nine X 1000-lb. inst. demo bombs were dropped on the target. Three bombs were salvoed at sea. 5100 X .50 caliber ammunition expended. Bombing was excellent. Native huts in Dagua Village to Cape Karawop strafed with no visible results. Photos were taken, and propaganda leaflets were dropped.

Lt. J.R. Jones flew in the #2 position on the 1st flight in A/P 082—Meany—taking off at 4:15 a.m.

Crew members were: Lt. R.L. Welch, S/Sgt. E.D. Welch, S/Sgt. E.D. Faulkner, S/Sgt. H.C. Aslin, and S/Sgt. M. W. Zenesky.

Thursday, April 20, 1944

Dearest Elnora,

Hi, darling—here's that man again. Gosh, more letters from you. Really a popular guy I am. The boys in the tent are trying to figure out how I can be from Indiana and have a southern drawl at the same time. It really has them baffled. Of course if they knew who I picked it up from they wouldn't be surprised. I thought I had lost it myself. I can imagine what I'll be like in about four years. My own Mother probably won't even recognize me.

You should see the food supplies one of the boys drug in today. We are set for a long war now. If we ever get weathered in we can hold out for days.

Our officer's mess finally opened day before yesterday, and it is quite an improvement. We don't have to go so far, and the food is 100 percent better. I think I could even get healthy again there. The liquor department should open soon, and then the joint will really do a booming business. We even had steak yesterday, and that amazed me to no end. It's wonderful how a little good food helps your spirits.

We have a show tonight that should really be something. It's Mae West and Victor Moore in *The Heat's On*. It should prove an entertaining evening that could only be exceeded by one with you.

Hmm—gained three pounds, eh? Putting on weight—I might have known. If you get too heavy I won't let you sit on my lap. I'll sit on yours.

We finally got a goodly collection of cigarettes in this tent. We picked them up all over the island. You can use cigarettes to buy anything around here. Well, almost anything. A quart of whisky will go a long ways too, only we seldom give any of it away.

So you like to think of that last night in Montgomery— funny, so do I. There'll come a day and look out. I should be in great shape after a year around this dump. That is if I'm not slightly buggy by then. I'm a little nuts anyhow, so maybe it won't show.

If you think you can smear me up better than you did at the end of that letter, then I'm ready. Fact of the matter is I have been for a long time. The first time I ever kissed you I wondered if you weren't playing for keeps. Sure enough, and there I was in the middle of it. I didn't have much of a chance, did I?

Did you say you had taken some more pictures? I'm ready for those any time in the near future. I'll have to check up on this weight situation. It's a good thing I have something to tease you about, darling. I can't let you have all the fun.

It's getting along about show time, and the boys are getting ready to go. Suppose I had better get going. Wouldn't you like to come along, then we could neck in the balcony like a couple of high school kids?

Night, dear. I'll be back in another letter shortly, and until then it's,

I love you, always, J.R.

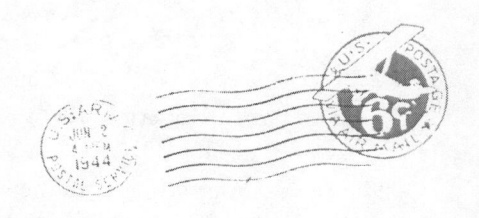

THE MUSIC BECAME SO POTENT: KOSTELANETZ TO JAZZ

Friday, April 21, 1944

Dearest Elnora,

I didn't think I would write this evening, but the music became so potent I couldn't resist. About all I've done this evening is sit and stare into space. My mind must be pretty far off.

What all did this fortuneteller fill you with, dear? Tell me more. I should think she has a pretty easy job these days as nearly all people are in the same situation.

I was rather wrong about that show last night. It turned out to be quite a stinker. Oh well, it's free, and we don't have anything else to do but gripe.

Now hearing "Time on My Hand" by Kostelanetz— very restful and very pretty. I wish I did have time on my hands and you in my arms. Now it's the "Touch of Your

Hand" from Roberta. His music certainly reminds one of better days.

Hi, darling—this is the next night. The lights gave up on me last night, and I didn't have a chance to finish.

I've just returned from the best show I've seen since I have been overseas. It quite surprised me as I really didn't expect much. It was *Lost Angel*. No really big stars in the cast, but it certainly turned out to be a sleeper. It had the cutest little girl [Margaret O'Brien] in it I've ever seen. She certainly made this audience sit up and take notice. I do hope you see it as I know you will like it more than anything you have for a long time. I think everyone present must have fallen quite in love with her.

We have a very nice number by Glenn Miller playing— "Rainbow Rhapsody"—ever hear it? On the reverse side is a cute little item called "It Must be Jelly ('Cause Jam Don't Shake Like That)." No fooling, that's really it. Only the latest in jazz, that's us!

Damn, this letter isn't getting anywhere. I must be getting out of form, darling. Every time I start to write a line, I begin thinking about you and I come to about half an hour later. When will the day arrive when we can sit down and talk this thing over? If we're together we won't need to talk then. Last night Sy, who lives with me, asked to see a picture of a girl who could write so much—that's you, darling. I hope you'll be able to meet some of the guys and their wives. We would be able to have some of the best times you've ever dreamed about. It's a date, darling.

Must close and get to bed, dear, as this war starts early. Night, sweet—Lord, but I miss you, and I

Love you always, J.R.

MISSION FFO 113-E: APRIL 22, 1944

The news of today was the landings made by the 6th Army in three places on the New Guinea Coast, Hollandia, Tadji, and Tanahmerah.

Nine A/P of this Squadron were to take off from strip #4 at Nadzab, form with two other squadrons of this group and the 38th group on course, and proceed direct to the target which was Tendayne Island via the Leron River. The Squadron was unable to attack the primary target due to weather and was forced to make an attack on the secondary target which was target 29-B near Potsdam Plantation on the south shore of Hansa Bay. Photos were taken, and bombing was excellent.

Lt. J.R. Jones flew in the #2 position on the 1st flight in A/P 064—The Wild Indian—taking off at 3:50 a.m.

Crew members were: Lt. W.W. Everett, S/Sgt. H. C. Aslin, S/Sgt. Sgt. M.J. Jones, and S/Sgt. M. W. Zenesky.

MISSION FFO 114-J: APRIL 23, 1944

The primary objective on today's strike was ack-ack installations in Target 20-B near Nubia Village at Hansa Bay. There was no secondary target. The target was bombed at medium altitude by nine A/P of this Squadron and the remaining three squadrons of the group and the 38th Group. After making rendezvous with one squadron of P-47's at Gusap, we proceeded direct to the target. The mission was carried out as ordered, although bombing was poor with only ten bombs dropping in the assigned target. Thirteen bombs fell on the land between the target and the Awar River and twenty bombs fell in the water. There was nil interception and no ack-ack of any kind seen over the Hansa Bay area. A/P 060 sustained damage on landing at home base and will be turned in to a service squadron. There was no injury to crewmembers.

Lt. J.R. Jones flew in the #2 position on the 3rd flight in A/P 064—The Wild Indian.

Tuesday, April 25, 1944

Dearest Elnora,

It's a wonder I'm writing this evening, as I had to censor the mail again. It wasn't so bad today though as I believe most of the men went to the show last night.

I might add that I was there myself. It was Frank Sinatra in *Higher and Higher* and, confidentially, I really liked it. It had three of the nicest songs I have heard in many a moon. "I Didn't Sleep A Wink Last Night," "The Music Stopped," and "Isn't This a Lovely Way to Spend an Evening?" I liked the first one best of all. That guy can really put a song over, but I don't particularly care for him in the movies. All that sweet music rather put me in the mood to woo a certain redhead I know. Got any ideas on the subject?

We got a new batch of records today, and somehow we managed to lay hands on one of those lifetime needles. It really helps with these old records. We also got some old recorded radio entertainment. Such programs as *Carnation Hour*, *Cavalcade of America*, *Truth or Consequences*—all old standbys. We do all right.

One of my favorites we have is an Alvino Rey recording of "It Isn't a Dream Anymore." Lord, but it's nice! Reminds me of that Rey record I told you about once. You and I should certainly have a great time collecting records some day. I can listen to them for hours on end. This tent of ours looks like a music shop these days. We even started playing Tommy Dorsey when we got up at 4:00 a.m. this morning. Of course we had a few complaints from the neighbors, but a little thing like that doesn't deter us. Start the day with song.

I have another new book and it's supposed to be very good, but I haven't started is as yet. It is *Driving Woman*, and I hear it's a best seller. At least I manage to stay up with the latest in literature around here.

Bill Davis's wife is going to have a baby soon. He lives with us. We are all set to have a long-range christening as soon as the news arrives. At present he is chewing his nails. I remember the last baby we brought into the world. Lord, what a party! I get a headache when I even think about it.

That mailman of ours today said that gal in Texas really must think a lot of you, and I says yep. You are really getting well known. Tough luck, men, but I saw you first, and that's the best thing that ever happened to me.

I received two letters from you today—April 8-10—pretty rapid service. Boy, does this letter smell sweet—like you were wrapped up in it or something. All the boys just had to take a sniff.

One thing that pleases me very much about you is the way you look at the times we're apart. Your attitude makes me quite happy. I surely was lucky the day you decided I was the guy.

You didn't sound very happy on Easter Sunday, darling. What's the trouble—blue? It's easy to get that way. I figure we are pretty fortunate though. We've already got something a lot of people have never heard of and that's faith in each other. Yours has been perfect, and I couldn't ask for anything more.

Well, sweet, best I had be on my way as it's up at 4:30 for me. Good night, darling, I suppose things will never be quite the same till I'm able to put my arms around you and say Elnora, I love you so,

Always, J.R.

Mission: April 26, 1944

Supply mission from Finschhafen cancelled due to weather. They flew to Finschhafen and returned.

Lt. J.R. Jones flew in A/P 084—Hung Lo—at 1:20.

Crew members were: Lt. T.H. Heidorf, S/Sgt. Sgt. S.A. Cortesio, S/Sgt. H. C. Aslin, and S/Sgt. M. W. Zenesky.

Mission FFO 118-K: April 27, 1944

Ten A/P of this Squadron were ordered to go on a supply dropping mission to Hollandia strip. Forty-two para-bundles and 16 free-falling cases dropped on Hollandia strip and around edges. Dropping of the supplies was staged at 150 ft. Photos were taken.

Lt. J.R. Jones flew in the #2 position in A/P 084—Hung Lo—taking off at 6:10 a.m.

Crew members were: Lt. T.H. Heidorf, S/Sgt. S.A. Cortesio, S/Sgt. H. C. Aslin, and S/Sgt. M. W. Zenesky.

Friday, April 28, 1944

Dearest Elnora,

I got started on this a bit late this evening. One of my old flying school buddies dropped in to see me. I hadn't seen him in ages. We talked over the old days at Maxwell Field, etc. We certainly covered a lot of ground.

Last night by some miracle we procured several cases of beer. It cost us plenty, but it was well worth it. It tasted better than anything I've had in a long time. Got quite a glow on before I turned in. Woke up this morning and wonder of wonders, I had two eggs for breakfast. As I didn't have to fly today, I spent a good part of it in bed. I enjoyed that too. The old grind starts again tomorrow though, and I'm going to bed rather early.

The show last night consisted of one of these cowboy jobs with John Wayne named *In Old Oklahoma*. It wasn't bad for a shoot 'em up. I guess I'm just easy to please. There don't seem to be any good ones coming up, but I'll more than likely go to them anyhow.

You'll have to excuse me, darling, but I just had to take time out for a bottle of beer. I hope you didn't mind waiting for me. You'll have to get used to it. In fact next to you, I love it best and that's saying something.

Ah, did I hear you say that you were going to take a few more pictures? I really have something to look forward to. Also, I can check upon this weight situation. You wouldn't fool me, would you?

Well, darling, as much as I hate to, I'm going to have to cut this short and take off for the sack. We seem to be arising very early for some peculiar reason.

Good night, dear—I'll try to do better next time, but the best I can do at present is to say I love you with all my heart.

Always, J.R.

Monthly Intelligence Summary No. 11, Period March 29 to April 28, 1944

Individual Cases:

It was reported in the last month's summary that a light burning at night half way up the mountains in back of our squadron area had been seen on two occasions. Also, an unconfirmed report had been received that a cache of tinned food and supplies had been discovered in this same area. Upon further investigation, it was revealed that a new searchlight battery had been installed in this area and would thus account for the above mentioned activities. CASE CLOSED.

At the request of the War Department transmitted through representatives of the MID, an investigation of the character of one of the enlisted men of this organization, Pfc. [name withheld], [serial number withheld], is being made. This man has been associated with Communist organizations in the past. A surveillance of outgoing mail is being carried out, and a report will be made to the MID. CASE PENDING.

Morale:

It was reported in the last month's summary that there had been a strain on the usual high morals of the squadron due to the apparently inadequate stores of food and supplies. This month, with the opening of a separate officer's mess and with a marked improvement in the enlisted men's mess, this situation has been fairly well eradicated.

The infrequency of leaves for the enlisted men is still a source of discontent, and any improvement that could be made in the transportation facilities would of course improve the morale of the men, many of whom have gone more than a year without a leave.

Positive Security Measures:

The reason and necessity for security in successfully carrying out our offensives have been carefully explained to our men with the objective of getting their cooperation in obtaining positive security and security discipline.

Remarks and Questions:

The undersigned devotes his entire time to intelligence duties.

There are several questions concerning combat photographs to which an answer would be appreciated. They are: (1) <u>Distribution</u>. This Officer would like to know if it is permissible to distribute combat photographs to the personnel of the squadron after these photographs are no longer of any military value. (2) <u>Censorship</u>. This Officer would also like to know what the policy is concerning censorship of these photographs to determine whether these photographs may be sent home by the men.

This Officer would also like a definite statement on the policy of maintaining a squadron photo library where the men can develop and print their own personal film, rather than send them to the theater photo laboratory on the Mainland. The establishment of such a laboratory would tend to have an excellent effect upon the morale of the men since there is such a great interest in photography in this Squadron.

Carl A. Strauss
1st Lt., Air Corps
Asst. Intelligence Officer

Mission FFO 120-G: April 29, 1944

Six A/P's of the 501st Squadron left with their primary objective being to act as protective cover to the 17th Recco. Squadron and to knock out ack-ack from Maffin Bay to Cape Verman. Our secondary purpose was to obtain photographs of the coastline along the same area. The other squadrons of the group and the 38th Group with us made rendezvous with one squadron of P-38's over Hollandia. Bombs were dropped in the vicinity of Sawar strip. There was interception by enemy A/P's, ack-ack was reported from several locations. The altitude of the fire was good, but it was inaccurate. There was nil damage to our A/P's and no injury to crew members.

Lt. Jones in A/P 335 was forced to land at Gusap due to mechanical troubles and was unable to reach the target. He was given combat mission and mission time as directed in the Fifth Air Force General Order #299 dated April 16, 1944.

Lt. J.R. Jones flew in the #3 position on the 2nd flight in A/P 335.

Crew members were: Lt. T.H. Heidorf, S/Sgt. J.A. Liparela, S/Sgt. H. C. Aslin, and S/Sgt. M. W. Zenesky.

Narrative Unit History For April, 1944

Combat Operations:

During April the 501st Bomb Squadron ran a total of 15 bombing and/or strafing missions. These fifteen strike missions entailed 124 sorties with a total of 620 hours flying time. Our crews dropped 135.6 tons of bombs on enemy installations and strafed him with 72,080 X .50 caliber and 11,800 X .30 caliber rounds of ammunition. Their SSF Jap planes were definitely destroyed on the ground at Hollandia Airdrome and an additional four fighters were heavily strafed, badly damaged, and probably destroyed. Numerous fires and explosions were started and other damage impossible to assess specifically was inflicted upon him. And all this with a loss to us of only one crewmember slightly wounded by enemy fire.

In addition to the fifteen strike missions, our Squadron flew 5 weather reccos of 5 sorties, 14 courier missions of 14 sorties, 2 supply drop missions of 20 sorties, and 4 escort missions of 4 sorties, giving us a grand total of 1,054 hours and 50 minutes of flying time for the month.

In comparison with missions this Squadron has flown in the past, there really were no outstanding missions during April. The long-awaited strikes on Hollandia proved this Jap-base to be *just another target* for our planes to plaster. The enemy has definitely reached an all time low ebb in his aerial warfare in this theatre of operations.

Local Interest and Personalities:

Our new Group chapel was completed, and our first services were held there April 2nd. This is a valuable and welcome addition to our home area here at APO 713 UNIT One. Also during the month, the mess hall and club for officers of our Group was opened for use. This has helped greatly. On April 15th, the 345th Group Softball League got under way. We have two teams entered—officer's team and enlisted men's team. Both teams are doing well, and are keeping the 501st right up at the top. On the 24th, we invited all personnel of the squadron to an *open house* in our Intelligence Section. Captain Connors, ALO for the 345th Bomb Group, was the principal speaker, giving a thorough and interesting picture of the war against the Japanese.

Benjamin E. Green
Captain, Air Corps
Unit Historical Officer

Tuesday, May 2, 1944

Dearest Elnora,

Hi, Red, how's my darling? I'm awfully tired this evening, and I miss you something terribly. You have been around in my dreams enough lately to drive me batty.

The beer was pretty good while it lasted. I've had a buzz for the past three days, but now the party is over. The club bar did open, and we have an occasional drink before dinner. Just a polite snort and that's all. It's a very nice place we have, and I'm going to hate moving on and leaving it. I think you have heard that song before if you know what I mean. Oh well, I'm getting used to it, but slightly tired of it. T'was bound to happen after nearly a year of this.

I imagine you think my letters have been pretty irregular the past few weeks, but these last days have been pretty hectic. You'd be surprised at how much I write compared with all the rest of the fellows in the tent. Of course I realize that I could never quite stay up with you. You have been far sweeter than I have ever dreamed anyone could be. I must have realized that quite a while ago though. It's been much more difficult to write you since I left last July. I can't tell you much of what I do. I can't tell you exactly where I am and what the place looks like. My hands are rather tied. All that I must store up to tell you at a later date. I never tire of telling you how lovely I think you are, and how much I love you—how happy I'll be when that one lovely ring becomes two. I think about all of those things constantly. It's something I never want to forget.

This has been a very dreary, rainy day, but it has its compensations in being cool. So cool in fact, that I only sweated half as much as usual. We are getting much too close to the equator for comfort these days.

I haven't had any mail from you in the past few days. I guess weather is holding it up. Couldn't be any other reason. I did receive two more issues of *Esquire* though. Wow! I often wonder if all those pictures of pretty gals build up or tear down morale. Maybe it wasn't so smart to send me such a magazine, dear. Oh well, I know where a much nicer girl is if I could only get there. I wish you could turn up between a couple of those pages. I would really get your fifty cents worth then.

I laid hands on a new book today that looks fairly interesting—*In Bed We Cry* by Ilka Chase. Mother says it is pretty risqué so I have an idea what to expect. I've heard and read that it's pretty good, so here I go. I'll give a fuller report later on. If you decide to read it, don't tell your mother that I informed you about it. I don't want to get in trouble so soon. As you have probably discovered, my reading is widely varied. You'll have to take all the blame, darling.

Your outing to Galveston sounded like fun, dear. Wish I could have been there with you. It would be a great pleasure to take you out of your *old maid* status as you put it. At least you have promises that I fully intend to keep. If you are seen without me then it will be all a mistake.

The show last night was pretty much of a stinker. Ted Lewis in something or other. The show I'm waiting for is Spencer Tracy in *A Guy Named Joe*. They tell me the

B-25 is rather prominent. It was filmed near Greenville. I thought for a while I'd have a chance to fly in some of the scenes, but I left too soon. Saturday night we are going to have *Madame Curie* again. It seems I'll be able to see the gal you look like after all.

Well, my darling, it's time to say good night again. I hope to get a letter from you tomorrow. It's going to be a great day when I know what you are thinking in the present instead of two weeks ago. But past, present, or future, for me darling, it's I love you always,

With all my heart, J.R.

Wednesday, May 3, 1944

Dearest Elnora,

Hi, darling, how are you? I'm writing this letter on a desk, and it doesn't feel right. At present I'm night operations officer, and everyone else is up having a party at the club. What a job this is. The phone has been ringing constantly since six. I hope it lets up soon so I can go to bed. The big executive type, that's me! I wish I had a babe sitting on my knee—redheaded too. What a secretary you'd make—good for my money any old day.

Still haven't received any mail from you. You aren't having more snowstorms, are you? I should get a pretty good batch one of these days.

This is a nice cool evening, strictly made for cuddling—how's about it? How come we always manage to get around where the weather is so hot? Doesn't bother us a great deal though. Pardon me—my mind just went on one of those Montgomery tangents. I really knock myself out thinking about that. Can't help it, darling—you were much too pretty those days—even if I did have to catch you falling down steps a few times. Every small thing we did was great fun.

Darling, being as how I have to get up at 4:00 am, I think I better turn in and get a little sleep no matter how much I'd like to spend the rest of the night making love to you in my day dreams. I would much rather have it a reality, but that must wait for a time. Do you think you'll be able to hold out a few more months, darling? It won't be so long now, thank God.

Night dear, I'm off to bed. Hope I hear from you tomorrow. Just want to know that you know I miss you and I love you –

Always, J.R.

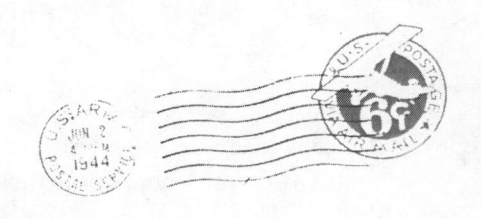

A PURPLE HEART AND PRECIOUS LITTLE SLEEP

MISSION: MAY 5, 1944

Eight A/P of this squadron were ordered to bomb Sarmi. This mission was incomplete due to weather. The planes turned back at Dumpu. All bombs were salvoed or returned to base.

An accident occurred on the line causing the death of one of our oldest and best crew chiefs, T/Sgt. Fred Decobellis. He came over from the States with our Squadron, and had always been one of the most reliable and dependable mechanics. It was with a feeling of respect and sorrow that the Squadron attended the funeral of Sgt. Decobellis at the Army Air Force Cemetery at APO 713 on May 6th.

FRIDAY, MAY 5, 1944

Dearest Elnora,

Hi, darling—how goes it in Houston? Things could be better here, but I won't go into that, at least not yet.

Nothing is doing as far as I know around here. I did receive one wee small letter from you and other than that, no word. You sound as if they are certainly working you these days—overtime and all that stuff. Just don't sit on the boss's lap. You're a big girl now and should know about such things—I hope!

Last night's show was really a dilly –*I Walked With a Zombie*. What a thriller. The things we do put up with. Didn't scare me a bit. In fact, I thought the zombie was kinda nice. Can't be too particular these days, you know.

Believe it or not it is nearly cold this evening—rainy and very blue. Every day that passes I would give more and more to get away from here. Believe me, darling, a year in this place is plenty, and a year away from you is much too much.

Sunday the General presents the medals; that should be good. I don't even know what one looks like. I suppose I'll get my Purple Heart then. I've a D.F.C. and a couple of Air Medals coming, but there's no telling when they'll come through. I've been told that the Purple Heart is the prettiest medal of them all. I'll soon be able to judge for myself about that.

I'm going to be ending this very shortly, darling, as I've had precious little sleep the past two days, and I have a bit of a headache.

The food has been excellent the past few days, and the club bar is in action—almost like civilization, except for a few minor items, such as the girl you're in love with and the wonderful places you used to go.

Night, darling—I'll write more of a letter tomorrow. How is the ring holding out? The mate is doing very well, only it looks kinda lonesome—like me.

Always—I love you, J.R.

Daily Log: Saturday, May 6, 1944

Lt. Col. Fridge, Deputy Group Commander, made official a day of M and T [maintenance and training] for this Squadron so all personnel in the Squadron could attend the funeral of T/Sgt. Decobellis, taking place at 10:30 this morning.

The formation of this Squadron with all other squadrons of the group for the presentation of various medals and awards to be made by General Whitehead in the group was called off. It will take place at some future date.

Monday, May 8, 1944

Dearest Elnora,

Hooray, I got the first letter in nine days from you. I was wondering where you were. Nobody has received any lately, so it isn't your fault. I was sure of that in the first place. I should really collect in a few days.

These past few days haven't been too much to rave about. Just sit around and smoke too much. My mouth is burned out, but I don't seem to be able to let up. Must be getting old since I can't be a day over a hundred at present.

The cinema is strictly on the blink these days, nothing worthwhile. A couple good ones are coming this week. One is *The Lodge* or the story of Jack the Ripper. That should be a thriller. More blood and thunder, that's what we need most of all. I'll tell you if it's safe for you to go after I've seen it.

I finished *In Bed We Cry*, and I couldn't give it much. Pretty thin stuff with a heavy layer of sophistication. Don't believe you'd care for it. I think you know the facts of life already.

The food is still great. If this keeps up I'm going to look healthy when I get home. You must look bad, or you can't go home at all. They tell me I still have some time to put in, so I'm not too optimistic.

It's not so bad now as it was in the days when we used to shoot up Rabaul, and Wewak. It seems odd to fly over Wewak and not be shot at. With the fall of Hollandia it rather narrows things down. Strafing is definitely more exciting than medium bombardment. You feel so naked way up there. I'm not too sorry the war has quieted down. Still plenty of work to be done though.

They postponed again the medal presentations that had been rescheduled for Saturday. I don't know when it will come off now. It seems I shined my shoes all in vain. I even got a hair cut for the general. I suppose he will get around to it someday.

I'm certainly going to hate to move again. You just get settled down and boom you're off again. Can't kick though—we're winning, and that's something. Better than getting chased back.

I hope you have taken those photographs by now. I'm rather anxious to see you again. I'm going to try to get a picture of me and a plane. It won't exactly be mine as it isn't around anymore, but it's a B-25.

Well, darling, I should be closing as we are still arising at an unearthly time of day. Things aren't what they used to be. I was meant for banker's hours.

Has Mrs. Smith heard any more from Roger lately? I hope he gets home one of these days. Give them all my best.

Good night, darling—I'm off to bed. Thanks for the letter—looked plenty good. I shouldn't need to tell you, but I will though—

I love you with all my heart, J.R.

Tuesday, May 9, 1944

Dearest Elnora,

Two more letters today. I'm back in the running again. Perhaps we'll have a steady supply again, I hope. The latest is dated April 13, so several more should be forthcoming.

Have you heard from Shields lately, dear? I wonder what he is up to these days. I'd give plenty to see one of those guys over here, but I'd hate to wish this place off on them. It's been a long time since I left school. You ought to know. There wasn't even a war then, and that was long ago.

It's getting pretty lonesome without you, Red. Speaking of being lonesome, the most lost I ever felt was one evening at Hamilton Field, just before taking off for Hickam, nearly 2,500 miles and worlds away. Seemed odd the next morning to be sailing past the Royal Hawaiian Hotel and Waikiki Beach. I'll never quite forget how those amber lights on the Golden Gate Bridge looked as I saw Frisco for the last time.

It was Abilene where I stopped in Texas. I suppose I might have made Houston, but it would have made things a little tough for both of us. It was quite a temptation though. I also stopped at Phoenix with engine trouble. Luke Field is certainly a nice place—had quite a chat with some general there. After that we spent a week in Sacramento enjoying ourselves. That's a very lovely town, dear. I think you would like it very much. McClellan Field is one of the prettiest places I've ever landed. Sure would love to be stationed there. We could really set the world on fire there.

Of course I was writing you from Honolulu. It was a break to stay there nearly three weeks. It's just too bad you weren't along to enjoy it with me. I had absolutely nothing to do and was making $16.00 a day. We could have just sat on the beach and had an easy life. Of course the mosquitoes are quite a bar to romance, but that fact doesn't seem to have worried anyone in the past. They have quite a moon there, and I believe we could have put it to full use. If you were around I could make my own moon like that big number that used to turn up in Texas last May. That year mark has certainly rolled around quickly. Let's hope the next one finds us together.

I'll tell you more about my trip later on, darling, as it's growing late and time to hit the hay. They allow us to tell quite a bit about it these days. Perhaps I can make my letters a bit more interesting. Night, darling—back in a flash. Miss you so, and I love you,

Always, J.R.

Escort Mission FFO 132-M: May 11, 1944

Two A/P of this squadron were ordered to escort C-47's to Hollandia and en route back were ordered to strafe targets of opportunity. Mission was 100 percent complete as ordered. Strafed canoes and villages along Sepik River with unobserved results. 5600 X .50 caliber ammunition expended.

Lt. J.R. Jones flew in the #1 position in A/P 069—Herky Betty—at 7:10 a.m.

Crew members were: Lt. W.G. Willard, Lt. E. Davis, S/Sgt. L.M. Carlton, S/Sgt. H. C. Aslin, and S/Sgt. M. W. Zenesky.

Daily Log: May 13, 1944

On the 13th of May, a long awaited event occurred—the official presentation by Major General E. C. Whitehead of awards and decorations to the members of our combat crews. There was a group formation on the parade grounds, which serves also as a baseball diamond for the group. Our Squadron was well represented, since Capt. Bailey was, next to Col. True, the *most decorated man* of the day. He received the Silver Star, the Air

Medal, and the Purple Heart. In addition to this, the D.F.C. was presented to 1st Lt. Symens; the Purple Heart to 1st Lts. Flanagan, Jones, Larsen, Shapiro, and S/Sgt. Itt. Air Medals were presented to Capt. Sacco, Lt. Kreidler, Lt. Flanagan, T/Sgt. Hill, Sgt. Albers, and S/Sgt. Itt.

Photo of ceremony where J.R. received his Purple Heart Medal courtesy of the Lawrence J. Hickey Collection.

Photo of Purple Heart courtesy of Lloyd Sullivan.

René Palmer Armstrong

Saturday, May 13, 1944

Dearest Elnora,

Ah, Saturday—my day off. We kept that date with the General, and he pinned the medals on us. I got my Purple Heart, and it is a beautiful job. As the General shook hands he said, "I'm glad you got out of it okay, and I hope you don't get any Oak Leaf Clusters on it." That makes two of us. They don't give medals out as freely as they do in Europe so don't expect me with a chest full. I'd settle just to come home. I'll have something to show the grandchildren and incidentally you too, darling. I wish the General would decide to let us go home someday soon. I yearn for a change of scenery and climate and mostly for my redheaded beauty—that's you.

The show tonight was certainly blood-thirsty. If you desire genuine thrills, go to *The Lodger*. It has a villain to end all villains. That Merle Oberon is certainly lovely too, and I must say she showed it to excellent advantage. If you go, you'll see what I mean.

Since I'm not coming home in the next few days, it seems that I may be going to Sydney in the next couple of weeks. It will only be my fourth trip. I do like it a bit better down there than New Guinea, can't imagine why. Perhaps this will be the last time. I think I've said that before, but if you'll bear with me darling, it may not be many more months longer. You have been heaven itself since I left.

Your excursion to Galveston sounded like great fun. You can only imagine how much I would have liked to have been with you. You'll never know how many times I've been alone in that town while I was at Wallace. Too bad you couldn't have been around then. Perhaps all would be different today, but it's pretty wonderful as it is. The best thing that ever happened to me was meeting you and the Smiths a short time before. I'll never be able to repay that debt to Shields. Actually, that made my first months in the Army nice as any that have followed—except for a few all too brief days last May and June.

It's too bad you couldn't have taken a few pictures while you were at the beach. A little leg art wouldn't go bad to a tired pilot, particularly with you around, darling. Besides, I could really check up on this weight situation—ahem! It says here you pulled that sweater girl act on me that second date I had with you. I've always wondered if that was intentional or not. You nearly brought the wolf in me out that fine day, my sweet. What would you have done then?

Speaking of pictures, one of the fellows in the tent managed to get his hands on a camera and much film. I don't know how they will turn out, but we are trying. The first shots seem to have me clad only in underwear, a little leg art myself. Perhaps I can arrange to have a few more clothes on in the near future. I believe you already have a picture of me sailing through the air in shorts. Nice figure, eh! We'll see how they turn out. Now you can shake out letters looking for pictures for a change.

You should have seen the moon last night, darling. I've never seen it like that in New Guinea before—a big, orange full moon. I guess the nights here are something you could never see at home. They are really beautiful, but alone they aren't so good. No night anywhere will be what it should till we stand together in it. Need I tell you I'm pretty blue this evening and that I love you dearly?

It's getting late sweet, and I have to get up very early tomorrow. I'd love to stay a little longer, but I'll return soon, I always do. Night my darling—

I love you—always, J.R.

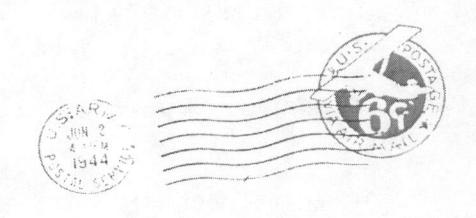

THE WAYWARD FOOTLOCKER

Daily Log: May 14, 1944

The first planning of the Advanced Echelon for our next move was done today, many changes will no doubt be made; the place will be Hollandia.

Mission FFO 135-D: May 14, 1944

Nine A/P of this Squadron were ordered to bomb Takar Village at an altitude of 6,000 ft. and strafe it at minimum altitude. 36 X 500 lb. bombs, inst. demo., were dropped on the target with five hitting off shore, six bombs were salvoed off shore due to malfunction of racks. 10,270 X .50 caliber ammunition and 800 X .30 caliber ammunition expended. Results other than bomb bursts were not visible. Several destroyed huts and bomb craters were seen on the strafing pass. Bombing that hit in the target was excellent. Photos were taken.

    Lt. J.R. Jones flew in the #2 position on the 2nd flight in A/P 036—Old Baldy.

Monday, May 15, 1944

Dearest Elnora,

I didn't write yesterday for a couple of reasons. First, I flew all day and second, as it was Mother's Day, I had quite a bit of correspondence. I wrote to my Mother, Mrs. Smith, and Mother Landes. That's quite an evening's work for me. I may be a day late, but please tell your mother that I send my best regards, and tell her thanks for having such a sweet daughter.

The mailman came through tonight and brought me four letters from you—pretty good work, kid. One of them contained Shields's letter, and I must say it puzzled me slightly. I can't figure out whether they got married, engaged or what. Tell Shields to please elucidate. Mary Ann [Lt. M.A. Cook] slightly outranks the boy, doesn't she? I wonder how I'd feel if you were a captain. Would you pull your rank on me? You'd like Mary Ann—she's a great deal like Haerle. Both of them are sort of screwy.

So you are making more snapshots? I'll be on the edge of my seat now till I receive them. It would be nice if both you and Daurice are in them. Perhaps I'll be able to dig up a few pictures myself. I'm trying—I might be able to take some in Sydney, but don't hold your breath too long. I hope the film we have isn't too old. I suppose the letter you put those pictures in will be one of those delayed jobs, it never fails. Happy day when we won't have to depend on pictures any longer.

We had another good show tonight. *Standing Room Only* with Paulette Goddard and Fred McMurray. Pretty crazy comedy—all about crowded Washington. Again, remember *The More The Merrier* in Montgomery. That was by far the best.

That will teach you trying to be so athletic at the beach. So you were all stiff the next day—that'll learn you. Do you mean to stand there and tell me you spent all day in the sun and didn't pick up an extra freckle? I have to see that to believe it. I can see where I'm going to have a lot of fun with you on that score. It would never do for you to spend seven hours in a plane. It would really fry you. It's just like a hot house, and I frequently burn slightly.

I'm still in the dark as to how Daurice's husband manages to stay in Texas and get to Houston so often. If I stayed in the Army twenty years I couldn't get off that much. I'll just have to take you around with me, which suits me fine.

This has been another rugged day for me, sweet, and I hear the old sack calling me. I've had a little trouble staying awake as it is. Why don't you drop around and see me in my dreams?

If you don't hear from me for a day or two, don't be surprised. The mailman is out of stamps and airmail envelopes both, and you are getting the last one in the tent. We should get some more in two days. Just wanted you to know it wouldn't be my fault.

Well, darling, I will say good night and be on my way. Thanks for the sweet letters, but you already know that I,
    Love you always, J.R.

Scan of cartoon from original "Warpath" courtesy of Lloyd Sullivan.

Escort Mission 137-F: May 16, 1944

Two of our A/P's also went on an escort mission to Hollandia, and strafed targets of opportunity en route back. Lts. Coffman and Jones took part on this mission.

Mission FFO 139-A: May 18, 1944

The primary objective of today's mission was supply and personnel in the Dagua and But areas. The secondary target was 1-B at Hansa Bay. Six A/P of this Squadron hit the target of Dagua with bombing results excellent. Fighter cover was reported as satisfactory. There were nil interception of enemy aircraft and no damage to our A/P nor injury to combat crews.

Lt. J.R. Jones flew in the #2 position in the 1st flight.

Thursday, May 18, 1944

Dearest Elnora,

As you can plainly see from this stationary, I finally received my footlocker. [J.R. mentions the fact that he missed his footlocker on Sept. 10, 1943, and hoped one day he would see it again. Looks like it only took nine months to show up from his landing in Australia.] I had given up hope till one of the boys came flying in with it. The only thing of any value was a good pair of pinks [pinkish-beige pair of slacks], and brand new pair of shoes, and of course, darling—your stationary. I won't get much good out of it here, but it's better than living out of a barracks bag as I have in the past. I'm going to use up that white paper first and save this for later.

Speaking of pictures, darling, how about this one? It was taken as the General pinned on the medal. Each fellow had his taken and was given three of them so this is yours to keep. I'm naturally sending one to Mother too. The

General is Whitehead of the Fifth Air Force. The man behind him is Col. True, C.O. of the 345th Bomb Group. Some class, eh!

The mail really came through in a rush today—four letters and V-mail from you. The V-mail was May 5, and that's pretty good considering the way service has been lately. I managed to get exactly three stamps from the mailman today, but he said perhaps he'll be able to get me a few more tomorrow. No stamps—no letter to you, darling.

I also wrote a letter to Shields today—pretty unusual for me. I thought I had best answer that note in person as I know both parties concerned. That letter still baffles me a bit, but I presume it will all clear up in due time. At this rate even I will be caught up with my correspondence soon. It sounds from your letters that you have been receiving quite a few letters from me. I'm glad—I never dreamed that I could write so many and never tire of the task. Must be love, and I've got a ring to prove it.

We had a fine show this evening—Kay Kyser in *Around the World*. Loads of music and laughs and no plot; just what the doctor ordered for this climate. I heard two new songs in it for the first time: "Candlelight and Wine" and "Don't Believe Everything You Dream." Both were lovely. It's quite odd to hear a new song for the first time in a movie. I believe I've heard you mention them before though.

Think I'll close for tonight, my sweet, as I've been flying again and I'm rather tired. I hope you like the picture, and I'm now eagerly awaiting those snapshots from you. You owe me for a change now. Night, dearest—I'll be back quickly, but until then I can remind you that I,

Love you always, J.R.

Mission FFO 141-D: May 20, 1944

The primary objective of today's mission was supplies and personnel in the area between Dagua and Karawop Plantation. There was no secondary objective. The target to be bombed at medium altitude by six A/P of this Squadron that performed over strip No. 4 at Nadzab with the other three squadrons of the 345th Group. Cloud coverage made the target not visible thus the results were undetermined. There was no damage to our A/P nor injury to personnel.

The 1st flight dropped their bombs on the lead plane's release. All three airplanes strafed huts along the shore from Dagua Village to Cape Karawop. Lt. Jones and Lt. Schade took K-21 pictures of strafing. Lt. Jones' crew reported three (3) serviceable trucks seen 1 ½ miles west of Dagua Drome at point 940250, as well as 10 thatched buildings, possibly in the vicinity of point 030227. They also reported seven (7) well constructed buildings seen at Karawop Village.

Lt. J.R. Jones flew in the #2 position in the 1st flight in A/P 082—Meany—at 4:15 a.m.

Crew members were: Lt. R.L. Welch, S/Sgt. E.D. Faulkner, S/Sgt. H. C. Aslin, and S/Sgt. M. W. Zenesky.

THE CHOW HOUND: EATING IN STYLE AGAIN

Sunday, May 21, 1944

Dearest Elnora,

Hi, Red—I have been rather off the ball the past few days, and I hope I'll be able to catch up soon. I just managed to lay my hands on a stamp, so I'm off. I started to write to you last night, but I found myself saddled with the job of O.D. and a large stack of mail to be censored. Damn it, darling, it just takes all the romance out of my soul after reading all that. I just gave up after I finished. I get more disgusted every time I get the job.

The night before, Davis's baby came through and we had to celebrate that. It's a boy, and that's all the information we have. We didn't drink much, though, as all of us had to fly the next day. Perhaps it's just as well because we don't want the kid to start out life as a drunkard.

The plane came in with the food from Australia [Chow Hound] last night, and we are eating in style again, even had eggs for breakfast. You have no idea how good one of those things looks after you haven't seen one for a month. I'm just letting you know that you'd better feed me or else!

We played a baseball game today, and I was no less than terrific. I didn't even see the ball, let alone hit it. I guess I'm slightly out of practice. I've played very little since leaving Greenville and believe me, darling, that's a long time ago. I hope I don't get stiff.

I should be off on leave in a week or so. I'm getting pretty tired again, and a change of scenery would do much to improve my state of mind. I hope I don't get sick again down there. It should be very cool down there at this time of year. It's winter in Australia, you know. I just need you along to take care of me. Lord, but I miss you more than ever when I get to a place like that. It seems only natural that you should be around where there is laughter and happiness.

The mail has dropped off again in the last few days, and none of it has been too recent. Service never has been too good at this APO. Must be getting too far from Texas. I can see now that I am going to have to prove to you that there are a few other states in the Union. I don't mean Indiana either.

Cinema Report—last night they played *Phantom Lady* with Ella Raines and Franchot Tone—pretty putrid. I don't think you would have liked your boy last night as he played an insane killer. Sorry I can't see the resemblance, but thanks just the same. I don't think the future attractions are going to be so hot, but I'll go just the same. I still want to see *A Guy Named Joe*, but it doesn't seem to be around in this part of the world at present.

I believe I had a date with you last night, or was it a year ago last night? It couldn't have been because it's all too clear. We've been engaged a year, my sweet. Nothing like a long wait is there? I think everything has worked out pretty well.

This V-mail tells me that I should have some pictures of you soon. I'm all for that. I want to see if you are skinny as you say. I just want to see you very badly, darling. That's the true story. They say one picture is worth ten thousand words, but I'd much rather have those words with you. Even those wouldn't be sufficient to tell you how much I love you. Really, darling, I'm most anxious to have those pictures. Did you receive the one I sent to you?

Back to work tomorrow, as much as I dislike the idea. Good night, darling—I hope this letter makes up for the past few days for

I love you always—J.R.

Photo of B-25 Mitchell *plane, the* Chow Hound, *used to bring food back from Australia courtesy of the Lawrence J. Hickey Collection.*

The following is an account regarding food Melvin Best shared with me during our December 2010 meeting:

Most of the food we ate was canned. For forty-two days in a row we ate Spam. Spam cooked every way you can imagine! And dehydrated potatoes...those dried flakes that you pour water over and make-believe they are real potatoes. Yuck! We had not had fresh foods for three months when we flew two butchers from our squadron to a ranch near Woodstock Field in Australia. While the butchers processed the beef, the rest of us went to Townsville for fresh vegetables. We bought onions and one other vegetable. The prize was the ten 10-gallon containers of fresh milk. The trip back to Port Moresby was at 15,000 feet to chill the milk and preserve the freshness of the meat. When we landed, the kitchen staff was waiting and began preparing the best meal we had had in months—fresh beef steaks, fresh vegetables, and cold, fresh milk!

It was the first fresh milk we had had in four or five months. That night we were the sickest four hundred men on the island!

Mission FFO 143-D: May 22, 1944

Six A/P of this squadron were ordered to bomb ack-ack positions around the But and Dagua areas. One A/P did not take off due to engine trouble. The mission was carried out as ordered. A possible ammunition dump was hit and two bombs hit around a possible ack-ack position one mile SE of But Village.

Monday, May 22, 1944

Elnora darling,

How about a short note this evening? I don't think I'm going to have time for much more. No, I'm not lazy, just in a hurry.

I'm slightly stiff after that ball game yesterday; that exercise will kill me yet! I honestly believe I'm getting healthy around here. At least I seem to be putting on weight for a change. Can't understand it—perhaps the fact that I ate two breakfasts this morning might account for something, one at 5:00 and again at 7:30. I just can't resist those eggs. I ate the second breakfast because something was wrong with my ship, and I didn't fly today.

Show again tonight. I don't even remember the name of it or who was in it. There was some awfully good music though. Some guy with a very slick voice sang "Wrong," and it very definitely appealed to me. Nothing like a good song to make me wish for a certain redhead.

It looks as if my leave is called off for a couple of weeks. I was all primed for that too. They have been flying the tail off of us, and I fear they intend to keep it up. The Jap is due for a very rough time in New Guinea. I wish he'd get wise and go home.

We have really been having the earthquakes lately. The joint really rocks while they are going on. They usually happen at night, and I just let them rock me to sleep.

Must run, my darling. I'll write again tomorrow, and then too I'll be saying—

Always, I love you, J.R.

Photo of baseball game courtesy of the Lawrence J. Hickey Collection.

Daily Log: May 23, 1944

No missions or local flying this date. Routine duties, 14 packages of Chesterfields were given each man and officer.

Wednesday, May 24, 1944

Dearest Elnora,

Finally dug up two letters from you yesterday. I wish they would get that European shindig in high gear so we could get a few items of pleasure. They seem to be getting the most of everything over there, but it appears that they will need it someday.

We got a shot in the arm yesterday for cholera, and it got slightly stiff from it all. I haven't had to take one of those things in a long while. You don't mind taking them over here with all the disease around. I was still rather sore from playing ball the other day, and what did I do but play again today. We won, naturally, but I'm still known as the hitless wonder. Maybe I'll get my eye back some day, but I'm beginning to doubt it. A little exercise goes a long way in this climate.

Say, darling, I just had a brilliant idea the other day. How would you like to go back to college after the war is over? Congress is attempting to pass a bill whereby they will pay your tuition for one to four years and give you an allowance of fifty dollars a month plus so much for dependents. I certainly would like to get my degree, and perhaps you might be able to transfer and get yours too. I should have plenty of money saved to see me through nine months. It would be wonderful fun—get an apartment and live the life of Reilly. It sounds good to me, but time can tell more about that. Just think, we could always be guests of the Delt House for dinner if the budget ran low. Some fun! What's your idea on the subject darling?

So you baked a cake. Getting plenty domestic, aren't you, dear? I like angel food cake fine, but don't you think it will be a trifle difficult to live on that exclusively? Things brighten up, however, as I find out little by little about your talents. You're beginning to sound rather versatile. I can see a lot of surprises are going to be pulled on me some fine day. Hot dawg!

I have just been informed of the happy news that I get up tomorrow at 5:15. That's the best part of the day for sleeping, and we invariably get up then. Hardships—I'll have to sing that little ditty to myself.

Night, sweet—be back with you shortly. If you knew how much I miss you, you'd strike out for New Guinea tonight, and I start half way just to tell you,

I love you—always, J.R.

Photo of Delta Tau Delta Fraternity House at Kansas University courtesy of the Delta Tau Delta Educational Foundation.

Mission FFO 146-E: May 25, 1944

Photo of B-25 Mitchell *parafrag bombing courtesy of the Lawrence J. Hickey Collection.*

Note: Lt. Jones, in A/P 076—The Jaded Saint, attacked the target with the 498th Squadron.

The primary objective of the strike was a supply area 1000 ft. west of Dagua Drome. According to photo interpretation reports, this area contained two stacks of fuel drums, each consisting of 300 drums. In addition to this, numerous boxes of supplies were reported to be stored under the trees there. This target was to be bombed and strafed at minimum altitude by six (6) planes, five with a maximum load of 22 clusters of 3 X 23 lb. parafrags, and on load with 12 clusters of 3 X 23 lb. parafrags.

Six (6) airplanes were to take off from Strip #4 at Nadzab, form with the other three squadrons of the 345th Group over the Leron River, and proceed from there to the target. There was no fighter cover, and our group was to be the only one on this target.

Lt. Jones, in A/P 076, which was delayed on take-off, failed to join our squadron before reaching the target. As he arrived in the area, he saw the 498th Squadron making its bombing and strafing run, and he joined their formation. He too strafed from But Village down the coast and dropped five of his clusters on Dagua Village with unobserved results. His remaining seven clusters were salvoed at sea, due to the fact that he could not find any suitable target.

Lt. J.R. Jones flew in A/P 076.

Crew members were: Lt. R.L. Welch, S/Sgt. E.D. Faulkner, S/Sgt. H. C. Aslin, and S/Sgt. M. W. Zenesky.

Friday, May 26, 1944

Dearest Elnora,

Here I am after a hard day of rest, slept till nearly 8:30. It was raining when I woke up, so I just stayed in bed. Since that time I have been doing a great deal of nothing. Pretty hard work if you ask me.

Tonight I go to Link Trainer [flight simulator] from 8:00 till 9:00. Even in New Guinea we have that damned contraption. I think they bring it along just to annoy us, and I might add that it does. I could use a bit of practice on instrument flying, however, and so I go. We usually get our instrument flying the hard way around here, and with the mountains we have, it's a trifle disconcerting to say the least. I'd much rather stay home and write to you.

I know you would take the news that I couldn't get home as soon I thought cheerfully. Somehow I can depend on you for that, and it's very comforting, my dear. If you think you have worn out a calendar, you should see me. I live by one, anyhow—the Varga one.

Glad to know the Smiths got their car back, but something tells me they are going to have a sweet time replacing that tire. Was it the Ford that we had such a merry time in one evening? They were certainly wonderful to us, weren't they, darling? I was truly happy to know that Roger had at last received some mail. He must have been overjoyed, and I know his mother was. I keep hoping that someday soon he will be home again. It has preyed on my mind since the first letter I received from you telling me about it. He has so much to get out of life, and I hope to God the day won't be too far off before he does.

I managed to lay my hands today on a record by Lena WOW! Horne singing "Where or When." Pretty, I thought I'd die. I don't know why that song occurred to me that evening with you, but it fitted so perfectly. How true.

I am still hearing about those snapshots, but as yet nothing has turned up. Honestly, darling, I'm about to burst with curiosity. I want to see you so badly in a snapshot, you can image how much I want to see the real you. You couldn't take my breath away again as much as you did one evening—or could you?

I think I'd better close, darling, and wind my way down to Link Trainer. It's a long walk, and I hope I can lay hands on a Jeep. I have more fun in Jeeps than a plane. I think we have more casualties in them.

Good night, darling—Always my love, J.R.

The Link Trainer was a pilot-training aid which provided a pilot the means to experience pitching, diving, rolling, and climbing. The army air corps purchased thousands of the trainers to assist pilots in learning how to fly at night and in bad weather condition, learning to rely only on instruments. These devices were the forerunner of today's flight simulators.

Saturday, May 27, 1944

Dearest Elnora,

Hi, darling—here I am hard at work in my office as you can see. I'm night operations officer, and I can hear the show going on down the road. Fine thing to do to me. Just for that I'll spend the evening making violent love to you. Am I kidding? Oh how I wish I wasn't.

Today being Saturday we had to polish up the brasswork for inspection—even in New Guinea! I had to cut the grass around the area. It's more like trees as this kunai grass grows about six feet tall. It's also sharp as a razor and as a result, my hands are rather sore. Anyhow, we can look out the sides of the tent again.

I received a citation for the Air Medal today. It was that jam I got in last December. I was recommended for D.F.C., but I guess I wasn't heroic enough. I got out all in one piece though, and that suits me just dandy. That's all I ever want. We get an Oak Leaf Cluster for every 100 hours of combat time. I have two of those and am now working on a third. I ought to have plenty of Air Medals to say the least. Phooey on all that business—I just want to get home and see my pretty redhead.

Next week I should be on my way to Australia, and if that falls through I'll choke. Back to good old Sydney—Kings Cross, Double Bay, etc. I can find my way around that town almost like a native now. And think I always get lost in Houston. I'd bet even money I'd have a devil of a time finding your house. That would be the last straw.

I'm really glad that Roger has finally begun to receive mail. Just think it's been nearly a year now. I hope he survives in good health. I believe he will. Give Mr. and Mrs. Smith my best next time you see them.

I am in dire need of a haircut again. It doesn't quite cover my ears, but almost. I had better get it done one of these days before the Major tells me to. Boy, I hate that job. I think my hair grows faster in this climate. At least I don't have to worry about being bald for quite a while. Doesn't that make you happy, dear?

Some more of the older men are going home soon. Lucky dogs! We have already received letters from several fellows back in the States. It sounds like a great life. I know I'm willing to try it at any time in the near future.

Really have an odd assortment of bugs flying around me this evening. Most of them defy description. This would be an entomologist's (bug hunter, to you) paradise about here, but I'd prefer they go somewhere else. Why couldn't they all have turned up when I had to make a collection of them in college? You should have seen me flitting around with my little butterfly net over the campus. I was really a choice article.

It's been fun being with you this evening, darling. Think how much more fun it will be when it's in person. We found that out in a few brief days last June. Somehow, it was just like I always imagined it would be. No disappointment there, darling.

Night, sweet—see you tomorrow. I wish, for I miss you so much, and I'll always

Love you, J.R.

WINGS AND A RING

Photo of ceremony where J.R. received his Air Medal courtesy of the Lawrence J. Hickey Collection.

Photo of Air Medal courtesy of Lloyd Sullivan.

Mission FFO 149-1: May 28, 1944

The primary objective of today's mission was ground support of Allied Forces in the Tadji-But areas. Enemy personnel reported to be within two miles Southwest of Cape Djeruan was our specific target and they were to be bombed and strafed at a minimum altitude. Six A/P of this Squadron took off from strip #4 here at Nadzab and proceeded directly to the target. This was a close support mission in which each of the four squadrons of the 345th were assigned specific targets and separate times for attack. There was no Group formation; each squadron went to and from the target area in single units. There was no interception by enemy A/Ps and nil damage to our A/Ps and no injury to our crew members. Lt. Jones also strafed a small 2 cabin boat near the mouth of the Danmap River with no visible results.

Lt. J.R. Jones flew in the #3 position in the 2nd flight in A/P 093—Special Delivery FOB—at 4:15.

Tuesday, May 30, 1944

Dearest Elnora,

Hi, darling—only one more day left of May and then we have June. A very good month, if I do say so myself. A very pleasant one to remember. In nine days, you will have possessed a ring a year. I had hoped to give you a new one before much over a year had passed. It can't be much longer now. Ninety days I should say—ninety, count them. I certainly am.

This has been quite a day. Rained all day long, and believe it or not I'm cold. The heck of it is that every afternoon I feel sleepy, it's boiling hot, and today I'm lively as hell. Such is life in the S.W.P.A. [Southwest Pacific Area]. At least we always have something to complain about—never a shortage on that!

Pretty good show turned up last night—Claudette Colbert and Fred MacMurray in *No Time For Love*. Screwy comedy as usual, but I liked it. I probably won't care a good deal about shows when I get home, but they have been a godsend over here. I often wonder what it would be like without those few brief hours of entertainment.

The mail has stopped dead again. I haven't received a thing in five days. Letters will probably be showing up here a year after I'm home. I won't need them then. I'll just pick up the phone and say, "Hello, darling, what's doing tonight, and I love you and what's more I'll be home in a few hours to prove it." Only you won't get me involved in any long conversations on the phone. Not while you are in reach.

I am still eating myself silly as the food doesn't seem to be petering out yet. I don't know where it's all coming from, but I'm not complaining. We also have a goodly supply of hootch [liquor], but we can't seem to get any mix, and it doesn't appeal to me straight. One of the boys has gone down to the mainland, and it is our fond hope that he will be able to dig up some beer. I've certainly got my fingers crossed on that deal.

I'm still sweating out that leave, and it doesn't seem to be getting any closer. I have flown a great many missions since the last one. I have forty-five of them now. I just hope I don't have to go over seventy.

'Scuse me for a couple of hours while I go eat supper. Bye now—

Here I am again, quite full and with a slight buzz. Four more of the boys are going home, and I have to go over and have a farewell drink this evening. It won't be a very long one, though, as I have to fly tomorrow. I hate to see them go, and yet I'm glad for them. They are a grand bunch of fellows, and they deserve it.

I just showed Sy that picture of you and I and the two kids taken in Montgomery. You remember the one where it looks like you are laying down the law. He said it looks as if you have the upper hand already. That's all right with me. I'm very agreeable at the present state. Know why? Sy just presented me with two letters from you at supper. Gee, it's swell to hear from you again, darling. No day will ever be as blue as the one I left Montgomery that Sunday a year ago—it can't be true. Yet it is—just as true as when you picked me up at Ellington last May, and I couldn't believe it then. It seemed we had only been apart a few days, and I know it will be the same this time. Only we won't be waiting till the next time, for it will be the last. We know what we want, and it will be ours. I know only that I love you with all I possess and that three years is much too long to have waited. We won't again.

I must close, dear, and join the boys to say good-bye—but as it is with you, it won't be for long. Goodnight, my darling.

Always—I love you, J.R.

Unit History for May, 1944

Recreation has been well taken care of in the group, principally by the formation of a Group Softball League. Our Enlisted Men's team is third in the league and our Officers are number two. All have shown a keen interest and competition has been stiff.

The Squadron has been alerted for moving since the 17th of May, so that since that date we have been packed and ready to go, as well as anxious. The whole Squadron feels that a move northward is a *step in the right direction*—toward the eventual end of the war.

Carl A. Strauss
1st Lt., Air Corps
Unit Historical Officer

Monthly Intelligence Summary No. 12, Period April 28 to May 30, 1944

Propaganda Activity:

There were no enemy propaganda activities coming to the attention of the Intelligence Officer of this organization other than the usual Jap radio broadcasts. It is the belief of this Officer that these broadcasts are having very little, if any, detrimental effect upon our men.

Morale:

The morale of this organization continues to be high. The spirit of the organization is being continually bolstered by the successful landings in Dutch New Guinea, Hollandia, Wakde, and now at Biak Island. The Squadron has been on the alert to move since May 17th, and all members of the organization seem to be eager to move northward, feeling that in this way the end of the war is in sight.

Positive Security Measures:

Periodic talks and lectures by the Intelligence Officer for non-combat ground personnel, in which the general program and background of the war in the area as well as in Europe, have been presented.

Carl A. Strauss
1st Lt., Air Corps,
Asst. Intelligence Officer

Narrative History for May, 1944

During the month, on the 21st, the Squadron suffered the loss of a plane and crew on a strike at Dagua. This was one of our few losses, and the fourth since we have been operating in New Guinea, and it was deeply felt by all the squadron. Missions for the month were not of a very outstanding or important nature, compared with some in our past. However, despite the not-too-favorable weather, we were kept busy running a total of seventeen (17) bombing and/or strafing missions against targets along the northeast New Guinea coast and also in Dutch New Guinea. Our greatest efforts were of a harassing nature in the But-Dagua area, which was hit eight times with a variety of bombs from both medium and minimum altitudes. Boram strip was rendered further unserviceable on one (1) mission, and one (1) ground support mission was executed in the area between But and Tadji. The remainder of our strikes were of a *pre-invasion* nature, as they were directed at targets in the Sawar-Sarmi-Wakde area. Sawar and Sarmi were hit on four (4) occasions, Wakde Island once, and Takar Village, on the shore opposite Wakde Island, also received its share of 501st bombs. In all these seventeen (17) strike missions, 107 sorties were entailed and 772.45 hours of combat flying time were *chalked up*. A total of 125 ½ tons of bombs were dropped on enemy installations, and 121,635 X .50 caliber and 19,700 X .30 caliber were expended in strafing his air strips, personnel, and generally not observable, although one possible serviceable Lilly [Japanese light bomber] was considered destroyed at Dagua; several large fuel fires were started at Wakde Island; numerous shacks and native huts were blown to bits; a lugger with Japs aboard was heavily strafed; and general devastation was carried out in the But-Dagua area.

*Photo of 501st Bomb Squadron's score board
courtesy of the Lawrence J. Hickey Collection.*

AIR MEDAL: COURAGE AND DEVOTION TO DUTY

Thursday, June 1, 1944

Dearest Elnora,

I received two letters from you today—both very short. Surprisingly enough, the last one was dated May 18. You said you were rather tired in them. Well, dear, I'm dead at the present time, and as a result this won't be too long itself.

I'm getting my share of flying. In fact, more than I'd like to be doing. If I'm not heard from for a couple of days, I'll be out doing a little work and facilities for writing won't be too handy. I hate to start roughing it again, but we're off again. I can't even keep track of what's going on any more.

It's certainly cool out tonight. I went to the show and shivered all the way through it. It was Rosalind Russell in *What a Woman*. She is too, and it was better than the average picture by far. We have *As Thousands Cheer* coming up next week, and that should be very good. I hope I'm around to see it.

Good night, my darling—I miss you—oh, how can I tell you how much? It seems an impossible task. I'll keep trying till the day comes. I love you always, my dear. It's been a long time, but I hope that time itself has proven it.

My love, J.R.

General Orders No. 348, June 5, 1944

Air Medal:

By direction of the President, under the provisions of Executive Order 9158, 11 May 1942 (Bulletin 25, W.D., 1942), amended by Executive Order 9242-A, 11 September 1942 (Bulletin 49, W.D., 1942) an Air Medal is awarded by the Commanding General, Fifth Air Force, to the following named officers and enlisted men.

First Lieutenant JAMES R. JONES, (0794421), Air Corps, United States Army. For operational flight missions from 9 September 1943 to 26 February 1944.

Home address: Mrs. Survetus Jones (Mother), Stratford Court, 12th & Indiana, New Castle, Indiana.

The citation is as follows:

For meritorious achievement while participating in sustained operational flight missions in the Southwest Pacific area, during which time hostile contact was probable and expected. These operations included bombing missions against enemy airdromes and installations and attacks on enemy naval vessels and shipping. The courage and devotion to duty displayed during these flights are worthy of commendation.

George C. Kenney
Lieutenant General
U.S.A. Commanding

Mission FFO 158-I: June 6, 1944

Ground echelon left Wakde for Hollandia. 5 A/P of this Squadron were ordered to bomb and strafe Biak Island in direct ground support of our troops (6th Army) that were there. Col. True, Group C.O., led the attack with Lts. Jones, Kirmil, Monaghan and Bedell. All planes reached the orbiting point off Biak Island and circled until given a target by the ground station. The target was given as 4 tanks, a dry run was made from across the assigned target and all bombs were dropped at a point given by the ground station. All bombs (10 X 1000 lb. 4/5 sec. and 8/11 sec. delay) were dropped at a pinpointed target. The explosion was seen, but the damage un-assessed due to high cliffs beyond the target and the speed of the planes. Two more passes were made before the planes left the target. One plane strafed the target during the pass.

Lt. J.R. Jones flew in the #3 position in the 1st Flight in A/P 437—Little Thumper.

Mission FFO 160-D: June 8, 1944

Eight A/P were ordered to strike Sorido drome on Biak Island and Col. True led our Squadron and the Group with Lts. Jones, Kirmil, Monaghan, Harper, Coffman, Bedell and Symens. All planes hit the target which was the drome and the area to the north of it. Two small flash fires were started, possibly dumps, and the area was heavily strafed. Ground station reported *Blew Hell out of Target*. Our planes stopped for refueling and preliminary interrogation by S-2 of 3rd Bomb Squadron at Hollandia and then with ground echelon proceeded back to Nadzab.

Lt. J.R. Jones flew in the #2 position in the 1st Flight in A/P 437—Little Thumper.

This would be the last mission for J.R. At the end of this mission, he had completed the required fifty missions and the flight surgeon grounded him after his debriefing. J.R. was truly ready to end his combat missions and after returning to his base, he was sent to Sydney for a much-needed rest.

Saturday, June 10, 1944

My dearest Elnora,

Hello, darling—sorry to keep you waiting a few days, but I've been up in the forward areas. It's definitely no picnic there either. I have never been so tired and dirty in my life. Hollandia and Wakde are no places for a vacation. We ate emergency rations all the while we were gone, and I have tasted better food in my lifetime. Hollandia is just about the dustiest place it has ever been my pleasure to land at. As soon as you touch the ground, everything disappears. Some fun, but I can think of better ways to earn a living.

When I got home again, I was shot [over tired]. The flight surgeon promptly grounded me, saying I had been flying too much. I guess I am pretty nervous. I have fifty missions now and 235 combat hours. As a result, I'm being sent to Sydney in the next few days. I'm not mad a bit about that. I have been ready for weeks. I'll probably go wild this time. God knows I could use a rest.

I have received many letters from you in the past two days, darling, and what lovely letters. I want to come home. I'll certainly have a time answering all these. The latest one dated May 27 surprised me no end. Of course the worst has happened. In one letter you tell me you are going to send those pictures the next few days. Then comes a lapse and a letter saying I've sent the pictures. Naturally I haven't received them as yet. They can't do this to me. I'm really anxious to lay my hands on those, dear. You have no idea how much I want to see you. I only hope I receive them before I leave for Sydney.

I saw a pretty good show the other evening. It was *As Thousands Cheer*, and I really liked it. José Iturbi was marvelous playing the piano. I also heard the ditty "I Dug a Ditch in Wichita" for the first time—quite a classy little item. How about Iturbi playing boogie-woogie for Judy Garland? Really got a kick out of that one.

We really pitched a party last night. At least it worked off some steam which was a pretty good cure, but I didn't feel so good this morning, however. We have loads of grapefruit juice and lots of gin to put in it. Nice hangover material.

So you think your brother will get home soon. That should be nice for everyone concerned. I wish I could be doing the same thing. Do you think you could entertain a poor soldier on leave, love starved as you once told me, and don't think I ain't?

I have also received quite a few letters from Mother, and from what I gather you two girls are still gossiping quite a bit. How am I holding up through it all? I think you are making quite an impression on her even though you two have never met.

Good night, dearest. I'm off to bed. I'll write tomorrow and tell all. Gee, I'm lonesome—

Always—I love you, J.R.

Monday, June 12, 1944

Elnora darling,

Five more letters today, but still not the one I'm looking for. Of course, dear, I look forward to all of them, but nevertheless I'm still extremely anxious to see those pictures. Of course you wouldn't know why. What startled me most was the fact that one of the letters was dated May 31. Now how did that happen? Perhaps today will be the lucky day.

June 12—I can't think of a better day to receive a picture of you. Does that date by any chance sound slightly familiar to you? One big long year now gone. It passed rapidly at that, but days away from you could never go quickly enough to suit me. But my pretty redhead, it won't be long now. Perhaps with the war going the way it is I won't have to return to combat. Wouldn't that be lovely? It certainly wouldn't break my heart.

I have just returned from getting a badly needed haircut. I was beginning to look like Tarzan. Fact of the matter is, the C.O. ordered me to get it in a nice sort of way, of course. I was going to do it anyway (it says here). Oh how I hate that task, and the barber we have is lulu. I think he delights in getting officers into his chair.

So, you heard from your old flame again—the pilot I mean. It would be odd if I should run across him. I often wondered how I would feel if I ever came on to any of your exes. I'd probably be very happy just to talk to anyone who knows you. He would probably share my opinion on how lovely you are. That's obvious if he was far enough gone on you to ask you to marry him. I often wondered what became of him and if I was the cause of it breaking up. You never volunteered any information on the subject, so I let well enough alone. I had an inkling once that all might not be going too well for me, and to say I was worried would be putting it mildly. I can tell you one thing, darling; if he loved you half as much as I do that would be plenty. I must have convinced you of that as you decided to marry me. Thank God for that.

That lipstick you smeared all over one letter looks familiar to me. Too bad it isn't on me. I surely wouldn't complain.

I ought to be taking off on leave in a couple of days. I wish all my clothes were clean. The Aussies aren't very speedy in their service either. Guess I'll just have to run around in my shorts a few days. I hear tell it's much too cool for that.

Must shut up for the present, darling, and be on my way. Be back presently, saying—I

Love you always, J.R.

Daily Log: Thursday, June 15, 1944

Lts. Jones and Erskine on leave to APO 927.

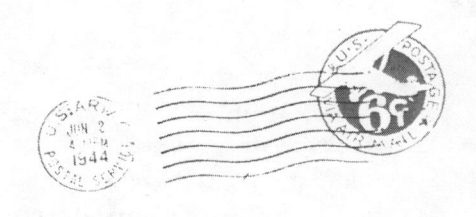

THE FRONT LINE AND THE FRAT BROTHERS

SUNDAY, JUNE 25, 1944

Dearest Elnora,

Hi, darling—remember me? Of course by now you must have guessed that I have been in Sydney again. Had a very nice time, but God it was cold. I shivered the entire week, and here I am again in New Guinea burning up. You can't win. About the only thing worthy of mention that I did was see Bob Hope and Betty Hutton in *Let's Face It*. I got a huge kick out it. I also ate plenty and drank huge quantities of beer, as you probably already suspect—just a nice, quiet vacation.

About the pictures—I have received all but three of them. I can't thank you enough for them, dear. A couple of them were marvelous. I like you best of all in that tan dress. Dear, you looked wonderful. You weren't kidding about being slim, were you? Perhaps I've been teasing you too much—looks good, though. Then there was that legs picture. WOW—what a thing to send to a man in

New Guinea. I can say truthfully though it was direly appreciated, wonder why? Pretty shapely, sweet—trying to lure me on, eh? Well, you did all right. This is something I want to see for myself. Another picture I like was with red toenails. Yes, they showed up plainly. As for me liking the hair—well, darling, I've never seen anything about you that I haven't liked, so you have no worries on that score. A very sweet letter accompanied the pictures I liked best. They were never out of my hands while I was in Sydney.

I'm glad you liked the picture I sent you. I'm afraid the others didn't pan out as the film was no good. One is the best I can do at present. Maybe you won't need pictures much longer.

I had a very pleasant surprise while in Sydney. I met one of my fraternity brothers at the airport—Preston Johnson. The biggest surprise was that he is stationed just down the road from me. He also told me Jim Bell is only a short distance from where I live. I'm going to look him up tomorrow. Jim's mother, father, and sister are prisoners of war in the Philippines. I'm anxious to know if he has ever heard from them. Also, Jack Moore, John Weatherwax, and Bob Keplinger are all in this area. I hope I'll be able to see them before I go home. These names may all be Greek to you right now, but they will all be definite personalities some day. I also met two other fellows from school while on leave. It was just like homecoming—nice word that.

I may have a very big surprise for you three of four weeks, darling, bigger than you think. Now don't go straight up in the air, but I think it's going to happen this time. In fact the orders are in. Think you could stand me around, darling? I wouldn't say anything about this. Let's keep it a secret. We've been wrong before, but I think it's our time now. I'll write more of this later.

Goodnight, my dear—I love you so very much, and soon I'll be able to prove it.

Always—my love, J.R.

Monday, June 26, 1944

Dearest Elnora,

Well darling, here I am back as promised. Pretty prompt, ain't I? Really had a good night's sleep last night, and I feel like a new man—well almost, anyhow. I wish this were about two weeks later, and then perhaps I wouldn't be writing this letter. I have been gazing at those pictures again, and I'm finding it rather difficult to get this letter started.

You never told me before until one of these last letters that you had decided to quit dating. Of course I imagined something of that sort when only names of females appeared in your letters. I was pretty sure you weren't suffering from B.O. [body odor]. If you were happy that way, darling, then it's quite all right by me. It only makes me aware that I must hold a pretty good position with you. Wonder how I got an idea like that? Anyhow, I think we'll remedy that situation, and you'll have a date every night to catch up. Think you could stand that much?

"I Couldn't Sleep a Wink Last Night" and "The Music Stopped" are catching on quite rapidly in Sydney now. It took me by surprise as they usually are pretty far behind. I don't think the Yanks will be in Australia much longer, and something tells me the girls down there aren't going to find life the same. It could never be so gay again—just one long party for them.

So you finally got a call from your brother. Did you talk to him or just go blank again? Perhaps he will be home again by the time you receive this. I certainly hope so as I know it would please you all very much. Can't say that I blame you; at the rate things are going, I may cross trails with him yet, but don't count too heavily on it. You never really know about those things. Maybe he can hold you down till I get there.

I get rather tickled at you and your financial difficulties, dear. What a bookkeeper you must be! What I can't figure out is how both of us are going to get along on $325 a month when you have such a terrible time with $125 or whatever it is you make. Oh well, it will all come out okay. A good many are doing it, so why can't we? We probably won't eat one week out of each month, but we'll get used to it.

I shall be leaving you soon to shave and clean up for dinner. A bath is really something to look forward to in this part of the world. It will be nice to do it with hot water again.

The last letter I have from you says we were together a year ago that night. I can imagine your mood because I was feeling the same way. It almost floors you when you think that anything could have been that good. It won't be long now, dearest. I must close, sweet, and attend to business. Will write again soon.

Always—I love you, J.R.

Photo of soldiers shaving courtesy of the Lawrence J. Hickey Collection.

Tuesday, June 27, 1944

Dearest Elnora,

I've been listening to the radio all evening, and I've heard a good many of the tunes you always talk about. Perhaps I won't be too far behind when I get home. Dick Haymes sang "You'll Never Know" a short while ago, and that hit me between the eyes. Much good music these days, isn't there? At present Guy Lombardo is giving me a little trouble though.

Aha, Bob Hope is now on—big night! Last night I turned up for the usual Monday show. Wasn't too good except for some dancing by Ann Miller. See what I mean!

This morning I went to see my college chum, Jim Bell. We had quite a chat about old times. He's coming up to see me one of these evenings. We didn't have too much time for chatter as he is a 1st Sgt. and pretty busy. Ah, I pity these boys who must work.

I took a sun bath today and sorta overdid it. I think I'll stay indoors tomorrow; don't want to get too healthy! Life is rather dull since I'm not flying any longer.

I suppose you are rather baffled by all this news of my coming home. It's like this—they suddenly decided to send us all home instead of keeping us overtime and flying the hell out of us. The C.O. told me that I could stay if I wanted to and I would make Captain in two or three months. But, that would mean staying perhaps five more months and perhaps flying 30 or more missions. I said no thanks, I have important business in Texas that can't wait. Being a captain doesn't mean that much to me and I'm quite sure it won't to you. Besides, I know I will have to go overseas in perhaps four months and I don't want to be stuck on this damned island. If I must go again, I hope it's China.

Perhaps I'll get a break in this Army some day. All that I want at present is to get home and see you. Does that make it plain enough? Look out, 'cause here I come!

I imagine you will be surprised when I do get in. It will probably be as sudden as your friend from England. They come and go quickly, don't they? So, he was complimenting you, eh? Well just wait till I get through with you. You ain't heard nothing yet.

Well, darling, I gotta go—to sleep I mean. It's getting pretty late in this part of the world. We probably won't know if it's day or night soon and wouldn't care less. What's the difference—we'll be together and that's all that will matter. Good night, darling. See you tomorrow—

Always—I love you, J.R.

Monthly Intelligence Summary No. 13 for June, 1944

Morale:

The morale of this organization continues to be high. The spirit of the organization is being continually bolstered by the successful invasion of Europe, bombing of Tokyo, and the further successes in this theatre of operations.

Positive Security Measures:

Security posters have been placed throughout the squadron area.

Periodic talks and lectures by the Intelligence Officer for non-combat ground personnel, in which the general program and background of the war in this area as well as in Europe, have been presented.

Expansion of Intelligence and Information activities with wider distribution of magazines, newspapers, press clippings, situation maps, and other items of general interest for all personnel in the squadron.

A Belloptican machine has been received and all combat pictures taken by our airplanes on strike missions are now shown regularly to all personnel in the squadron. This has a very good effect on ground personnel, particularly those who do maintenance work on airplanes and who load bombs and ammunition. They see visually the results accomplished by their own labor and thus realize the importance of their contribution to the war effort.

Of Local Interest Doings:

June, traditional *Month of Brides*, saw the Squadron celebrating its first anniversary *wedded* to the Fifth Air Force. The union has been blessed with no mean proportion of success, based, as all good marriages are, upon mutual understanding and common interests. It may have been coincidence, but the Squadron is rather proud of the fact that the batting average of the Fifth Air Force took a leap forward shortly after our arrival in the Theatre and the trend of S.W.P.A. events took a decided change for the better. In this first colorful year of combat, we've outsmarted, outguessed, and outmaneuvered the Jap, leaving him punch-drunk and reeling and, as far as the New Guinea Campaign is concerned, he has *kissed the canvas for the count*.

While little in the way of actual celebration marked the event, the launching of the Squadron into its second year of combat was commemorated by a mild beer bust in the enlisted men's mess. The anniversary saw the unit far removed from its original island base and found it stationed closer to the general direction of Tokyo, at Nadzab, in the beautiful Markham Valley.

No one could complain of monotony and routine during the month's operations as evidenced by the unusual incidents that occurred. On 4 June, just for a starter, the Squadron was alerted to move to Wakde Island. Due to crowded conditions, our planes were subsequently removed to Hollandia while the ground crews remained at Wakde. There they experienced a taste of the *real thing* when they had a *big night out*—out of their bunks and into their foxholes, due to the Jap breaking through our defenses and laying a few retaliatory eggs but causing no damage to our planes. One of our privates had the unusual distinction of spending several hours in the same foxhole with a Major General. Next day a Technical Sergeant, one of our A.M.s, [aircraft mechanics] was approached by a middle-aged and distinguished looking gentleman of no apparent rank with the request that he aid in the clearing up of the mess caused by the bombing. The Sergeant very laughingly replied that, due to his rank, it wasn't necessary for him to do that type of work. Whereupon the middle aged gentleman drew a cap from his hip pocket on which were pinned two glittering stars of a Major General. Needless to say the Sergeant was soon busying himself.

Quantities of *fresh meat*, as the *old timers* refer to our replacement, entered the Squadron during the month, bringing firsthand accounts of *what's what* back in the States. All were somewhat surprised at the advanced state of *civilization* we've reached in this *combat* zone. The swift advances of the Campaign point to our moving from this area, which will be hard to take, as we have established comfortable and pleasant living and working conditions. Filching a line from Mr. Fitzpatrick of Travelog fame, "it will be with reluctance that we leave beautiful Nadzab, the Jewel of the Markham Valley."

Benjamin E. Green
Captain, Air Corps
Intelligence Officer

Unit History for Month of June, 1944

Our squadron continued at the same base during June, although the great speed of Allied drives against the enemy had pushed him so far back that we were unable to reach him from our Nadzab base. All strikes carried out by our planes had to be staged from forward bases, our crews making four trips to Hollandia during the month to run a total of seven strike missions against enemy installations at Biak, Manokwari, Jefman, and Samate.

There was, however, one big strike of the month. The targets were Jefman and Samate Airdromes, the last remaining and the most westerly Jap air bases in Dutch New Guinea. The squadron was placed under the operational control of the 310th Bombardment Wing (M), and on June 15th, six planes went up to Hollandia to stage from that base. The mission was to be a coordinated one with our squadron following the 38th Bomb Group over the target. The two groups were to be led by Col. Hall of V Bomber Command. Group briefing was held at the briefing room of the 3rd Attack Group, and the squadron was briefed on the morning of the 16th.

Our squadron, leading the 345th Group, took off from Hollandia Drome at 0900/K/16, with Major Marston as Group Leader. We made rendezvous with the 38th Group at Wakde Island at 1010/K and proceeded there to Mios Woendi Island south of Manokwari where, at 1155/K, rendezvous was made with the fighters—P-38s. The strike force continued then, across the Vogelkop Peninsula, to the target. The 38th Group, leading, made a strafing pass on Samate Drome from the southwest, continued on a northeasterly heading to bomb and strafe Jefman Island. Our group was to bomb and strafe Samate Drome and then to strafe Jefman. Our squadron approached Samate Drome from the southwest at a heading of 22 degrees, but was unable to drop their bombs there due to the nature of the terrain—a ridge due south of the drome making it impossible to see the target until too late to bomb. Samate, however, was strafed heavily, as was the personnel area designated 6-X.

Our squadron was intercepted by five or six OSCARS [Japanese plane] and HAMPS [Japanese plane] between Samate and Jefman Dromes. Several passes were made, but attacks were not too closely pressed, and in each case the attacking planes were driven off by the superior cover of the P-38s. One HAMP was definitely shot down by Lt. Kortemeyer in A/P 078.

Continuing on the Jefman Island, the squadron, still flying six planes abreast, dropped 68 x 100 lb. Parademo bombs on the southwest portion of the island and in the dispersal area northwest of the drome. Two twin-engine bombers were hit by these bombs, and one was strafed and damaged. Bombs also hit among at least six twin-engine bombers in the dispersal area, of which three are thought to be definitely hit. A fuel dump southwest of 3-W was hit starting a fire with an explosion and flames up to 500 ft. An ack-ack position at 3-W was hit and probably destroyed. Both Jefman and Samate were thoroughly strafed with 12,450 x .50 caliber and 2300 x .30 caliber expended in the strafing. The two dromes were covered with heavy black smoke as our squadrons pulled away from the target.

The entire strike was most successful and upon returning to the targets on the following day, the crews reported both Jefman and Samate looked deserted and desolate.

Major Fain was relieved of command of the squadron and has returned to the U. S. for a well-earned rest. On June 4th, Captain Darwin G. Neuenschwander succeeded Major Fain as Squadron Commander. Captain Neuenschwander has been with the 501th Squadron from the very beginning, coming into the squadron as a member of the original cadre. He is an excellent pilot and has over thirteen-hundred hours flying time. After attending the University of Utah, he received primary and basic flight training at Cal. Aero. Academy, taking advanced training at Luke Field, Arizona. His superior skill and ability as a leader of men as well as of aerial formations are certain to result in a highly successful tour of duty for Captain Neuenschwander as our Commanding Officer.

Daily Log: Wednesday, July 6, 1944

The following Officers and EM received their orders to go back to the States today: Lts. Coons, Jones, Bedell, Flanaghan; T/Sgts. Anderson, Giroux, Krauss, Foster, Davis; S/Sgts. Bauman, Martinez, Bibeault, Hansworth, Spencer, Taylor, Egich, Ogle, Augusta, Adams, Helvey, Hilhelm, Safarowitz. 9 EM left today on leave to Mackay.

Thursday, July 6, 1944—V-mail Letter

Dearest Elnora,

Perhaps this won't come as too much of a shock as I have already told you that I might get to go home. I should be home in two weeks, perhaps less. This will be the last you hear from me till I'm with you. I don't know what my immediate plans will be, but we'll soon find out.

I never did get the picture of you in shorts, but I think the idea can be improved upon soon. Perhaps your brother will be home by the time I get there. I hope soon.

I'm about out of space so I'll close. It won't be long till I can say in person that I

Love you always, J.R.

Letter Dated July 26, 1944, to Elnora from Mrs. Survetus Jones, J.R.'s mother

Dear Elnora—

I suppose by now you have all your nails chewed off.

I, too, am rather in a dither, but Mr. Jones said last eve that lots of the airboys were coming by boat. So maybe that is it, but while he is riding a boat, he is resting up and isn't in combat.

I was so very glad to get the clipping as I had no idea who his C.O. was.

It seems as if I have been so busy. Last Friday I had to go to Muncie, Indiana, to the hospital as Mr. Jones's mother was having some surgical work done on her neck. So I went over to be with her through the first night and day. She got along fine and went home Tuesday of this week, but has to go back in two weeks for another operation. But don't say anything about it to J.R. if you see him first, as it might worry him and it wouldn't do any good. We certainly don't want him to have anything but a nice time when he does get here.

Yesterday I drove out to Indianapolis with my neighbors who are going to Alaska. They had to buy some trunks, and I didn't realize how high things were. It looks to me like you would have to do your big buying at Woolworth's Five & Dime. I imagine they have started most brides off in housekeeping.

The first cost of things doesn't seem so great, but the tax is what gets one. I wouldn't fret about things, as nice things come with the years. As for dishes, I get more use from a cheap set of dishes I use all the time than I do from my Havilland. About all I have is just enough to get along with. After a few long moves one really cleans house. I would much rather live in apartment hotels, but it seems as if I am queer.

We have to go to South Bend again this weekend as Mr. Jones goes up there to a doctor, so I always go along.

My neighbors are starting to Alaska this weekend. They have been selling furniture and junk. I only wish it was the Jones family.

Well, I will see you later.

Love, Mrs. Jones

WINGS AND A RING

Photo of J.R. and his father, Survetus Jones, courtesy of Suzie Jones Neff.

Photo of J.R.'s mother, Mrs. Gordia Jones, courtesy of Suzie Jones Neff.

Saturday, July 29, 1944

Dearest Elnora,

I guess you're surprised to hear from me again in New Guinea. I don't like it myself. They have lost our orders, but they finally turned up yesterday. I'll be coming home by boat and that won't be any two-day trip. From Frisco I'll be sent to Chicago, and then I'll go home for a week or ten days, and then comes the good part. The rest of the time is ours, darling. Think you can stand the strain? I'll be in Houston as soon as possible. We can spend a week in New Orleans and then we'll probably go to Miami where the relocation center is. We should really have a time there. It's all on the government. At least you'll get a honeymoon out of it, which is more than most brides get.

I'm going crazy around here waiting to get home. All I do is think about you and the good time we are going to have. This is really killing me. The food is lousy here, and we have nothing to do all day. We just live for the picture shows that they have nearly every evening. I finally received all the pictures, and darling, some of them were marvelous, almost as pretty as you really are. To say you look good to me will be putting it mildly. At least we know it won't be long now. Too long to suit me, but nothing compared to the time already gone by. I had hoped to be home by your birthday, but such is luck. You'll be twenty-two when I get there instead of the twenty when last seen. You're getting to be an old maid, aren't you, darling? But I can fix that in a hurry. I probably won't be writing again till I get to Frisco, but you'll know that I'm with you every minute of the time.

It hardly seems possible that I'm waiting to come home. I wonder how it will be. Disappointing in some ways, I guess, but you'll make it be better than it ever was before. This past year has been one I won't forget for quite a while.

I'm glad I know what it's like though, and it won't be so bad should I have to go over again, just so it isn't these damned islands. If I should get a little dopey at times, just blame it on the heat. It's not as bad as all that, but it must be wonderful to have anything you want to eat, all forms of entertainment in reach, and most of all, being with the one you're head over heels in love with. My imagination has really been on the loose lately. I close my eyes, and I see cool bottles of beer and redheads running by, something like Dagwood (in shorts, too—oh boy). That's something I'll have to see for myself.

Don't make too many plans till I get there because I haven't the least idea what is going to happen, except that we'll be doing it together. It will probably mean a lot of traveling, but I don't think you'll mind that if you like to tear around as much as I do, and it seems you do.

From all your last letters you seem slightly put out by a lack of mail—can't understand it, darling. I know by the time you receive this you'll think I've deserted you, but never fear—I'm always turning up. Thank God I won't have to write any more letters, but I've missed yours terribly these last weeks.

I'd best close, darling, as it's getting dark and we don't have lights. Lovely place this. Next time I tell you I love you, I hope it's in person, and I will too. Darling, I must run—these next days are going to be awful, but it won't last long.

Always—I love you, J.R.

P.S. I saw Jack Benny, Carole Landis, Martha Tilton, and Larry Adler the other day. Pretty good show too.

Love again—me.

Monthly Intelligence Summary No. 14 for July, 1944

Of Local Interest Doings:

The first few days of July were very quiet in our Nadzab *home*. Some men having a hard time finding anything to do but catch up on their sleep. Everyone knew, and had known for some time, that in the very near future our new *home* would be well up in enemy territory, Biak Island, and the combat crews were being interrogated constantly about conditions.

After days of maintenance and training and slopping through oceans of mud from the sudden torrential rains, so common to the Markham Valley, the advance echelon left for the newly captured, but not yet cleared, island of Biak. Men were packed into trucks in the middle of the night and hurried to the transport strips where heavily loaded C-47's took off in steady streams at dawn each morning. Jeeps and their little trailers were bouncing along the roads to the waiting transports. Entire walls and tents and some buildings that were portable were loaded with tables, file boxes, camera equipment, or anything loose. The various sections thought they would need to start business anew.

By the latter part of July those bearded veterans of the first landings of the Squadron had cleared a huge area about three miles from Mokmer Airdrome (also under construction by the Engineers who were widening and smoothing it) which was near the middle of the shoreline road full of mud and water about the consistency of half melted ice cream. The entire cleared area was hard on the eyes due to the glare of the sun on the white coral rock, and the dampness very seldom allowed clothes to dry. However, with all of the *hardships*—sore backs and sunburn and the constant warning by the medics to be careful of bites and scratches which might lead to the dreaded typhus—the area began to shape up in a hurry. Fresh from a furlough in Sydney, First Sergeant Kelly directed the stream of trucks filing day and night into the area with their loads of coral rock for the tent floors; men hurrying the construction of the mess hall, orderly room, and communications. Part of the men were living on the *line* in order to keep the busy planes serviced. All seemed to be a mess of conflicting plans and orders. Order comes out of chaos, so they say, and the orderly life we knew at Nadzab soon began to take place in easy strides. At the month's end the 501st had the most complete and best appearing area of the surrounding sites. The Mokmer area seemed to groan and writhe with new life and expansion. The dozens of Jap skeletons, which were strewn all over the place, were buried. The natives, under their *drill instructor*, Pfc. Peter (Jungle Jim) Foley, chop-chopped their way through insect ridden brush, clearing paths and tent sites. New combat crews arrived to stare at the place they were to call home. Captain Green and Captain Erspamer held forth, directing all sorts of work; Captain Shetron, Advance Echelon Commander, was bringing the construction crews so that they worked faster and better.

Our planes made trip after trip to Nadzab, bringing men, mail, meals, and money and necessary equipment. The pet phrase among officers and enlisted men alike was, "Oh Boy, you should have been here when it was tough!" accenting the last syllable. New arrivals quickly set up a temporary place to live—some in the mess tent, some in the orderly room, others under rickety tents—anything to keep out of the rain, which poured down in gallons every afternoon.

Photo of camp site on beach courtesy of the Lawrence J. Hickey Collection.

Traditionally, 501st men strived to outdo their fellow soldiers in tent construction. Some were built without center poles, others were hard packed coral floors and one or two boasted wooden floors. An order was issued by Captain Erspamer that all tents must have wooden frames, which pleased most of the men no end. Others grumbled, as is the usual procedure. Squadron streets were laid off and each tent given a much larger space than they had been previously. Jeeps plowed over and around humps of coral the bulldozers couldn't cut, bringing food and water from the Quartermaster. Chow was excellent, better than what we had at Nadzab, and it was all consumed by tired, hungry, *construction-engineers* with lots of comments (All good!) thrown in the direction of the hardworking cooks.

Captain Darwin G. Neuenschwander, our Commanding Officer, was transferred to Group, to take over the job as Operations Officer for the four Squadrons. Captain Edward H. Erspamer was made Squadron Executive Officer, and Captain John

B. Nusbaum was made Squadron Commander. The job of Adjutant went to 1st Lieutenant Martin H. Holtzmann and that of Squadron Operations Officer went to 1st Lieutenant Charles E. Coffman. A new arrival, 1st Lieutenant I. E. Baker, filled the vacancy left by 1st Lieutenant Carl A. Strauss as Captain Green's assistant in S-2. Many of the *old timers* went on their merry way, bound for home to *rest and rehabilitate*. Colonel True awarded medals to those who had them coming and shook many hands as the camera clicked off some of the best shots yet produced. New arrivals among the officers and enlisted men were wide-eyed at the stories told by the departing men. Ground echelon replacements arrived in spurts, swelling the T/O [Technical Officer] to near full strength. The new men fell into the swing of things, quickly saying, "I never thought New Guinea was like this!"

Photo of an operations unit courtesy of the Lawrence J. Hickey Collection.

The European war fronts were plotted and discussed, with all eyes eager to see the latest moves on the map. Bets were out as to how long, how soon, when and where the war would end.

The war in the S.W.P.A. and C.P.A. [Central Pacific Area] carried headlines of the Saipan and Guam situations. The B-29s were blasting away at the Japanese homeland, and the operations of our own 5th Air Force in the Manokwari and Halamaheras area—that long awaited *last mile* into the Philippines, kept every heart eager and all spirits high.

July, probably more than any month since the Black Panthers came to the S.W.P.A, will be remembered by the men as the month they moved 900 miles in one hop, knocking at the back door of the Philippines. Raids were experienced every night for a week and Japs were three and one half miles in back of them at all times (a constant back-itcher). To get rid of that tired feeling, they went swimming in the ocean, where the water is as warm as a bath back home. Best of all was the smooth manner in which the mail came up on those here in Biak, ahead of all the others, scarcely a day passed that we weren't called out by the welcome voice of the assistant *mailman*, Sgt. Norton Blaylock. M/Sgt. Passodellis could be seen coming into the area at any hour to get a few minutes rest. The Ordnance men and Armorers had to load at night so that the bombs would not remain in the ships overnight. Engines could be heard at any hour, with missions going on all night and sounds of the bulldozers and scrapers were chugging and choking on gnarled stumps and underbrush, clearing a road for the high speed unloading of the freighters out on the reef. *Duck* and LST's were humming along in the bay area, to and from the ships, with everything it takes to fight a war successfully.

July was a busy month, with the business of moving, but everyone agreed on one subject: "We would move every day if it would get this war won and get us all home by Christmas."

Benjamin E. Green
Captain, Air Corps
Intelligence Officer

Personnel Cited
Air Medal (Oak Leaf Cluster)
1st. Lt. James R. Jones
William E. Henley
1st. Lieut., Air Corps
Citations Officer
General Orders No. 144
Air Medal (Oak Leaf Cluster):

By direction of the President, in addition to the Air Medal Awarded, the following named officers by the Commanding General, Fifth Air Force, as published in section I, General Orders 345, Headquarters, Fifth Air Force, dated 5 June 1944, Bronze Oak Leaf Clusters are awarded to them by the Commanding General, Far East Air Forces, under the provisions of Executive Order No. 9158, 11 May 1942 (Bulletin 25, WD, 1942), as amended by Executive Order No. 9242-A, 11 September 1942 (Bulletin 29, WD, 1942).

Oak Leaf Cluster:

First Lieutenant James R. Jones, (0794421), Air Corps, United States Army. For operational flight missions from 26 February to 18 May 1944.

Home address: Mr. Survetus Jones (Father), Stradford Court, 12th & Indiana, Newcastle, Indiana.

George C. Kenney
Lieutenant General
U.S.A. Commanding

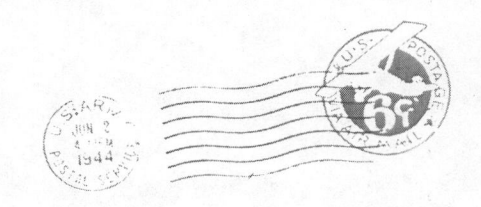

THE LONG BOAT RIDE HOME: DAYDREAMS OF A CERTAIN REDHEAD RUNNING THROUGH MY MIND

As in the telling of their eleven days together at the beginning of this book, I can only imagine J.R.'s thoughts as he made the long boat ride home. He flew over in a matter of days, but the boat ride home could have taken up to a month. His last letter to Elnora was dated July 29, 1944. With such a lot of time on his hands, I'm sure he reminisced about those eleven days together and daydreamed of the days ahead when he finally could be with his redhead. So close, yet still so far away!

J.R. hoped to make it home by August 14th to celebrate in person Elnora's birthday. Reality was that he wouldn't make it there in time and he wouldn't be able to send her a letter or card during his journey home.

On the surface, it would seem that J.R.'s troubles were over. He had flown fifty missions, been shot at, been bitten by creatures he had never studied about in school, was half starved to death, sustained injuries and survived a crash landing. However, the war was still on, and Japanese submarines were a reality. Large troop transports were prime targets for the enemy, and I'm sure that his stress level was great. I would be willing to bet the closer he got to home, the more anxious he became.

In one of his letters to Elnora from Maxwell Field, J.R. wrote that the mail clerk had tacked a small note on the back of one of Elnora's letters explaining he had a difficult time reading J.R.'s address. J.R. supposed that one of the mail clerks at Maxwell was responsible. The tacked note said as follow: "Dear Pinkie, tell this guy that if he doesn't give you a better address, I will." The mail clerk then signed his initials. J.R. kidded Elnora that she had a silent admirer and wanted to know how she did it. He didn't like the name Pinkie because it was too close to Stinkie. Suzie Jones Neff told me that nickname resulted when Elnora was in high school due to a bathing suit malfunction, exposing much more than she cared. That clue made me chuckle and wonder if Elnora had ever told J.R. what the true meaning of Pinkie was, or did he just assume it was a nickname because of her hair color?

Once he returned home, J.R. knew they would marry immediately. Elnora was employed at Brown Shipyard and she would have to quit. Since he loved to tease her, I'm sure that he gave her a bad time about his visions of a lady riveter being his true love. He jokingly hoped that she didn't have bulging muscles, very unbecoming a lady of such upbringing. He also teased her by asking why it was that bomber pilots couldn't have hostesses aboard their plane? You know, someone to do the cooking and sewing. For his plane, he nominated The Texas Redhead.

With such close quarters on the return ship, J.R. surely spent time on deck. In several of his letters he wrote about the night sky he saw in such faraway places. The stars were so bright it was blinding and he saw more shooting stars in one evening there than he had in all his life in the U.S. He also reported that even though it had a very romantic look, it was rather deceptive on account of the mosquitoes. He described a sunset that looked something like Walt Disney might want it to, saying he'd never seen such colors in his life.

J.R. surely reflected on the endless days of jungles, bugs, mud, and missions. One of his escapes was writing Elnora while listening to music. He began many a letter at the precise hour of 4:30 in the afternoon because he always felt this time of day was when he and Elnora should just be returning from a picnic or a tennis game. He said the grass would have been just the right shade of green and the sky couldn't have been bluer. He dreamed they would both clean up and dash out to eat at some quiet place, take in a movie and then perhaps a few dances afterward. He wanted to take her home and kiss her good night and never wanted to leave her again. Boy, could that J.R. dream a dream, and it was easy to see why Elnora so easily gave her heart to J.R. As I read his letters, I find myself falling in love with the images he created so vividly in my mind.

Since music and dancing were such a big part of both of their lives, *music that haunted your mind*, as J.R. would say, he often wrote and thought about what it would be like to be with Elnora again. He teased her by telling her what he wouldn't give to dance with a girl who hasn't dated so many cadets that she was practically a professional hostess.

J.R. was comforted to know that one of the big guns in his Pop's company said there would be a job waiting for him any time he walked in, and at least he knew they wouldn't starve once he got out of the Army Air Corps. However, he realized it would be rather tough to find another job that paid $300 a month right away. J.R. had always wished he could buy a car, but he realized that, because of the war, there were few cars to be had, and he knew one would be rather difficult to maintain. He daydreamed that he would get a Jeep when the war was over. He wrote that he could see them sailing down Main Street in one, but had to warn Elnora, however, that skirts were very impractical in one. They had so much to do some day. Everything would be new to them and was bound to be fun. He suggested that when the war was over, they should go back to college together and be two of the oldest and happiest freshmen on campus.

Romantic that he was, he told her several times he would have liked to make love to her in a way that any man should. Probably, when he saw her, he would have liked to get married in the first thirty minutes, but he knew that wasn't too practical. He said that from the sounds of her letters, she seemed pretty eager about getting married. J.R. preferred a short and sweet ceremony with the fewer in the audience the better. Then, he wanted to leave on a dead run. He teased her that she must feel like she was really getting something when she got a name like Jones—just think of all the people who would try to keep up with them!

In one of Elnora's letters, she told him she was going to kiss him like he'd never been kissed before. Now, he said, that was what he called "something to look forward to." His response was, "By the way, dear, have you ever had a date with anyone who had been in New Guinea for a year? You may be in for a few surprises yourself. Those Japs had no idea what they were keeping me from or they'd have quit fighting yesterday."

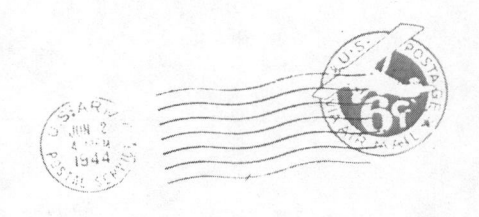

MRS. JONES, MEET THE NEW MRS. JONES

J.R. only had ten days from his return to the United States to his ordered reporting date in Florida. Due to the short schedule, his parents were not able to attend the wedding; thus, the honeymoon letter to his mother. My friend, Glenna, and I found their marriage license at the Harris County Court House in downtown Houston, issued September 5, 1944. According to J.R.'s letter, shown below, they married on September 7. Mrs. Smith provided a pre-wedding luncheon rehearsal for them at the Rice Hotel in Houston. We do not know where they were married. The ever-so-generous and gracious Mrs. Smith provided a small wedding reception for the newlyweds at the famed Warwick Hotel. Just as J.R. had spoken of in his letters, he took his new bride to New Orleans for their honeymoon.

The following are the first pages of the actual two letters J.R. and Elnora wrote to his mother while on their honeymoon. Transcriptions of their letters follow each of their handwritten letters.

René Palmer Armstrong

Envelope

1st Lt. J.R. and Mrs. Elnora Bartlett Jones
Jung Hotel
1500 Canal Street
New Orleans
To: Mrs. Survetus Jones
Stratford Court Apt. 1
New Castle, Indiana
Jung Hotel Stationary

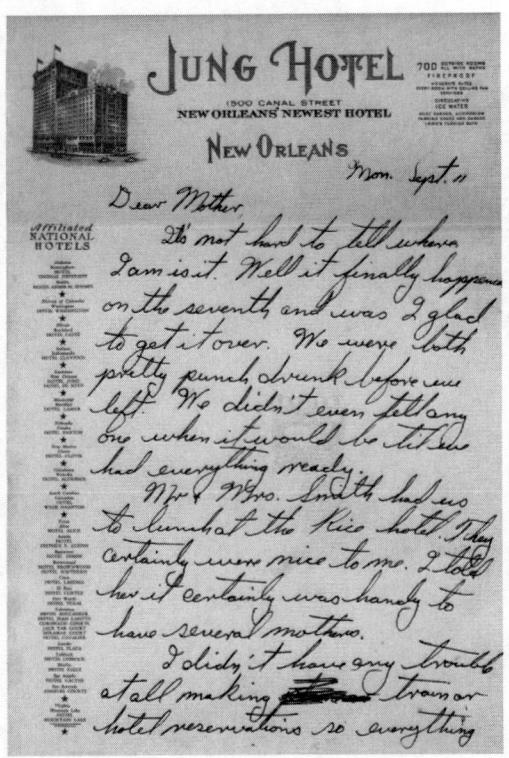

Scan of J.R.'s honeymoon letter to his mother courtesy of Lloyd Sullivan.

Monday, September 11, 1944

Dear Mother,

It's not hard to tell where I am, is it? Well it finally happened on the seventh and was I glad to get it over. We were both pretty punch drunk before we left. We didn't even tell anyone when it would be till we had everything ready.

Mr. & Mrs. Smith had us to lunch at the Rice hotel. They certainly were nice to me. I told her it certainly was handy to have several mothers.

I didn't have any trouble at all making train or hotel reservations, so everything has gone very smoothly.

It has been very cool here, which came as a relief after boiling hot Houston. Elnora and I have walked miles and have been every place in town. I've eaten shrimp till it runs out my ears. This is certainly a wonderful town for having a good time although it was a mad house over the weekend. You should have seen this joint Saturday night. It looked like Grand Central.

We leave the 13th for Miami and that should be quite a ride.

Things couldn't be better for us and we are having the time of our lives. When you see her, you'll know why. Please write to me at Miami, and I'll write again soon. You have my address I think. Cadillac Hotel, Miami Beach, Florida. I suppose it will really be crowded there as I think they send the whole Army to rest there. I'll never kick at having to be in this country again though.

I guess that's all from me. Elnora wants to put in her nickel's worth so Mrs. Jones meet Mrs. Jones.

Love, J.R.

René Palmer Armstrong

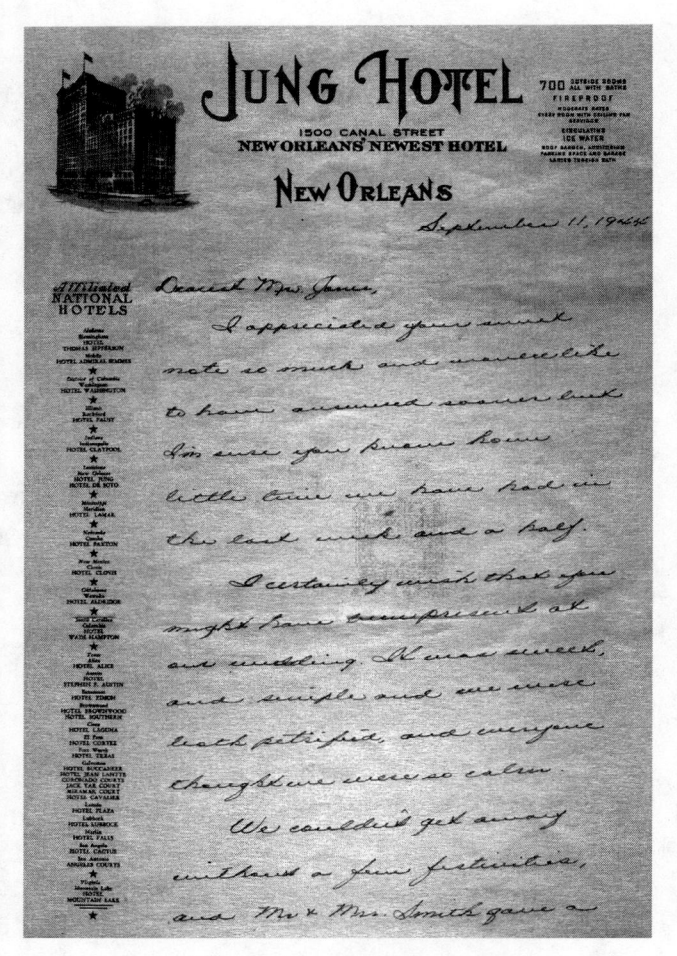

Scan of Elnora's honeymoon letter to her new mother-in-law courtesy of Lloyd Sullivan.

Monday, September 11, 1944

Dearest Mrs. Jones,

I appreciated your sweet note so much and would like to have answered sooner, but I'm sure you know how little time we have had in the last week and a half.

I certainly wish that you might have been present at our wedding. It was sweet and simple, and we were both petrified and everyone thought we were so calm.

We couldn't get away without a few festivities, and Mr. & Mrs. Smith gave a luncheon for us, and we had a dinner at the Warwick immediately after the ceremony. We wished for you and Mr. Jones, but I can understand how inconvenient it would have been for you to make a trip at this time. I first hope that it won't be long till we are settled someplace and you all can come to visit us. I'm so very anxious to meet you all. I wish I could have before we married, but I don't suppose it will make too much difference.

I want to thank you again for the lovely little lace handkerchief. It did help so much to make our wedding day a happier one, and it really added the finishing touches to my gold gabardine suit, brown hat, gloves, and alligator bag and shoes. (P.S. the bag was a gift from my aunt—and I wouldn't take anything for it, as it was a gift to her from my grandfather.)

Guess you can tell from the tone of this letter that I'm the happiest girl in the world, and will continue to be as long as that handsome guy over there goes around with a smile on his face.

I'll try to take good care of him—although it's all a little new right now.

This is a wonderful place to spend a honeymoon, and we have really been taking in the sights. This food is killing. It hasn't changed a bit since the last time I was here and the coffee—still just as thick.

   Write us soon.

   Always love—Elnora

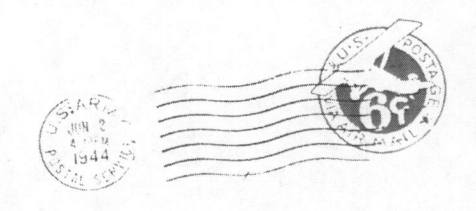

THE REST OF THE STORY

The honeymoon letters from New Orleans were the last of the letters found in the box. Obviously, with no more letters, the story might have ended there. However, after searching for two and a half years, I was able to find their daughter, Suzie Jones Neff. She supplied the following information regarding her parents' life after his return from the war front and after her parents' marriage. The information she provided is sketchy, but based on comments she heard them make or private jokes they shared. Suzie was only sixteen when her father died and twenty-eight when her mother died. Most of us at those ages have not had the meaningful discussions that we would like to have with our parents regarding life's major events.

Photo of J.R. and Elnora Jones courtesy of Suzie Jones Neff.

J.R. had so often written to Elnora that he couldn't wait to get her in his hands and dance the night away. I can only imagine the happiness they both felt as they attended the dances on the base. Big bands would be playing, refreshments would be plentiful, and sweet music would haunt their minds. J.R. would have a hard time keeping his eyes, and his hands, off of his new bride. Finally, his wish had come true and he no longer had to regret not marrying Elnora before he left for war.

Photo of J.R. and Elnora Jones courtesy of Suzie Jones Neff.

The war was still raging at the time of J.R.'s and Elnora's marriage. After their honeymoon in New Orleans and three weeks of debriefing in Miami, Florida, J.R. was reassigned to Turner Army Airfield in Albany, Georgia. Finally together, I am sure they shared many hours talking about J.R.'s experiences in New Guinea—now that there weren't censors to stop him. J.R. used to tease Elnora about her deepening southern accent. She suddenly was pronouncing Albany (short a, accent on the first syllable) as Al-Binny (accent on the second syllable). He also kidded her mercilessly about her pronunciation of graham crackers. He thought she'd never get rid of that Georgia-peach accent.

Family base-housing was hard to come by during the war. Elnora used to tell Suzie stories of how they had to *jump* when it was available. The only way to get a bigger place was to have half their stuff packed and ready to move when someone was posted elsewhere. The soldiers had a joke about knocking on their own doors and calling out before entering a house because they never knew if their wife had up and moved while they were gone on a mission.

J.R. relayed the story to Suzie of the first jet engine he'd ever seen. While he was stationed in Albany, he had to take his turn in the radio tower. He was talking to a pilot who gave his location and ETA [estimated time of arrival]. Being a pilot himself, he did the math and told the pilot his calculations were off. He was trained well enough to not reveal much information on the radio. The pilot insisted that his calculations and ETA were correct. J.R. finally asked, "What are you, a flying saucer or Santa Claus?" J.R. warned Elnora that he would be doing a lot of armchair flying with the boys at the air base clubs and that she would need to be ready to hear these stories for the rest of their lives. I so love hearing their stories at the reunions each year of the 345th Bomb Group. Upon hearing of their tales, I do not understand how any of them survived and how they can even today laugh at some of their escapades.

Photo of J.R. and Elnora Jones courtesy of Suzie Jones Neff.

J.R. got to see his first helicopter in Albany. He came home later that day and told Elnora that was the day he was getting out of the air force. He'd rather be court-martialed than go up in one of those things.

The war ended on August 14, 1945, with the surrender of Japan. It would be several months before the discharge papers would be processed, and J.R. and Elnora would have many decisions to make. Once again, life would change completely for them. Freedom to go wherever and to do whatever would be a wonderful concept for J.R. again, but it would come with a price. No longer would the United States government be supplying lodging and a steady paycheck. Would jobs be scarce with the volumes of servicemen being discharged at record numbers? I'm sure that they spent many hours discussing their options.

After J.R. was discharged, they moved to Indiana to complete their degrees at Indiana University. While they were in Indiana, they lived in a walk-up apartment in Hagerstown, Indiana. Suzie remembers her mother relating a few stories about how difficult it was to navigate the stairs in the building carrying groceries, purse, and cold weather gear.

Suzie also remembered a few stories about family gatherings with the Jones-Doty clan. It seems Grandmother Stella Doty had a "pet" bull that gave the family endless nightmares. The bull would charge the fence every night to see Stella and get a treat. The family was certain the bull was going to trample her. A good pilot had to possess a certain daredevil kind of attitude, and it looks like J.R. came by his kind of attitude quite naturally after learning about his grandmother.

There was another family story about the preacher and the mashed potatoes. Most Sundays the local preacher was invited to supper, and everyone in the family was expected to attend. Of course, the food was always passed to him first, and he had a miserable habit of taking the butter off the top of the potatoes. This did not endear him to Grandfather Doty or Bud Jones (J.R.'s father) since the buttered area of the potatoes was their favorite part. They had a standing family tradition that the men in the family were passed the potatoes first and were served with her grandmother's laughing comment that the preacher wasn't there to take the butter.

J.R. stated in his letters that he couldn't wait to get home and have a steak and a Coke. He often warned Elnora that she was going to have a hard time keeping him full as he never seemed to have enough to eat while in the jungles of New Guinea. J.R. was extremely underweight when he left for home. It was a good thing he had a long boat ride home so he would have a chance to put on some weight before seeing Elnora, as I am sure she would have been alarmed to see him that skinny.

I asked Suzie why her parents chose to complete their college at Indiana University instead of returning to J.R.'s beloved Kansas University. She believed there were several reasons. Primarily, Elnora and her mother, Mary Bethany Bartlett, did not get along. It was our understanding that someone else had been hand-picked by the family to marry Elnora; J.R. was not the chosen one. This created a lot of tension with her mother who though it important that Elnora marry into the right social status. Since Elnora did not know her new mother-in-law, she wanted to spend some time with J.R.'s side of the family and found this to be a great way to escape her mother's constant oversight. In the mid-1940s, Indiana University had a really good home economics department and Kansas University didn't. Besides, Elnora was always adventurous enough to enjoy trying new things and J.R. was much more conservative. It just made sense to move.

Photo of J.R. and Elnora Jones courtesy of Suzie Jones Neff.

Secondly, Mrs. Gordia Jones taught Elnora how to cook. One would think that, being a home economics major, Elnora would have been a good cook. While she was growing up, Elnora learned the theory but needed a lot of practice since Jane, their maid, kept running her out of the kitchen. Elnora's mother couldn't cook anything but tea cookies and the occasional pie. Suzie reported that Elnora could literally burn water. So, Suzie thought J.R. may have had an ulterior motive in moving closer to his mother. He knew he'd get a decent meal now and again and get his favorite pork-tenderloin sandwiches. Elnora eventually did learn how to make pork tenderloin sandwiches, poached eggs, and that disgusting orange Jell-O mold with raisins and carrots—a favorite of J.R.'s.

It was amusing to Suzie that Elnora got her degree in home economics with an emphasis in foods and yet she couldn't cook. Elnora received three teaching certifications: home economics, her primary one; English; and science. What she really wanted to be was a dietician. Fortunately, she was a fantastic seamstress, and all of the family's clothing was made by Elnora. Because her creations were of better quality than the store's, the only things bought were J.R.'s suits and shirts.

J.R. really wanted to be a lawyer, but times were tough and money was tight. It didn't take long for them to go through the money J.R. had saved while stationed in New Guinea, even with the assistance of the newly legislated Servicemen's Readjustment Act of 1944. Commonly known as the G.I. Bill of Rights, this legislation was signed by President Franklin Delano Roosevelt and was meant to provide educational benefits for the returning soldiers along with assistance for housing. J.R. graduated Phi Beta Kappa from Indiana University with a degree in business. Suzie still has his key.

Over the years, Suzie asked her parents' reason for the move from Indiana to Houston after they completed their education. She received several replies. One was Elnora's family was in Houston. Her father was older and occasionally Elnora was needed to help out. The second reason was probably more accurate; J.R. did not like living in rural Indiana. He was a city boy by temperament and education. He also disliked the Congregationalist Christian (Quaker) church the family attended and promptly converted to the Presbyterian Church. He said the little church house they attended in the backwoods of Indiana gave him nightmares. Suzie visited the church in 1984 after the death of her grandmother, Gordie Mae Jones. She stated she could see why her father disliked going to that church as it was a tiny, one-room white church backed by a huge country cemetery. The back of the cemetery was bordered with ancient willow trees. She did not know if it was the locale, the topography, or just the day they were there, but a fog seemed to cling to the cemetery long after mid-day. The impression was more Louisiana swamp than Indiana farm country.

Suzie suspected the real decision was made because J.R. wanted to shake the Indiana farm dirt off his shoes and move to a city more suited to his abilities as a businessman. Many of their friends had moved to Houston after the war and the nightlife in Houston was much more appealing than Hagerstown.

Suzie shared that J.R. was also not inclined toward blue-collar labor. J.R.'s father warned Elnora to keep J.R. away from anything mechanical as J.R. was not mechanically inclined. Of course, since J.R.'s father had owned and operated a garage and then later sold specialized parts to the teams on the Indy car circuit, this was always somewhat of a mystery to the family.

J.R.'s only mechanical ability was with kites. He could design and build incredible kites that they would fly. His pride and joy was a red and green box kite he would re-paper every year with Christmas tissue. If not familiar with box kites, they are especially hard to build and even harder to fly. By the time the kids were old enough to hold a kite string, J.R. had them building their own shield-shaped kites. It was a tradition every spring to assemble them and play. Memories of this are what make our childhoods magical. I'm sure that J.R. took great delight in seeing his children master the skills of flying a kite and dreaming of being up there in the sky like he once had been.

After returning to Houston, Suzie suspected they lived in an apartment for a while, then bought their first house on Wendell Street in Bellaire, not far from her grandparents' house at 6633 Mercer Street. Getting on with life, buying a house, having kids—life was to be full for J.R. and Elnora after the war. They quickly settled into reality and purchased their first home in the early '50s in Bellaire, Texas. One of their favorite places to dance was the Hi-Hat, the very place they went on that fateful blind date in August 1941.

Photo of J.R., Elnora, Jay, and Suzie Jones courtesy of Suzie Jones Neff.

J.R. accepted a position with the National Biscuit Company (Nabisco) in Houston as an accountant. In '48, J.R. obtained a position with Shell Oil in human resources and remained with them for the remainder of his career. Making a living required J.R. to work long hours at the refinery; and since he was in management, he was mandated to work when the union workers were out on strike. He had his twenty-fifth anniversary with Shell in '73, shortly before his death.

J.R. and Elnora had a dog named Stinky. Elnora teased that he was their first child. Stinky was a terrier and something mix, with him appearing to have a little poodle or spaniel in him as well. J.R. and Stinky used to play with a fireplug toy that jingled. Later, they got Frika, the family dachshund. Frika was a lovely black and tan standard dachshund and was a tiny terror. Elnora said that J.R. and Frika played ball so much that Frika didn't have any whiskers left as J.R. had accidentally pulled them all out during their playtime. Frika also climbed fences. Frequently, they would come home to find she had scaled the chain link fence and was waiting for them in the front yard.

In J.R.'s letters to Elnora, he hinted he was not really injured. In reality, J.R. would suffer lifelong physical problems due to antiaircraft ammunition hitting his plane and the subsequent crash landing on December 26, 1943. Suzie related that every so often, a piece of shrapnel would work its way out of J.R.'s knee. In spite of this, J.R. and Elnora both loved to dance and at some point, Suzie thought they ice-skated quite a bit because there were two pairs of ice skates in the garage closet for years. People normally wouldn't buy expensive ice skates unless they planned on using them regularly, especially in Houston. J.R. wrote to Elnora several times in his letters from the heat of the New Guinea jungle about wishing they were ice skating.

In the '50s, Elnora was a home economics and English teacher of the eighth and ninth grades at Lanier Junior High in Houston, Texas. A. J. Foyt, the famous race-car driver, was one of her students. She quit teaching in November '55 with the birth of their son, Jay. Suzie was born in May '57, her being one of the hurricane babies of that year. Elnora resumed teaching in '63 at Hartmann Junior High, teaching eighth-grade science and home economics. She took a year off to care for Suzie who was in a motorcycle accident. She then resumed teaching at Pershing Junior High as the eighth-grade earth science teacher.

J.R. either couldn't or wouldn't cook. Most men bonded over barbeque, but he left the outdoor grilling to Elnora. Suzie thought it brought back memories of New Guinea. J.R. even developed a violent dislike of houseplants after the jungles of New Guinea. Nothing green and growing was allowed in the house. Elnora would tote them in and then find them out on the back porch a little while later. It ended up that Elnora had quite a collection of pots on the back porch. She did manage to sneak in an ivy plant, and Suzie thought it must have been related to Louise of *Little Shop of Horrors*. It seemed to know that J.R. didn't like it, so it grew up the wall in its spot in the corner and then started across the ceiling toward the light. Of course the light was right over the spot on the couch where J.R. would sit and read. It then started growing downwards toward him. Suzie relayed they all waited to see when he would notice it. He eventually did and the "thee's" and "thou's" came out in abundance. J.R.'s grandparents were Quakers and Suzie said that when he got upset, he reverted back to some of their words.

That complete avoidance of any outdoor activity extended to camping or weekending at the Bartlett family cabin. He did love swimming and they took advantage of the Evergreen Park pool in Bellaire; later, they joined a country club and spent most of their summer hours there. Clean pools and beaches were great, but lakes were to be avoided.

J.R. played golf fairly well but didn't really have the time. He was an electronics buff and loved going to the store and looking at the new television sets, stereos, and all the latest gadgets.

J.R. and Elnora visited the Shamrock Hotel on anniversaries and frequented local dining spots like Gaido's, Kaphan's, and Sonny Look's Sirloin House. While talking with Suzie, I realized that it was possible I could have actually seen the couple, as I worked at Sonny Look's just before J.R. died. Isn't that amazing?

Besides raising two children, J.R. and Elnora mostly worked, visited with their friends, the Powells and the Stanuells, and helped start the St. John's Presbyterian Church in Westbury, a suburb of Houston. Elnora and J.R. wrangled the three-year old nursery at the church for years. Elnora told Suzie that J.R. was not well-suited to handle babies, but the three-year olds were more his speed. Suzie had a few pictures of what Elnora called J.R. doing the "daddy drop." J.R. never could get the hang of holding an infant.

Music was still a very important part of their lives, and Suzie said the radio was always on at their house. Elnora would do housework, singing and dancing her way through laundry, mopping floors, and cooking. J.R. loved to whistle and apparently was quite accomplished at it. Suzie recalled the refrain that J.R. used to whistle—"Full Moon and Empty Arms," recorded by Frank Sinatra in '45, based on Rachmaninoff's Piano Concerto #2. They had a good stereo, possessing a fairly extensive record collection which included everything from Stan Kenton to the classics.

J.R. loved basketball and Indy car racing. After all, he was from Indiana where both are requirements or you're kicked out of the state, according to Suzie. He also loved to go to the Hobby airport and watch planes land from the observation deck.

J.R. had his share of traveling during the war, so summer vacations were usually trips to Galveston where they stayed at the old Jack Tar Hotel or to San Antonio in some Holiday Inn.

The family took the occasional trip to Indiana, but they usually didn't have the time to take vacations for several weeks in duration.

Photo of J.R. Jones courtesy of Suzie Jones Neff.

J.R. was a lifelong and avid reader. He always had a book, newspaper, or magazine in hand. He had an interest in the Civil War and had several Civil War encyclopedias, reading anything he could find on the subject. However, his literary taste ranged from biographies to popular fiction, from Leon Uris to Michael Crichton.

Truly, theirs was a love affair to last a lifetime. J.R. suffered a massive heart attack and died suddenly in '73. What a difficult thing to face when a spouse dies at such a young age. I can only imagine the duress felt by Elnora with the loss of the love of her life and the prospect of having to take care of her family alone, without J.R. at her side. Elnora died of bone cancer in '85. It was at the time just before Elnora's death that she told Suzie her hope of someday someone taking their love letters and writing a story about them. Suzie thought the letters might have been destroyed in her house fire, not knowing that her brother had taken them to his home. Although the details of what happened next with the letters is somewhat of a mystery, the box of letters found its way to an auction house in Dayton, Texas, and were bought by an antique dealer as part of a lot that included historical newspapers. It was the newspapers that caught my husband's eye, but it was the box of letters upon which this book evolved. Suzie has told me several times how much she appreciated what I was doing in writing about her parent's love story. Our hope is to place the original letters along with some of her parent's memorabilia into a center for the study of WWII, perhaps at a university, enabling future generations to study and learn from J.R. and Elnora's letters. Surely they provide a unique glimpse into life at home in America and abroad in New Guinea during wartime 1941-1944.

The following is a quote from Suzie Jones Neff:

> They were the average American post-WWII couple. He came home, they got their education and they started a life. They worked hard and had kids and tried to give their kids a good life. For the most part, they tried to put the war behind them and focused on what they could accomplish rather than what troubles they faced so early in life. They didn't seem to think anything that had happened to them was very extraordinary or special.
>
> I remember Mom showing extra respectfulness to the Polish, Jewish gentleman who ran the shoe shop in Westbury. I remember Dad making a special trip to give him his business. Mom pointed out, after we had met him the first time, the numbers on his arm and what

significance they had. And that we were never, ever to show disrespect to him or any of his family because of what they had endured. In their minds, the real heroes of the war were these survivors.

JOURNEY OF DISCOVERY

THE BOX OF LETTERS

My husband, Ken, is a consummate treasure hunter, and I refer to him as a licensed dumpster-diver. While he was digging around in the Treasure Box in Texas City in 2002, he came across a stack of newspapers that caught his attention. Of the eleven he purchased, one was published the day after the attack on Pearl Harbor. As he negotiated the purchase of the newspapers, the owner conveyed, that at the time she acquired them at an auction in Dayton, Texas, the newspapers were sold as a lot with a box of old letters. My husband asked what the letters were about, and the proprietor said she didn't know. Since he really wanted the newspapers, he took the box of letters too and placed them in our storage area.

In 2006, I was looking for something in that storage area and found the box of letters. Since I didn't know their origin, I asked my husband where he found them and he told me of his experience four years previously in purchasing the newspapers. He told me he had not looked at the letters and had no idea about their content.

René Palmer Armstrong

I can remember quite vividly the day my friend, Glenna Racer-Riggan, and I sat down and began to explore the hidden treasures found in that box of letters. We randomly picked up letters from the pile and excitedly read J.R.'s words as he tried to woo Elnora. We decided to put the letters in chronological order so we could begin to understand his attempt to communicate to Elnora what it was like to be separated. At one point I said to Glenna, I'll bet we find Elnora daydreaming by doodling what hopefully would be her married name, *Mrs. J.R. Jones*—and we did! On the back of another envelope we found the handwritten initials of the possible new bride *eJb*.

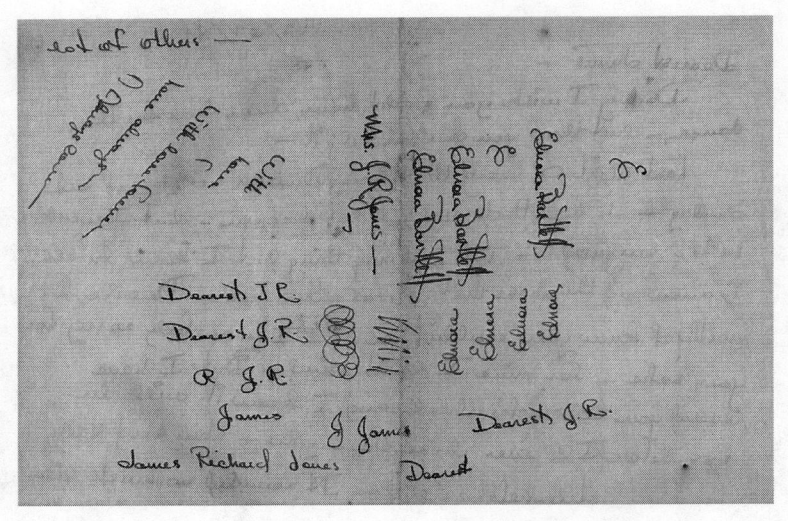

Scan of Elnora's doodling of what would be her married name courtesy of Lloyd Sullivan.

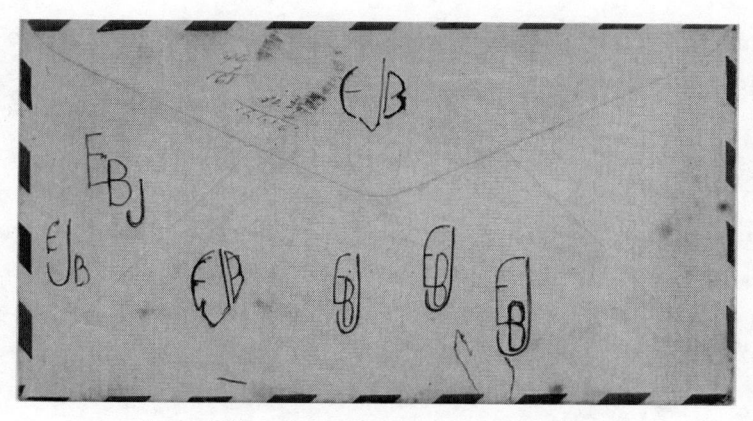

Scan of Elnora's doodling of what would be her married-name initials courtesy of Lloyd Sullivan.

Glenna and I spent two days, eight hours a day, standing side-by-side at two copy machines in our local office supply store, copying the letters and envelopes, painstakingly handling them one-by-one to preserve the letters. You can imagine our excitement when we would open up a letter and find a picture. Sometimes we would pause and read something in the letter that particularly caught our eye. At times, it was almost overwhelming and we would find ourselves in tears as their story began to unfold. It wasn't long before we realized that this wasn't only J.R. and Elnora's journey; it had becomes ours as well.

Upon returning home from copying, we decided that we would divide up the fifteen-hundred plus handwritten copied pages and transcribe them. You cannot imagine the excitement we experienced as we typed the letters. We were burning up the phone lines between Texas and Ohio as we excitedly shared the tidbits of information we discovered. We soon realized that our cell phone bills were going to be enormous, so I secured another cell phone on Glenna's service, enabling us to talk daily for as long as we wanted. So, we too found out what it was like to communicate from a distance. Of course, that was no comparison to their struggles in '43 wartime.

Communicating during that era, and especially during war, was definitely not what it is today. It would be very difficult to send a letter and not get a reply back to that letter for anywhere from three weeks to six weeks. Today, we have the luxury of e-mails, text messaging, and video links with our family and friends. Think of the heartache felt by a sweetheart after being told that her soldier had been killed in battle, only to continue receiving his letters for weeks or even months after his death. Additionally, since the soldiers were constantly on the move with the advances made during the war, their mail was frequently delayed or delivered to the wrong location, just missing the soldiers sometimes by days. As you read J.R.'s letters, you will find his constant frustration of missing *mail call* or hearing from someone who just arrived from his last duty station and learning that they had seen mail addressed to him.

Marshall Riggan

As my friend Glenna was helping me transcribe the letters, she related that her father-in-law was in WWII. She told him of the letters and our desire to learn as much as we could about New Guinea and the war. Much to Glenna's delight, she discovered that Marshall arrived in New Guinea on December 14, 1943. He celebrated his nineteenth birthday aboard ship in the harbor at Townsville, Australia. Mr. Riggan was a Radar Operator T/5 and a member of the 574th Signal Air Warning Brigade assigned to the Fifth Air Force. Although J.R. and Marshall were not assigned to the same units, it is possible their paths may have crossed. Based on the pictures he provided, the scenery and living conditions were similar.

Glenna wanted to thank her father-in-law for sharing his past and present with a daughter-in-law who loves him.

Photo of Radar Operator T/5 Marshall Riggan courtesy of Marshall Riggan.

Learning Firsthand at the Foot of an Expert

I quickly found out that I knew nothing about WWII and even less about planes, geography, and life in the wartime '40s.

It is amazing to me that I am usually only a few people away from the person I need to meet or who has some bit of information I need to know. I discovered that there are a lot of kind people out there who want to help you be successful and who are willing to sacrifice some of their own precious time to make things happen.

As I began my research to equip myself with the knowledge I needed to make this story come alive, I was given what to me was the single most important advice by a WWII veteran: "Buy Lawrence J. Hickey's book, *Warpath Across The Pacific*, and you will learn what James Richard Jones went through in the Southwest Pacific Theater of Operation." Once I acquired his book, I was delighted to discover that the very events that J.R. wrote about were right there before me. It even chronicled a very important event that happened to J.R. on December 26, 1943. I was able to speak directly with Mr. Hickey and explained my desire to tell the *human* side of war and the romance of J.R. and Elnora. I boldly asked if I could visit his library and find pictures that would illustrate what I had been reading about in J.R.'s letters. I also read a few excerpts to him from J.R.'s letters regarding some of the information I had found in the *Warpath Across The Pacific*.

Miracles never cease, and in a few short weeks another friend, Janine Burks Crenshaw, and I were on a plane bound for Boulder, Colorado, for a several-day visit with Mr. Hickey. We were graciously welcomed by Larry and soon introduced to one of the researchers who worked for him. After being shown binders of photographs, Janine and I quickly began to find pictures relevant to the story. Before leaving, Larry gave me about a five-inch stack of papers to copy, explaining they were the mission logs, intelligence reports, and unit histories for the 345th Bombardment Group for the time period when J.R. was in the SWPA. I quickly realized the gift I had just been given, and it then became clear to me that J.R.'s wartime experiences would allow me to write the rest of the story.

Censorship during wartime greatly hinders a soldier's ability to accurately describe what he was experiencing. J.R. could only say that he had a bad day. In reality, after reading the mission report, you realize the significance of what a bad day really meant.

Found At Last

That visit to Boulder provided more than just J.R.'s war experiences. It also provided the single greatest lead to me in trying to find the Jones family. Sue Hickey, Larry's wife, was able to take the information I provided her regarding J.R. and Elnora's date of birth and full names, and in less than thirty minutes, she was handing me the data I had searched for since '06. I now had their date of death, location of gravesite, and the name and address of their daughter, Suzie Jones Neff. Of all things, Suzie lived not more than an hour away from where I was living.

During my trip home, I was overwhelmed with emotions and questions. What should I do? What should I say to the daughter? How will she receive my visit? Why did the letters end up in an auction and eventually in an antique/junk store in Texas City? Too many questions remained, and I felt they needed to be answered.

I decided to visit with Suzie and see what I could find out. Armed with *The Warpath Across The Pacific* as my tool, I approached Suzie's door and knocked, not knowing what to expect. I explained that I was doing research on the crash-landing incident mentioned in the book as I showed her the page and asked her if this could possibly be her father. I didn't want to tell her I had the letters because I didn't know how they had turned up in a junk store.

Much to my delight, Suzie invited my husband and me into her home. We sat down and I began to ask her about her parents. I asked to see pictures and if she had any memorabilia related to her father's wartime experience. She explained there were items like his type A-2 flight (bomber) jacket, his attaché case, his metals, and other assorted items, including a box of letters that her father had written to her mother. Trying to remain calm, I asked her if I could see these items, but she explained that her brother had asked for items after her father passed away and her mother had given them to him.

After meeting with the brother, we realized the items were no longer in the brother's possession. Due to some unfortunate circumstances, the newspapers and letters were auctioned off in Dayton, Texas, and purchased by the owner of the antique/junk shop in Texas City. It was that *dumpster diving* husband of mine who purchased the letters that enticed me to writing this story. I am always amazed at the pathway that leads you into life-changing circumstances.

Armed now with the knowledge of how the letters came into my possession, I called Suzie and asked for another meeting. I explained that I had purchased the letters and announced my intention to write a book to document not only their love story, but also to provide the reader with a unique prospective of the '41-'44 lifestyle and the phenomenon known as *wartime romance*.

To my surprise, Suzie explained that her mother expressed to her that a book needed to be written about their wartime romance. After a brief pause, Suzie told me I had her approval to proceed further. Since that initial meeting, we have met several times, and she let me hold and photograph many of the artifacts surrounding their story. I am forever grateful to Suzie for allowing me the privilege of bringing her family's wartime experiences to light.

THE 345TH BOMBARDMENT GROUP—THE AIR APACHES

While visiting with Larry Hickey, he informed me that the president of the 345th Bombardment Group Reunion was living right there in Boulder. He asked if I would like to visit with Lynn Daker, and we jumped at the chance. After many hours of visiting, I was overwhelmed with information and personal accounts of their wartime contributions and experiences in New Guinea. What an extraordinary man and what bravery shown in such difficult circumstances. Mr. Daker invited me to attend the next reunion in Washington, D.C., as his guest.

In September '08, I had the privilege of being in the presence of the very group I had read about in J.R.'s letters. Overwhelming emotions flowed forth as I stood before them and explained who I was and of my intention to write a book about one of their members, with hopes of educating a new generation about the amazing acts of bravery they performed. They graciously welcomed me and shared some of their firsthand experiences. I felt like I was on hallowed ground.

It was on that trip that we were given a private tour of the National Air and Space Museum—Steven F. Udvar-Hazy Center at Dulles Airport. Our docent was the individual charged with the restoration of the Enola Gay and the archival of the Manhattan Project. I watched the amazement of this man as he heard firsthand of the feats of the 345th Bombardment Group. I learned that the 345th was given the honor of participating in the final official mission of WWII. This group escorted the Betty Bombers carrying Japanese peace emissaries from Mainland Japan to Ie Shima prior to the official signing of the surrender by the Japanese. When you watch the historic filmstrips, look a little closer and you will see two B-25 Mitchells of the 345th escorting the white planes—this is the fabric of which freedom is made.

I attended their reunion in Dayton, Ohio, in '09. Looking around at this reunion, I saw younger faces—now the second and third generation of the 345th. It is encouraging and inspiring that the next generation is trying to capture history before our greatest generation is no longer with us.

Photo of Lynn Daker with original A-2 bomber jacket courtesy of René Armstrong.

I met with Melvin Best in December '10. Melvin was a member of the 498th Bomb Squadron. Since he was with the 345th Bomb Group from the beginning to the end of operation, he was able to provide the needed information to complete more of the story. It was such a pleasure to learn of the many details of their everyday life. At eighty-nine, he still does school presentations to inspire the next generation. What a gentleman.

WINGS AND A RING

Photo of Melvin Best with his original A-2 bomber jacket and crusher hat courtesy of René Armstrong.

I cannot begin to express my gratitude to the 345th for the privilege of getting to know these fine gentlemen and to learn of the heroic things they did in WWII.

The Rita's Wagon picture easily illustrates how war and comedy can clearly coexist. Note the markings above their heads showing how many planes and ships had become their victims; then, note the kitchen sink. They had been so successful in moving the Japanese farther back by throwing everything at them, that someone decided they should throw the kitchen sink at them too!

Photo of B-25 Mitchell Rita's Wagon crew with kitchen sink courtesy of the Lawrence J. Hickey Collection.

FRATERNITY BROTHERS

In March '08, I had the privilege of meeting a fraternity brother of J.R. Jones in Lawrence, Kansas. Glee Smith was present the day another fraternity brother, Ed McComas, woke up J.R., waved the induction notice over J.R. and told him, "I know where you are going." All three men became pilots in WWII. Edward O. McComas became a famous Ace, shooting down five Japanese Zeros in one day. Glee performed some of his training at Ellington Field, Houston, Texas, right up the road from where I live. Glee became a flight instructor at the San Marcos Air Base, San Marcos, Texas, the very facility that houses the Central Texas Commemorative Air Force. It is this group's efforts to keep the war birds alive and provide a living history museum for future generations that prompted me to dedicate, in part, this book to them.

Spending time in Lawrence, Kansas, was amazing. This was the first time I had spoken with someone who actually knew J.R. Along with his wife, Jerry, they told me of panty raids on the Kappa Kappa Gamma sorority house and of the everyday life of a college student at Kansas University in the early '40s. Jerry showed me the ballroom in a small hotel in downtown Lawrence where J.R. and other Delta Tau Deltas would dance the night away. I couldn't believe I was standing where J.R. danced and was talking with his friends. I thank them for sharing a part of their lives with me.

In J.R.'s, letters, there are many Delta Tau Delta Fraternity brothers mentioned. Often they met by accident when on R&R [rest and recuperation breaks] in Sydney, Australia. Many times they discovered they were just up the road from each other, but they never had the chance to visit with each other due to the intensity of the war and the rapid pace in which they moved the Japanese back toward Japan. After the war, many of his fraternity brothers became distinguished physicians, attorneys, and magazine editors.

My Personal Journey of Discovery

My knowledge of WWII grew tremendously as I began to research the background for this book. I learned what *ack-ack* was, where Cape Gloucester was, and I learned that I had a lot to learn. However, one unexpected avenue led me to learn of my father's experience in WWII. He never spoke of the war, but only told funny stories of something he experienced, and once shared a picture of him in full uniform with his pants legs turned up and a hula skirt around his waist. He was dancing with a USO showgirl on stage. My only memories of his wartime experience were entertaining, but he never opened up and told me what he really experienced.

It was only after examining a stranger's journey of wartime relationships though his eyes from his writings, that the discovery of a part of my father he never shared with me became reality. With newfound knowledge, I poured over my father's service records and discovered the motivation behind some of his actions. There was no room for whining, no place for complaining, no excuses—just get it done. In my quest of discovery of J.R., my father's story began to unfold as well. It was very early one morning that I read over those service records and found that my father was part of the 234th Engineering Combat Group. He landed on White Dog section of Omaha Beach—D-Day. He literally went to hell and back—and I never knew that.

One's perspective on life changes and the urgency of moving on, and hopefully forward, propels you into a life of struggles to do just that. My father had little time for insignificant things. After all, he had faced death on a daily basis. However, sometimes, one fails to stop and realize what really is important. Or perhaps, could it be that you are afraid that if you stop, your emotions and the realities of wartime just might catch up with you?

I never would have taken that journey of discovery about my father had I not embarked on the mission of finding who J.R. was. To the daughter of James Richard and Elnora Bartlett Jones, I will forever be grateful for your helping me discover more of who my father was.

I would like to encourage you to take that journey if someone in your family or one of your friends served in any war. Take time to talk with them and find out firsthand what they went through.

We must never forget that our freedom came with a price of great personal sacrifice.

One of my personal friends is Bill Buchanan. Mr. Buchanan is ninety-two years old. He was the final inspector of the P-61 Black Widow Night Fighter at Northrop Aircraft Incorporated in Hawthorne, California, prior to enlisting in the army air corps during WWII. Amazingly, he earning three sets of wings in one year and was working on another. Volunteerism is the number one priority in his life—he currently serves three days a week at Clear Lake Regional Hospital, handing out candy as he visits patient rooms, and greets visitors from around the world five days a week at Space Center Houston. He purposely lives on the third floor of an apartment complex that doesn't have an elevator. He goes up and down those thirty-eight steps several times a day, keeping his body as fit as his mind is. What an inspiration he is to me and to others as he encourages everyone to get out and volunteer their time to help others. If a ninety-two-year-old veteran can do it, why can't we?

Photo of Bill Buchanan and René Armstrong courtesy of Lloyd Sullivan.

Take time today to say thanks to a veteran—go out of your way to shake their hand and tell them how much you appreciate their sacrifice.

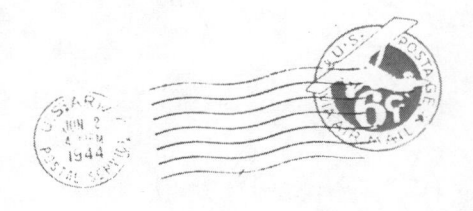

AFTERWORD

345th Bombardment Group

Photo of Air Apaches 345th Bombardment Group board courtesy of Paul Van Valkenburg, www.345thBombGroup.org

Who Were These Men?

They were the kids fresh from the backwoods and the farms and the tank towns of our land...young men from the business world of the skyscraper cities...from the mountains and plains, the Atlantic coastline and the Pacific slope and all the places in between...summoned up and thrown together to train in the South Carolina winter, and into spring...honed to a fine edge and thrust into combat on the far side of the world as a formidable fighting unit. They were the guys who did what had to be done, and what had to be done was just about anything you could think of or imagine.

They were the guys who had to learn to fire M-1 rifles and carbines, 45s and machine guns—and know when not to fire them; who saw that everyone had shirts and pants and shoes, gas masks and bed rolls and mess kits, razors and barracks bags and ponchos; who prescribed aspirin, atabrine, and penicillin, and drove the ambulances, issued medicine and bandages, cared for the sick and wounded and patched the pieces back together. They were the guys who navigated the bombers, watched the instruments and their hack watches and the ocean currents and the air speed, and took the formations to the targets and back; who kept the records straight, and wrote the official orders, and ran the mimeographs and typewriters, wrote regulation letters and maintained the official files; who patched up the planes when they staggered home with bullet holes and shrapnel gouges and stone-dead, shot-up systems and corked-out engines; who painted and polished, inspected and replaced the rivets and wires and hoses and gauges, and improvised to keep the birds in the air.

They were the guys who set the fuses, mixed the napalm, loaded the big bombs and the parafrags and hung the racks of delayed-fuse clusters in the bomb bays; who laced the strings of .50 caliber shells in the machine guns fore and aft and above and below; who manned the radios and grabbed those .50 caliber guns and fired 12 million rounds at enemy ships and installations and at planes in the air and on the ground, at targets scattered across 10,000 miles of strange and violent landscape; who drilled and filled and filed teeth and pulled them when they had to be; who tuned the motors and changed the tires, nursed the balky vehicles in the motor pool and drove the trucks through dust and mud and jungle trails and over land that had never seen a truck before; the guys who once even fashioned their own Group laundry to wash their clothes, and put together a lumber mill in the jungle to spit out rough boards for shacks and tent floors and storage shelves.

They were the guys who strung the telephone and communication lines over coral landscapes, across brushy wastes, and through coconut groves to connect the diverse, separated units with their strands of copper wire; who peered down the sophisticated bombsights and at the precise moment squeezed the button that rained all hell down on the target below; and the glamour guys up front who flew the birds...in tight formation to the pre-determined targets or targets of opportunity, and peeled off to take on enemy fighters, or send the payload down the pipe...or held the formation through screaming low-level runs across far-flung airstrips that threw up skies full of ack-ack...and, if they were lucky, they flew them home—sometimes intact, sometimes damaged, and sometimes barely held together by the scantest of faith, hope, and a prayer—completely shattered—flew them in whatever condition to safe landings or crash landings at their home base or to one of another friendly outfit as a last resort.

They were the guys who took what mediocre food was issued and prepared it under difficult conditions at any hour it was needed...in the pre-dawn hours for the flight crews scheduled for a mission or the flight line personnel who worked all night getting the planes ready to go with their bombs and fuel and ammunition. They did their job in makeshift tents or crude shacks that were called mess halls, and more often than not with the barely edible food they had to work with; who laid the pipelines for water and strung wires for electricity, and monitored the generators that furnished flickering lights for tents and shacks and repair sheds; who erected temporary buildings for Group and Squadron Headquarters, and for any other function necessary...then tore them down and moved them to the next location and set them up again, and tore them down and set them up as they moved a dozen or more times to new, advanced bases.

They were the guys who provided old movies on hastily built screens in an open clearing, found equipment for softball and volleyball and whatever recreation could be generated ...and found the extra little amenities of candy bars and cigarettes and 3.2 beer; who took the combat films and quickly processed them for intelligence purposes, for target evaluation, and kept the cameras operational for that all-important function; who were God's representatives, who offered spiritual comfort and counsel, and put together little chapels and conducted services for men of every faith, and performed the last rites for those who slipped away to everlasting sleep; who set up tents and tried to keep them dry inside during torrential tropical storms...or free of knee-deep mud, or just staked down and stationary in the blasts of devastating typhoons; who held the briefings and planned the strikes and carried out the strategies before each mission; who saw to it that there were showers, sometimes crude at best, and latrines, and did what they could to maintain such facilities.

They were the guys who censored the outgoing mail, and when the call went out, eagerly gathered for mail call when new sacks arrived from the States, hoping for word from that world that was so far away; who made the best of a bad deal at times like Thanksgiving and Christmas...and who saw a different kind of fireworks on the 4th of July...and May...and October...and February and September; who interpreted the strike photos and interrogated the crews after major missions and disseminated the information for use in future operations; who inspected and packed the parachutes, hoping that they would never be used; who suffered bouts with dysentery and dengue fever, hepatitis, malaria, diarrhea, skin rashes, jaundice, typhus, tetanus, and ailments and infections the medics had never heard of before.

They were the guys who experienced the merciless tropical rainstorms, the mind-softening 130-degree heat of the mid-day sun at the equator, and who hung on through twisting typhoons that wrenched the entire landscape; who felt the percussion of enemy bombs exploding nearer and nearer in an ever-increasing succession of sounds like no other...attacks which sent them scurrying into foxholes dug beside their tents or running for whatever cover was at hand...who knew the ghostly glow of incendiary and phosphorus bombs and the frightening scream of strafing guns that froze the heart of the bravest soldier... and, against all laws of averages, they were singled out as captive targets for direct hits by fanatical pilots of the Imperial Kamikaze Corps whose unbelievable strikes left a mind-shattering scene of injury, destruction and death beyond comprehension.

Scan of an American cemetery in New Guinea clipping which appeared in the Houston Post June 1, 1944, courtesy of Lloyd Sullivan.

But they were also the guys who witnessed savagely beautiful sunsets and the full moon over seemingly tranquil southern hemisphere seas...cooled off in wide jungle rivers and swam, at times, in the warm waters breaking on distant island shores; who spent endless lonely hours halfway around the world, thinking of pretty girls back home and of loved ones in their families, of baby sons and daughters they had never seen; who stretched out on their cots at night and joked and bitched and swore and talked to tent mates about a thousand things...and sometimes sat alone in the darkness...and cried...wondering if they would ever see their homes again. They sent letters back to the States, letters that were smudged and ink-stained because the sweat ran off their wrists and fingers as they wrote under the yellow light of an atabrine dipped bulb in the humid heat of the tropic clime...and there were no ball-point pens in WWII.

Paradoxically, they were also the guys who found a way to laugh in the face of adversity and make the best of a lousy situation. They each carried their part of the load and maintained their poise in a proud organization...and, most of all, they clung to their sense of humor when their world had become a monotonous, constant struggle to stay alive.

Maurice J. Eppstein, Colonel USAF Ret.
Former Adjutant, 345th Bomb Group

[From Col. Eppstein's remarks given as Master of Ceremonies at an Air Apache Reunion. Special thanks to Lawrence J. Hickey, author of *Warpath Across The Pacific*, for graciously allowing me to reuse this speech along with many of the original photographs and official government documents.]

RENÉ PALMER ARMSTRONG

"To commemorate victory and in appreciation of the splendid spirit and fine work of the men of the 345th BOMBARDMENT GROUP (M) You contributed materially to that victory!"

Glenn A. Doolittle
GLENN A. DOOLITTLE
LT. COL. A.C.
COMMANDING

Photo of VJ commemorative courtesy of the Lawrence J. Hickey Collection.

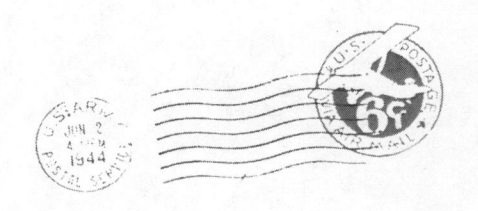

BIBLIOGRAPHY

Letters of James Richard Jones—1941-1944

Mission Logs, Unit Histories, and Intelligence Reports were taken from official, now declassified, government documents provided by Lawrence J. Hickey and found at the official website of the 345th Bombardment Group at: www.345thbombgroup.org

Hickey, Lawrence J. *Warpath Across The Pacific: The Illustrated History of the 345th Bombardment Group During WWII*. Boulder: International Research and Publishing Corporation, 1996.

University Archives, Spencer Research Library, University of Kansas Libraries, Lawrence, Kansas.

Glee Smith, Delta Tau Delta Fraternity brother—1939-1940.

Delta Tau Delta Educational Foundation, Fishers, Indiana

345th Bombardment Group members:

Melvin Best

Lynn Daker

Frank Dillard

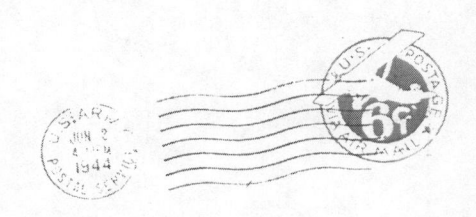

CONTACT INFORMATION

I appreciate your purchase of my first book and trust that it has in some small way educated, entertained, or perhaps enlightened you. I encourage your comments regarding the story by sending me an email at:
   rene.armstrong@comcast.net
   Happy reading!
   René

e|LIVE

listen|imagine|view|experience

AUDIO BOOK DOWNLOAD INCLUDED WITH THIS BOOK!

In your hands you hold a complete digital entertainment package. In addition to the paper version, you receive a free download of the audio version of this book. Simply use the code listed below when visiting our website. Once downloaded to your computer, you can listen to the book through your computer's speakers, burn it to an audio CD or save the file to your portable music device (such as Apple's popular iPod) and listen on the go!

How to get your free audio book digital download:

1. Visit www.tatepublishing.com and click on the e|LIVE logo on the home page.
2. Enter the following coupon code:
   e966-f621-0218-3b47-ad63-46ed-1cc4-179b
3. Download the audio book from your e|LIVE digital locker and begin enjoying your new digital entertainment package today!